THE USER EXPERIENCE TEAM OF ONE
2ND EDITION

Leah Buley
Joe Natoli

NEW YORK   2024

"My advice: Even if you're a cog in a huge UX team, ignore 'team of one' in the title and get this book. Get it whether you're just starting out in UX, a seasoned veteran, or merely UX-curious. It's always been one of the best books on UX, and this excellent new edition brings it up-to-date with the dramatically changed UX landscape."

—Steve Krug
author of *Don't Make Me Think: A Common Sense Approach to Web Usability*

"Essential. *The User Experience Team of One* distills the knowledge acquired from a career in UX and delivers it in plain, useful language. Whether you are a professional, a student, or looking to make a career change, this book explains how to approach a problem, what tool you should use, and why you're doing what you're doing."

—Isaac Gertman
Chair, Graphic Design, Maryland Institute College of Art

"*The User Experience Team of One* by Joe Natoli and Leah Buley is a must-read for anyone in design, whether you are just starting out or are an experienced product designer trying to push your organization forward. This book is packed with practical approaches that will help your organization, no matter the size, deliver significant impact through design."

—Andy Vitale
Chief Design Officer at Constant Contact, speaker, educator

"I recommend this thoughtful guide for anyone who needs to do UX work in a constrained environment, or who needs to advocate for the value of the practice while growing their own skills at the same time. It delivers a solid set of principles and methods without suggesting perfection is required, and sets you up for success with great advice on everything from choosing the right battles to exercising influence remotely."

—Cyd Harrell
Author of *A Civic Technologist's Practice Guide*

"Leah and Joe successfully deliver a rich compendium that balances the concrete with the intuition necessary for making a real impact."

—Kevin Bethune
Founder of dreams • design + life and author of *Reimagining Design*

"Where to begin? Wide as the ocean, deep as the deepest sea, the discipline of user experience overwhelms. So let's make it simple (but not easy). Start here, with this singular book, and never stop."

—Peter Morville
Information architect, animal philosopher,
and coauthor of *Information Architecture: For the Web and Beyond*

"The first edition of *UX Team of One* by Leah Buley came out when I was a budding UX researcher. I still have my dog-eared copy riddled with notes and highlights. While I was never a UX team of one, this essential resource made me a better researcher. It deepened my understanding of the broader context of design work and equipped me with effective tools and techniques to advocate for quality UX and collaborate effectively with stakeholders.

"This comprehensive new edition by Joe Natoli parallels the quality of Buley's classic, with an additional decade's worth of wisdom for today's unique UX challenges—notably an expansion on the role of UX in achieving business goals, the importance of interpersonal skills and collaboration, and updates to fundamental UX methods and frameworks for a new era of product development.

"Joe is one of our community's most prolific UX voices and contributors, and this new edition reflects his deep expertise and generosity. Were time travel real, I'd gift this to my past self. Now as a UX career coach, it is at the top of my required reading list for my growth-oriented clients, no matter their UX role or level of experience."

—Amy Santee
Career strategist and coach for UX professionals

"I don't know why they call this book *The User Experience Team of One*. It is brimming with excellent advice for UX professionals in any circumstance—from the lone wolf designer in a start-up to the individual contributor on a multitiered enterprise team. As a collection of methods organized by objective, it's easy to grab just what you need for whatever situation you may find yourself in. And if you're one of those folks who thinks wireframes are dead, you need to check out Joe and Leah's advice on making them, using them, and sharing them."

—Dan Brown
Curious Squid Design Lab

"*The User Experience Team of One*, 2nd Edition is an essential book for designers as it provides the necessary tools to perform their jobs effectively. Joe and Leah help designers understand how to create user-friendly, accessible, and inclusive experiences, making it an indispensable resource."

—Reginé Gilbert
James Weldon Johnson Professor, author of *Inclusive Design for a Digital World*

"An insightful guide on how to maximize impact as a UX designer from seasoned pros. Comprehensive and approachable, Joe and Leah have synthesized knowledge and tools with clarity and straightforwardness. It's an invaluable resource for both new and experienced designers."

—Jon Yablonski
UX designer and author of *Laws of UX*

The User Experience Team of One
2nd Edition
By Leah Buley and Joe Natoli

Rosenfeld Media, LLC

125 Maiden Lane

New York, New York 10038

USA

On the Web: www.rosenfeldmedia.com

Please send errata to: errata@rosenfeldmedia.com

Publisher: Louis Rosenfeld

Managing Editor: Marta Justak

Interior Layout: Danielle Foster

Cover Design: Heads of State

Illustrator: Joe Natoli

Indexer: Marilyn Augst

Proofreader: Sue Boshers

from Leah

For Ted Neptune and Frankie June.
Thank you for teaching me that there's more to life
than work work work coffee coffee coffee.

from Joe

For Eli, who built every inch of the ground I am so fortunate
and grateful to walk on. Without your love, support, patience,
guidance, and example, this would all be a dream
unfulfilled. Words absolutely fail.

HOW TO USE THIS BOOK

Who Should Read This Book?

While many people are attracted to the field of user experience because they want to be champions for users, being passionate about advocating for users isn't nearly enough to guarantee that you'll be a successful user experience team of one.

UX teams of one certainly *are* people who love and advocate for users. But they also make sure that designs get tested, business people's questions are answered, design problems receive an appropriate amount of creative exploration, UX specifications are implemented according to plan, the product is continually monitored and improved upon, and support for UX is ever-growing.

They do all of that without a roadmap or a blueprint, and they *don't* do it alone. They cannot succeed in bringing better user experiences into the world without the help of a much larger cast of people in very different roles—who may or may not be active supporters of UX themselves.

This book is for anyone who is interested in taking on the challenging and rewarding work of spreading a user-centered mindset to places where it's never been before. Because as ubiquitous as the term *UX* seems to be these days, as you'll see... we still have a *long* way to go.

This book is intended to be approachable for anyone who picks it up. Maybe you're new to UX and product design altogether. Maybe you're already working on product teams in another role but are interested in transitioning into the field of UX. Or you might be an experienced practitioner seeking ways to work more effectively within a cross-functional team.

Whatever the case may be, we're confident that you'll find practical, actionable, and useful information, as well as advice and methods that will serve to get you to wherever it is you're headed.

What's in This Book?

The user experience team of one ethos is equal parts philosophy and practice (see Figure 0.1). It focuses on having the right attitude, seeking out opportunities, being patient and inclusive, and doing the best work you can. Between philosophy and practice, we'll cover not just the guiding principles, but also the nuts and bolts of how to successfully run a UX project as a team of one.

Accordingly, this book is organized in two parts: Part I is *Philosophy* and Part II is *Practice.*

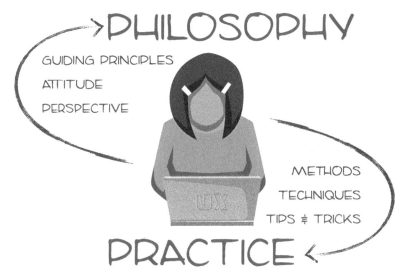

FIGURE 0.1
Being a successful UX team of one is equal parts thought and action, head and hand, philosophy and practice.

Part I, "Philosophy," is a frank walk-through of the UX team of one's concerns, from start to finish. In this section, we'll explain what it means to be a UX team of one, how to establish a successful foundation, and how to involve others and build support for UX along the way.

- **Chapter 1, "UX 101,"** gives an overview of what UX is, how it came to be, and what it takes to be a UX practitioner.

- Chapter 2, "Getting Started," focuses on how to begin, including the fundamentals of user research and design for the new and aspiring UX team of one.
- Chapter 3, "Building Support for Your Work," addresses some of the most challenging parts of life as a team of one: how to build support and do great work in spite of real-world organizational and interpersonal constraints.

In Part II, "Practice," we'll focus on the nuts and bolts of user experience work. This half of the book is intended to function as a ready reference, full of practical methods that have been selected and, in some cases, adapted to fit the realities of a UX team-of-one's situation.

What is this reality, you ask? Well, most importantly, teams of one must rely heavily on their non-UX colleagues to help them get work done. That means there's a preference here for methods that can be done in a rapid, rough fashion, and an even *greater* bias toward methods that invite collaboration and cross-functional participation.

In some cases, these methods may already be familiar to you, but our approach and tips are adapted for the work of a team of one.

- Chapter 4, "Planning and Discovery Methods," helps you set up a UX project for success. It includes planning and discovery of the team's requirements and expectations. It also covers techniques for establishing a shared UX strategy with the team.
- Chapter 5, "Research Methods," as the title implies, is all about research. This includes research with users, the centerpiece of a UX practice, as well as research into competitors and best practices.
- Chapter 6, "Design Methods," covers methods and techniques for inclusive and participatory user experience design.
- Chapter 7, "Testing and Validation Methods," provides methods for validating that your strategy, research, and design work has led you in the right direction.
- Chapter 8, "Evangelism Methods," brings our discussion of philosophy and practice full circle and finishes up with approaches for building support and awareness of UX throughout your organization.

- Chapter 9, "Growing Yourself and Your Career," is a blueprint for thriving and flourishing as you grow yourself and your career in user experience.
- Chapter 10, "What's Next," closes with a personal challenge for you to think critically about where you're taking your work in UX and how it aligns with the growth of the field overall.

Parts I and II are heavily cross-referenced, so methods that are described in detail in Part II are explained in context in Part I and vice versa.

The book is designed so that you can dip in and out as needed when you face a specific challenge or are working at a particular point in a project. That said, reading Part I from start to finish will give you a sense of the common growth path for a UX team of one. And reading Part II sequentially will give you a complete plan for how to run a UX project.

What Comes with This Book?

This book's companion website (🐘rosenfeldmedia.com/books/the-user-experience-team-of-one-second-edition/) contains a blog and additional content. The book's diagrams and other illustrations are available under a Creative Commons license (when possible) for you to download and include in your own presentations. You can find these on Flickr at www.flickr.com/photos/rosenfeldmedia/sets/.

FREQUENTLY ASKED QUESTIONS

What is a user experience team of one?

A UX team of one is someone who works in a situation where they're the key person advocating for a user-centered product design philosophy. If you're the only person in your company practicing (or aspiring to practice) user-centered design with little to no support, you are most definitely a UX team of one. However, even in organizations with multiple UX professionals, you may find yourself part of a team where you are the *only* UX person...which makes you an honorary member of the UX team of one club. **Chapter 3** explains the kinds of challenges that UX teams of one commonly face—and explains what to do about them.

I'm a freelancer. Is this book for me?

The User Experience Team of One, 2nd Edition focuses primarily on people working in or with organizations. But while it's not explicitly geared toward freelancers, consultants, or contractors, much of this book is still very relevant for independents, because they, too, must often work with the cross-functional teams of their clients. And if you're considering going out on your own, be sure to check out the section "Going Independent" in **Chapter 9**.

What's different about life as a UX team of one?

Working without the support of colleagues in the same profession, or without a high degree of UX maturity inside your organization, presents several unique challenges:

- **You feel like a jack-of-all-trades, but master of none.** You do a variety of work: probably some design, some research, some writing, some testing, and some evangelism. You care about your work, and you want to do it well. But being a generalist, you likely feel as if you're being spread increasingly thin. You may also wonder at times if you're "doing it right," or why all these techniques you read about every day on social media don't seem possible in your environment.

- **You need to evangelize—or justify.** You probably work with or for an organization that doesn't yet "get it;" they haven't fully bought into the value and purpose of UX. Or, even if they do value user experience, they may not be in a position to fully fund and build a robust UX practice. Either way, this means that in addition to your daily workload, you're constantly tasked with fighting for the UX improvements you propose, as well as trying to influence and increase the UX maturity of the organization as a whole. That's a pretty tall order.

- **You're learning on the job.** You don't have anyone to turn to for advice, so you need to figure out how to do your work on your own. You may have UX or product design professionals on social media or professional communities that you can turn to for peer-to-peer advice, but in your day-to-day work, you're on your own. Quite often, the best you can do is make an educated guess—and then trust and defend your hunches as to the best next steps.

- **You're working with severely constrained resources.** The biggest challenge for teams of one is time. There's enough work on any given day to keep an entire team of UX folks busy—but there's only one of you.

- **You're charting your own course.** No one in your organization has done this before. So, you're figuring out your own career path without a guide or a manual to follow, trying to build the airplane as you fly it.

What makes this role interesting is the dramatic tension between needing to inspire through expertise and trying to build your own expertise at the same time. That dynamic means you have a very unique set of challenges that go well beyond simply trying to do good UX or product design work. It makes skills like facilitation, flexibility, assertiveness, and persuasiveness central to the team of one's toolkit. This tension requires both practical and philosophical considerations—and that simple fact is the inspiration for this book.

Chapters 2 and 3 explain the working conditions that a team of one often experiences, while Chapters 4 through 9 provide specific methods that are optimized for those challenging working conditions.

Is this just an "intro to a UX" book?

Yes and no. While this book is intended to be accessible to people who are just starting out in user experience, we believe the advice and techniques here apply equally to seasoned practitioners. For example, Chapter 1 provides an overview of user experience and can serve as a basic introduction to the field. But the methods in Chapters 4 through 9 aren't the same typical UX methods you see, read, and hear about every day. We've chosen them specifically because of their power to educate and involve others who may not be familiar with or supportive of user-centered design, while requiring less time and fewer resources than their more formal counterparts.

CONTENTS

PART I: PHILOSOPHY

FOREWORD

"Jack of all trades, master of none."

—English expression (ca. 17th–18th C.)

I've never much cared for this phrase. It seems to carry the scent of a warning, either to the earnest young Jacks and Jills eagerly surfing from interest to interest or (more likely) to their hiring managers: Investing in breadth sacrifices depth. But in the world of design—and especially in the unique world of the user experience team of one— the creative professionals who thrive are the ones who can work without blinders on. Being able to see the big picture, to draw the connections others don't, means going broad.

"Specialization is for insects."

—Robert A. Heinlein's character Lazarus Long in
Time Enough for Love (1973)

Specialization is brittle. Specialization is highly optimized for specific circumstances. Specialization makes extensive assumptions about the problem at hand, the context in which it must be solved, and the characteristics of a viable solution. Specialization, sooner or later, eventually meets its own exceptions.

The team of one doesn't have the luxury of brittleness. The team of one must flex with the ever-fluid requirements of the role. So, if we are to embrace possibility, if we are to embrace potential, we must also reject specialization. Specialization comes with boundaries, comes with a leash.

Inherent in our rejection of specialization, then, is a necessary refusal to be boxed in. A refusal to place constraints on what you can bring, or limits on what you can accomplish. To be bold, to engage fully and without reservation, and not to stay in your lane.

"When all you have is a hammer, everything looks like a nail."

—paraphrased from Abraham Maslow,
The Psychology of Science (1966)

An important idea underlying Maslow's famous hammer is the notion that what we do affects what we see—and therefore what we can see. Different ways of doing things instill in us different ways of seeing. Every tool is also a lens.

A collector of tools must also be a curator of a great toolkit. The hidden acumen of knowing which tool to choose in the moment and why is what a generalist can bring that no specialist ever will. True wisdom comes when you can choose a tool not just for what it allows you to do, but for the possibilities it allows you to see.

"It's dangerous to go alone! Take this."

—Takashi Tezuka, *The Legend of Zelda* (1986)

So, let's all celebrate the generalist, the can-do problem solver who single-handedly—what's that you say? What do you mean, you're not ready?

Oh, right. The tools. The lenses. The resources to do the job (or jobs).

That's where Leah and Joe come in. This book is the toolkit, and the roadmap, and the warm fire to pull up to for reassurance and direction when you're lost and confused in the dark. The unease and uncertainty are part of it too; you can't move toward the new without also facing the unknown.

But you have resources: right here. You have tools. You have guidance.

Use them well.

Jesse James Garrett
Oakland, California
May 2024

WHAT'S CHANGED: A NOTE FROM JOE

The first edition of this book appeared in 2013. And more than a decade later, UX practitioners still praise its usefulness, usability, and value. Many report that Leah's book served as an indispensable guide in the earliest stages of their careers, and that they still routinely return to it for that same guidance. At the same time, the practice of UX has changed quite significantly since the book's inception—as has the business landscape it calls home. And in all honesty, that change has occurred faster and has been more far-reaching than any of us could ever have predicted.

Like so many people in other tech-driven professions (which at this point is all of them), the pressure to do a whole lot more with a whole lot less has intensified at the same pace. And in all honesty, too many of the prescribed, tried-and-true methods for UX improvement require far more time, effort, and resources than management is willing to entertain. And yet these same methods are still held up as best practices, still taught at universities and bootcamps, still suggested in countless courses, articles, and videos—despite overwhelming evidence that they *just don't work.*

Which brings us to this second edition and my involvement.

The challenge at hand was to bring the simple, effective principles and practices that Leah had introduced up-to-date, and retire a few that simply had outlived their usefulness. The goal for this new edition was also to address the often-difficult situations practitioners find themselves in—for example, the struggle to do good work in corporate environments where speed and urgency routinely trump importance or value. Not to mention the increasing need for UX practitioners to be generalists, executing across multiple areas of the discipline at a very high level.

I wanted to offer encouragement instead of cynicism—but still be 100% real about the challenges that practitioners should expect and prepare themselves for.

And above all else, I wanted to keep the spirit of Leah's work intact, as a voice who cared enough to communicate with people in a clear, down-to-earth manner that felt kind, generous, and personal.

I believe that mission has been accomplished. Leah and I truly hope you find this book useful.

INTRODUCTION

In June 2011 (which feels like forever ago), this message appeared on the Interaction Designers Association (IxDA) discussion list:

> I am at a point in my life where I know I want to do UX design after doing Web design for so long and then reading about usability testing, etc., 6 years ago. But my issue is I'm tired of working for organizations who say they care about their customer but don't do testing to even know what their customers want from them...I'm kind of fed up with working for people who don't get it.

This frustrated plea perfectly summed up the challenge that many passionate user experience professionals still face today, so many years later.

As far as we seem to have come, at a time when it seems UX is indeed a household name, many organizations still either have only a modest understanding of user experience, or none at all. In either environment, if you are the key person driving for a more user-centered way of working, you are a user experience team of one. And that's true whether it's your official job title or not.

But this is about more than just professional frustration. While this book is intended to be a practical resource for people who do user experience design without the support of a large UX team, we'll tip our hand right here at the beginning and confess something:

We firmly believe that being a UX team of one is much more than just a job.

It's also a critically important avenue for *doing good in the world*. The UX team of one is as much a professional circumstance as a constructive philosophy. And here are its founding principles:

- **UX is a force for good.** In an increasingly technological world, designing products with real people in mind helps you make sure that technology integrates in your life in a human-centered, ethically responsible way. It's a voice of reason, arguing that products and technology can support and even enrich our collective, fundamental humanity. And finally, it's a responsibility to be ever vigilant in watching for ways in which the technology you help bring into the world can be used to harm people instead of helping them.

- **The world needs more of it.** As the boundaries continue to blur between the technological and analog worlds, everything that you buy, use, and do will need this user-centered perspective. Companies that never thought of themselves as being in the user experience business before will realize that they are now. *We all are.* And with the rapid advance of powerful, cutting-edge technology like AI, VR, and AR, this field—and all the ways it shapes and influences the tech that increasingly runs our lives—can only grow exponentially.

- **You can make that happen.** Yes, *you*. The person reading this book right now, whatever your job title, whatever your career aspirations, you have it in your power to increase awareness of (and respect for) the user's perspective in the work that you do and with the people that you work with.

This book can help you spread knowledge and understanding of the power of good product design and user experience, one person, one team, and one company at a time. And what you'll find is that once people *get it*, those first moments of discovery about UX can often feel like a revelation. To many who end up becoming UX practitioners, it feels as if they've finally found their calling. The weight of that moment—and the passion it ignites—makes these crossovers enthusiastic ambassadors for user experience.

And, of course, your humble authors have stories of their own, which made them equally passionate about this discipline and all it is capable of. The spark that started the career of many seasoned UX professionals, just like us, was simply seeing an opportunity to improve something—and seizing it.

 Here's how I discovered UX. When I was growing up, I always wanted to be a writer. When I graduated from college, I got a job in what seemed like the most logical field—working at a magazine. The trouble was, I kept nodding off over my copyediting. There was one part of my job that I loved, however, and that was updating the website. I had picked up some rudimentary HTML skills in college. Soon I found that my favorite part of each week was the time I got to spend on the website. So, I decided to take the leap and look for a job making websites full time.

It was the early web tech bubble and HTML skills—even rudimentary ones—were in high demand. I tinkered around as a front-end coder for a few years but couldn't shake the growing conviction that I would really rather be doing what those people with that funny title "information architect" were doing. Not writing code but thinking about things from the human perspective and designing systems that were intuitive. So, I went back to school to study information architecture.

While I was working on my master's degree, I took what I now realize was my first "team-of-one" gig. My title was "tools developer" for a small company that helped law firms manage all the data that they have to keep track of when companies filed for bankruptcy.

Glamorous stuff. They hired me presumably because of my technical skills, but they liked and benefited from the fact that I was interested in design and usability, too.

It was a good training ground because they had a lot of funky, home-grown applications that needed plenty of UX help. It was a great place to test out the principles I was learning in school. I designed a slew of software interfaces. I spent time thinking about solutions for navigating large repositories of information. I conducted usability tests. It also exposed me to the challenges of getting people to prioritize user needs and design when there were so many other fundamental and urgent business issues to be addressed.

And, finally, it was where I learned the hard lesson that not all companies need or are ready for their team of one. That's okay. Eventually, I knew it was time to move on. What I learned there I put to good use in my next job as another team of one.

So, what skills and experiences got me on the path? Just a handful:

- Familiarity with the concept of user experience
- Interest in how people think, understand, and see
- A little bit of technical know-how
- An opportune environment to tinker and practice
- Just enough education to fuel my experiments

JOE'S CROSSOVER STORY

 I had artistic talent from the time I was old enough to hold a crayon, and I drew on anything that didn't move (including school tests). I grew up in a very small town in Ohio that you could drive through in three minutes, which is a tough place for a sensitive artist to grow up in. But where this all started for me was a meeting with my high school guidance counselor, when I was about to graduate. I went to this guy and said, "I want to do something art-related with my life." He looked me straight in the eyes and suggested I join the Army. He said people like me "are better off taking orders from other people." Again, this is a small town, so to him I'm just another useless dreamer. I said some very bad words, stormed out of his office, and decided I'd figure it out myself. I found Graphic Design in the Kent State University catalog and took a shot at the program; it sounded creative, and it sounded like something I could get a job doing.

Kent's program was extremely tough and rigorous: both a sophomore and junior review determined whether or not you could go on in the program. If you failed, they suggested you find another career. My great stroke of luck being there, though, was that the emphasis was on design as a problem-solving discipline. On human cognition and expectation. And while "user experience" wasn't a thing yet, the questions we were taught to ask were UX questions: Does this communicate to the intended audience? Does it meet their expectations? Does it motivate them or help them to act? Is it helping or hurting in terms of their ability to get what they need?

In other words, all the tenets of UX that we know now were there—but at the time, we just called it *design*.

Anyway, I graduated with a degree in Graphic Design. I worked at an agency the last two years of my college tenure, which was invaluable on-the-job learning. I bounced around a few design and ad agencies, and then this thing called *THE INTERNET* happened. I couldn't convince the old men who ran the agency I worked at that it wasn't a passing fad or trend, and that we needed to get into this work. They thought I was crazy. So, I jumped ship and started my own "Experience Design" firm.

It was the Wild West then; nobody knew anything about designing or building for the web because it was all so new. So, we said "yes" to every "do you know how to" question our clients asked, even when we had no idea how to do what they were asking. We figured it out as we went along, like everyone else at that time.

A big part of what enabled that jump was due to being exposed to people like Alan Cooper and Jesse James Garrett, who were talking about interaction and UX. To me, everything they talked about was exactly what design was, as I knew and practiced it—just applied to a digital medium, meaning websites, software, and Internet-based Software-as-a-Service (SAAS) products.

So, all I did when I crossed over to UX—all I've ever really done—was apply what I'd learned about graphic design: pushing clients to take a harder look at the *people* their communications and products and services needed to serve. To design those things around their expectations, needs, and cognitive behavior, so that value was communicated. So that value came back to the business from use of those products.

I grew that company, Natoli Design Group, to six employees, and then sold it to an IT firm in 2004. A few years later, I went back to independent consulting, speaking, writing, teaching, and product team training. Which is what I do to this day.

PART I

Philosophy

What makes a team of one special is that you find yourself in situations where not only do you see an opportunity for a more user-centered approach, but you also need to lead the charge, bringing others along with you. A team of one has to challenge the mighty forces of the status quo, inertia, and other people's ways of doing things. That's brave and ambitious work. It requires not only technical know-how, but also vision, conviction, and a soft touch.

This part of the book will arm you with all of the above. The approach outlined here can help you enter, impact, and evolve this exciting field. And it may just help you convert the masses as well—one person at a time.

CHAPTER 1

UX 101

Talking about user experience (UX) can be a bit like looking at an inkblot test: whatever matters the most to you ends up being what you see. People find their way to this industry through a variety of pathways, and they naturally apply their own lenses to how they think about and describe the work of UX. What's more, the definition of this field and the work involved varies widely across the industries and organizations who hire people to improve the experience of using their products and services. As a result, user experience is a famously messy thing to describe. This chapter will attempt to balance out the picture by giving you a simple definition of UX to work with, a little more information about where it comes from, and an understanding of how it's different from other fields.

Defining User Experience

UX, despite having been around for quite a while now, remains a controversial concept. At this point, hundreds of thousands of people have offered their own definition, and yet no single one has prevailed as the clear favorite. Part of the confusion stems from the fact that *user experience* is a general term that describes not only a professional practice, but also a resulting *outcome*. Another part stems from the fact that there's a lot of disagreement about what people who do UX work should call themselves (see sidebar, "What's in a Name?"). The situation is further complicated by the fact that the companies who hire people in UX roles don't always know what to call them either.

Essentially, to work in user experience means to practice a set of methods and techniques for researching what users want and need, and to design products and services for them. Through good UX, you're trying to reduce the friction between the task someone wants to accomplish and the tool that they are using to complete that task. But the job of doing that is bigger than it sounds.

The degree to which people find an app, site, or system useful, usable, or valuable is dependent on any number of influencing factors, and that list is so vast that no one person, team, or even technology can claim to be responsible for it (see Figure 1.1).

As a simple working definition, you might say that a user experience is the overall effect created by the expectations, perceptions, and interactions that someone has when using a product or service (see Figure 1.2). The quality of UX is often determined by how large the gap is between what a user expects (how they expect it to work) and what the product delivers (how it actually works). People usually describe the size of that gap—and the experience of using the product—with words like *love* or *hate,* or phrases such as *easy to use* or *pain in the butt.*

FIGURE 1.1
Often, the term user experience refers to the encounters that people have with digital products, from apps to websites to software to gaming and beyond.

FIGURE 1.2
User experience is not just restricted to what you do on your phone or your laptop. This bank ATM has an interactive user experience that impacts how easily people can withdraw, deposit, or transfer money.

 For as long as I've been doing this—three decades now—not a week goes by where someone doesn't ask me to define UX, to explain what it means to me. The answer to that question is a model I've developed that reflects a reality almost always left out of the conversation. This piece that we don't talk enough about is the critical relationship that makes UX, design, and development efforts successful; it ensures that we design, build, and deliver something of value. I call it the *UX Value Loop*, and it works like this (see Figure 1.3).

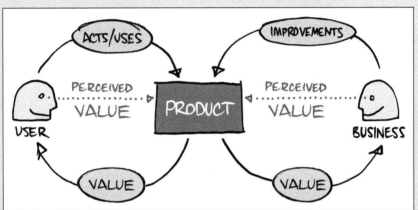

FIGURE 1.3
Joe Natoli's UX Value Loop.

You've got a *product* in the middle: a site, an app, a system, a printer, a guitar, whatever the case may be. On one side, you've got a *user*, the person who is going to use this thing. And on the other side, you've got the *business* that created it, who spent the money necessary to make it a reality.

The first critical part of the loop is that the user has to perceive there is value for them in this product. Let's say you and I are talking about work, and I say, "You should check out this app; it's totally helped me get organized." From that conversation, you perceive that this app may help you as well. So, you read some reviews that convince you to download and try it, or even buy it.

Once you take that action, here's what has to happen next for the loop to work: the very first time you use or interact with that app, it's got to give value *back to you* in some way. Something has to happen, almost immediately, that makes you think, "Wow, this is really cool." Or "Wow, that was easy." Or "Wow, this is going to make my life so much easier because I won't ever have to do A, B, C, or D ever again—I can do it here in this app!" **Value of some kind has to come back to you from that first use.**

That's half the loop. The other half is this: In addition to the value that goes out to the user, **value also has to come back to the organization as a result of that use** (or download, trial subscription, or purchase). This value is usually in the form of money made or money saved, but it can also be in the form of greater awareness of the product in the marketplace, more people signing up for something, or more social media followers. Whatever it is, it's got to help that business in some measurable way that every stakeholder in that organization is tasked to care about.

So, value has to come back to those stakeholders and to the company as a whole. Performance or efficiency metrics met, sign-ups increased, money made, money saved, etc. If that happens—if they get some positive result from people using what they put out there—now *they* perceive the product is valuable. Which is critical to enabling the next part of the loop.

Now they're willing to invest in improving, redesigning, or otherwise updating it. This could mean improving existing features, simplifying and streamlining processes, or increasing speed and performance. Now they roll out successive, updated releases that make users or customers say, "Wow, this just keeps getting better and more awesome!" Which ensures that those people keep using it and keep paying for the upgrade or subscription. Which keeps this entire cycle going.

I want to stress again that **the business side is the side we all forget about all too often.** Some people believe (for reasons I don't understand) that only people with the title "product designer" are supposed to care about business goals, which is both untrue and ridiculous. If you design *anything* in any way for an organization, you had better have some understanding of what the business folks who work there *need* from that product's existence. *All* UXers and designers are responsible for designing well for both sides of the value loop.

Why? Because if value doesn't come back to the business from that product, they will have no reason to want to improve the experience of using it.

Given that we transact so much of our lives through technology, how easy or difficult something is to use is what really matters. And that's what user experience is all about.

But while user experience is obviously about meeting the needs of users, it's also about meeting the needs of the businesses who fund the creation of these products and services. This part isn't talked about often enough, but it's of critical importance. Any investment in improving UX or product design comes with an expectation that there will be a return on this investment. Joe describes this need to serve both users and businesses with what he calls the *UX Value Loop*.™

As a field of professional practice, UX encompasses several disciplines. The main contributors are user research, information architecture, interaction design, and user interface design:

- **User research** is about understanding users and their needs, not just what they want or expect, but why they want or expect it.
- **Information architecture** (IA) is about uncovering and determining how information should be labeled, organized, prioritized, and related.
- **Interaction design** (IxD) is designing how people move through that information onscreen, how they interact with content or data, and what the system does in response (and when) to their actions.
- **User interface (UI) design** is designing what people see on the screen—fonts, colors, images, buttons, menus, etc.—and how those elements serve to create and reinforce understanding and guide the user through screens, content, and interactions.

As a result of this interdependence, it's become common to see people and companies mixing and matching these terms into inventive (and often confusing) titles. A rather large percentage of those titles have been adopted for user experience roles. Which one you use depends largely on what terms your employer believes are appropriate. The professional UX community, at the time of this writing, is extremely divided on the topic of what we should call ourselves.

And things get even trickier when you start talking about the subdisciplines that make up UX. Historically, the user experience community hasn't done a great job of standardizing its job titles, so the confusion that people new to this profession have is understandable. By way of example, a quick scan of user experience job postings will unearth a grab bag of job titles:

- UX Designer
- UX Architect
- UX Analyst
- UX Specialist
- UX Researcher
- UX Writer
- UX Engineer
- UX Developer
- UX/UI Designer
- UX/UI Developer
- UI Designer
- Experience Designer
- Product Designer
- Service Designer
- Business Designer
- Behavioral Designer
- Interaction Designer
- Content Designer
- Human Factors Designer
- Human Factors Engineer
- Usability Analyst
- Usability Researcher
- Usability Engineer

To add to the mix, there are other disciplines and roles that directly contribute to the resulting experience that a user has with a product, even if they may not fit as snugly into the job description of a user experience designer. Roles that impact and shape the UX of a product include *Product Owner, Product Manager, Project Manager, Business Analyst, Front-End Developer, Software Architect, Engineer, Programmer, Database Architect,* and many more. And for the sake of brevity, we're not even going to get into the influence of Sales and Marketing departments!

In this field (and especially online), you'll find no shortage of heated discussions about who gets to claim ownership of the user experience. Without fueling the flames, let's just say that for the purposes of this book, if you do *any* of these things, you're contributing to the user experience of your product. As such, this book is for you.

Along with that rather complicated list of titles, there are also infinite permutations on all of the above. Ultimately, though, these roles all address product design. They all require an understanding of the needs of users and customers who use the product, as well as the goals of the business that funded the creation of the product. The bottom line here is that no matter what the job title may be, the work that people do in UX typically falls into one of the following categories:

- **Interaction Design and Information Architecture.** Someone who designs the structure and detailed interactions of a site, app, or system. This person decides where people can go, what they can see and interact with, how they get from one place to the next—along with what signposts and controls should exist, where they belong, and how they'll be used. Once upon a time, these were separate roles, with good reason, but it's become commonplace for one person to be responsible for both.

  You could certainly argue that interaction designers focus on screens, detailed interactions, and workflows, whereas information architects focus on information structures, controlled and uncontrolled metadata, and ultimately, findability. However, both roles share a fundamental goal: designing how a user moves through a complex information system from moment to moment. So, for the sake of simplicity, we've combined them together here.

- **Visual or User Interface (UI) Design.** Someone who focuses on the visual layer of an application or product, employing clear and intuitive elements, such as buttons, icons, menus, and navigation, making it easy for users to understand how to interact with the product, guiding them through the interface seamlessly, reducing cognitive load, and minimizing the learning curve. A visual or UI designer establishes clear visual communication, hierarchy, and provides cues to act, using techniques like size, color, contrast, proximity, and alignment to emphasize important elements and guide users' attention. This allows users to quickly understand the relative importance and relationships between different interface elements.

  UI designers create interactive elements, animations, and visual feedback to provide users with a sense of control and response. They create interfaces that are responsive and adaptive to various devices and screen sizes, so that the UI remains usable and visually appealing across different devices. Finally, a visual or UI designer ensures that the UI is usable, inclusive, and accessible for all people. Considerations like contrast, color, typography, screen reader compatibility, and assisted navigation allow a wider range of users to interact with the product effectively. But the key part of a UI designer's job actually isn't the visual output they create; rather, it's the *appropriateness* of those visual decisions, informed by an understanding of how and why people respond to what they see on the screen in various ways—psychologically, emotionally, and physically.

- **User Research and Testing.** Someone who conducts research into user needs and behavior, along with testing products at various stages of completion with actual users to determine what needs improvement. This research could be *qualitative*—for example, one-on-one interviews with a handful of people to gain a rich understanding of their motivations and experiences. This research could also be *quantitative*—for example, sampling large pools of people to uncover broad trends in attitudes, behaviors, pain points, and the like.

  The research usually spans up-front discovery of user needs all the way through to product validation and usability testing. A researcher is like a demographer that uncovers who really lives in these spaces, how they use them, and what important factors characterize and inform that use.

- **UX Writing and Content Strategy.** Someone who thinks strategically about the role of content across the entire product, including the language and labeling used in interactive onscreen elements and navigation menus. Content strategists consider what messages are being delivered to users, how the language should be framed, what the voice and tone of the product is, and how and when the content will be created (and by whom). UX writers write UI text for elements like menus, labels, error messages, or chatbots to support the user as they interact with, or experience, a product.

  Basically, the content strategist sets the tone for the tenor of conversations that take place here. What topics do people talk about? What's the local dialect? What stories get told? How do the people who live here ultimately communicate with each other?

Most UX teams of one act as generalists, blending some or all of the above roles together. More often than not, if you see the title UX designer or UX/UI designer, it's usually a catchall role that requires working in all of these areas.

UX in Context: It's Not Just One Thing

Personally, we think it's easier to understand UX when you think about what it's like to actually use a product. For example, maybe right now you're sitting on the couch with your tablet, hopping around from your favorite note-taking app to checking your social media apps to researching in a browser to cueing up playlists in your music app. Your perception of each of those apps is impacted by how each looks, how it functions, and how well it serves its purpose in the personal need that it satisfies (helping you think through your to-do list, promoting your content via social media, managing your personal and professional communications, and listening to some tunes that keep your toes tapping as you work, respectively). In any of these apps, a thousand little decisions were made by someone—or more likely, *many someones*—to create what you experience as a flowing, seamless experience of working (see Figure 1.4).

PHOTO COURTESY OF COTTONBRO STUDIO

FIGURE 1.4
A user's experience is the cumulative effect of many factors, some that you can control, and some that you can't.

And that's just the software. Your user experience is also impacted by the physical hardware of the tablet: How big and bright the screen is, and whether it feels like "enough" to help you effectively use all those apps. For example, the texture of the protective case you're using, along with how you need to hold or position it; the feel of the glass as you tap, swipe, or scroll; and the responsiveness of the stylus as you increase the pressure or use it to change settings or switch apps. These are all user experiences, too.

And what about the products and services that are connected to that iPad? Maybe you've set up an in-home music system that plays tunes from the music app on your tablet or smartphone via Bluetooth? You can control the volume from your phone and hear the music get quieter or louder on the speakers in the other room. This is great execution on the part of the music system manufacturer, to be sure. But it also casts a warm glow back on your tablet and mobile phone, for being well-designed to support such integration.

The point here is that a user's perception of the product is often beyond the control of any one manufacturer; instead, it's the cumulative effect of *many* (see Figure 1.5).

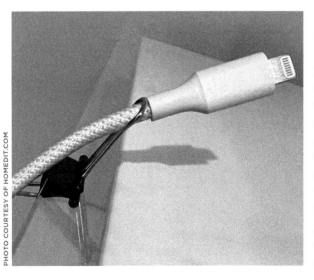

FIGURE 1.5
In the absence of better alternatives, users will try to hack together their own solutions, as this remote worker has, but the companies who make the products that we love do a better-than-average job thinking about the complexities of the user experience.

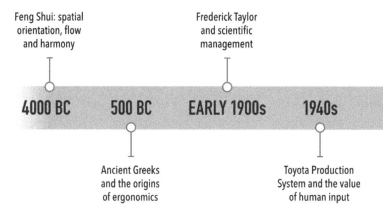

FIGURE 1.6

UX has a long and storied history that intersects with other business, design, and technology developments that your colleagues may be familiar with.

Where UX Comes From

As a team of one, knowing the history of user experience can help you reassure people that it's not just something you dreamed up (see Figure 1.6). If we were to sum up the history of UX in a few short sentences, it might go something like this, which comes from Leah:

> Villains of industry seek to deprive us of our humanity. Scientists, scholars, and designers prevail, and a new profession flourishes, turning man's submission to technology into technology's submission to man.

Pretty exciting stuff.

Now here's the longer version. User experience is a modern field, but it's been in the making for more than a century. To see its beginnings, you can look all the way back to the machine age of the late 19th and early 20th centuries. At that time, corporations were growing, skilled labor was declining, and advances in machine technology were inspiring industry to push the boundaries of what human labor could make possible.

The machine age philosophy was best exemplified by people like Frederick Winslow Taylor and Henry Ford, who both pioneered ways to make human labor more efficient, productive, and routinized. It's worth noting, however, that they were criticized for dehumanizing workers in the process, treating people like cogs in a machine. Still,

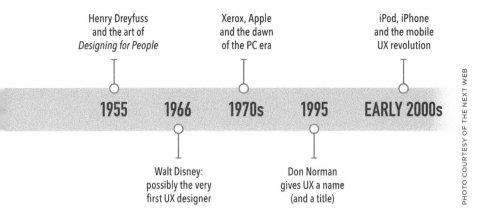

Henry Dreyfuss
and the art of
Designing for People

Xerox, Apple
and the dawn
of the PC era

iPod, iPhone
and the mobile
UX revolution

1955   **1966**   **1970s**   **1995**   **EARLY 2000s**

Walt Disney:
possibly the very
first UX designer

Don Norman
gives UX a name
(and a title)

Taylor's research into the efficiency of interactions between workers and their tools was an early precursor to much of what UX professionals think about today (see Figure 1.7).

FIGURE 1.7
Frederick Winslow
Taylor, the father of
Scientific Manage-
ment, pejoratively
known as *Taylorism*.

The first half of the 20th century also saw an emerging body of research into what later became the fields of human factors and ergonomics. Motivated by research into aeromedics in World War I and World War II, human factors focused on the design of equipment and devices to best align with human capabilities.

> **NOTE** THE ORIGINS OF ERGONOMICS
>
> In the late 1940s, research into pilot errors in the cockpit by Lieutenant Colonel Paul Fitts (who was also a psychologist) led to recommendations for the most effective organization of cockpit control knobs. Several years later, Fitts would coin Fitts's Law, one of the basic laws of physics for user experience designers (especially in the era of handheld smartphones). Fitts's Law states that the time required to move to a target is determined by the distance and size of that target.

By the mid 20th century, industrial efficiency and human ingenuity were striking a more harmonious relationship at places like Toyota. The Toyota Production System continued to value efficiency but treated workers as key contributors to a continually improving process. One of the core tenets of the Toyota philosophy was respect for people, which resulted in inviting workers to help troubleshoot and optimize the processes that they were a part of. For example, workers at Toyota factories could pull a rope to stop the assembly line if they saw a defect or a way to improve the process. Their feedback was encouraged, valued, and used.

Around the same time, industrial designer Henry Dreyfuss wrote *Designing for People*, a classic design text that, like the Toyota system, put people first. In it, Dreyfuss described many of the methods that UX designers employ today to understand and design for user needs, as shown in Figure 1.8. In *Designing for People*, Henry Dreyfuss wrote:

> When the point of contact between the product and the people becomes a point of friction, then the [designer] has failed. On the other hand, if people are made safer, more comfortable, more eager to purchase, more efficient—or just plain happier—by contact with the product, then the designer has succeeded.

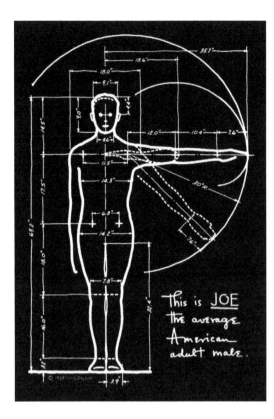

This is JOE the average American adult male.

FIGURE 1.8
Dreyfuss created Joe (and a companion diagram, Josephine) to remind us that everything we design is for people.

At the same time, some interesting parallel movements were taking shape. A small handful of academics were doing research into what we now describe as *cognitive science*. As a discipline, cognitive science combined an interest in human cognition (especially human capacity for short-term memory) with concepts like artificial and machine intelligence. These cognitive scientists were interested in the potential of computers to serve as a tool to augment human mental capacities.

Many early wins in the design of computers for human use came from PARC, a Xerox research center founded in the early 1970s to explore innovations in workplace technology. PARC's work in the mid-1970s produced many user interface conventions that are still used today—the graphical user interface, the mouse, and computer-generated bitmap graphics. For example, PARC's work greatly influenced the first commercially available graphical user interface, otherwise known as the *Apple Macintosh*.

The term *user experience* probably originated in the early 1990s at Apple when cognitive psychologist Donald Norman joined the staff. Various accounts from people who were there at the time say that Norman introduced *user experience* to encompass what had, up to that point, been described as *human interface research*. He held the title *user experience architect*, possibly the first person to ever have UX on his business card.

Norman actually started out in cognitive psychology, but his writing on the cognitive experience of products, including technology products, made him a strong voice to lead and inspire a growing field (see Figure 1.9). He described the origin of the term like this:

> I invented the term because I thought Human Interface and usability were too narrow: I wanted to cover all aspects of the person's experience with a system, including industrial design, graphics, the interface, the physical interaction, and the manual.

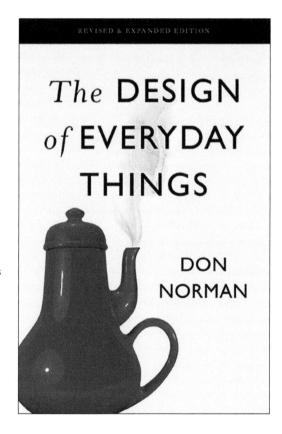

FIGURE 1.9
Norman's book *The Design of Everyday Things* is a popular text that deconstructs many of the elements that contribute to a positive or negative user experience. It's still pretty much required reading for anyone who is interested in UX.

With the rise of personal computing in the 1980s and then the web in the 1990s, many of these trends converged on each other. Graphical user interfaces, cognitive science, and designing for and with people became the foundation for the field of human-computer interaction (HCI). Suddenly, more people had access to computers, along with a greater need to understand how to use them effectively and efficiently. HCI popularized concepts like usability and interaction design, both of which were important forebears to user experience.

UX AND UI: WHAT'S THE DIFFERENCE?

You may find that the average person is more familiar with the term *UI* than *UX*. UI refers to the *user interface*, or the screen through which a person interacts with a computer or device. Because most people have used computers at one time or another and have had encounters with UIs that were both good and bad, they often have some idea of what a UI is and why it matters. UX, on the other hand, is a more intangible concept that encompasses not just UI, but also the hardware, the user's context of use, and the user's goals and motivations. That's a lot harder to cram into one mental picture.

And what isn't talked about nearly enough is the fact that UX and UI are very dependent on one another. Good UX is impossible without equally good UI design, because those visual attributes make it easier for people to interact with what they see on the screen. UI design serves as visual evidence of what exists and what's possible: it determines whether they know what to tap, swipe, or click—and whether what happens meets their expectations and moves them closer to their goals.

When people open an app or visit a website, they already know what they want and expect from it before they do so. Because of this, the job of UI design and designers is to make sure that every element they place onscreen tells those people that it's all here, as expected, and it shows them where to start while guiding them along the way. Designing appropriate visual cues so people know where and how to take action is very much a user experience concern.

continues

To explain the difference to others, it can be helpful to provide a tangible example. For example, PayByPhone is a service that integrates with parking meters to solve a basic problem: paying for parking even if you don't have change. The picture on the left in Figure 1.10 is the mobile app's user interface or UI. The picture on the right conveys some sense of the broader user experience of needing to pay for your parking, discovering that there's an alternative way to pay, and then trying to figure out how to do it.

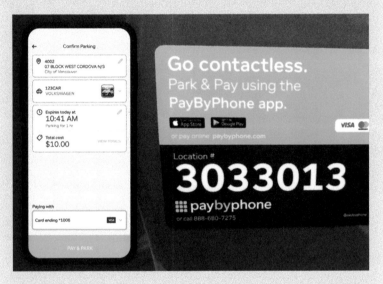

FIGURE 1.10
With the PayByPhone service, the user interface is just one part of the overall user experience.

In the internet bubble of the mid and late-1990s, new jobs with titles like *web designer, interaction designer,* and *information architect* began cropping up. As people became more experienced in these roles, a deeper and more nuanced understanding of the field of user experience began to develop. Today, UX continues to evolve in step with advances in the fields of accessibility, inclusion, and AI-driven technology, with an ever-expanding number of online on-demand courses, bootcamps, and university programs to train future genera-tions of UX and product design professionals.

Where UX Professionals Come From

The field of user experience grew primarily out of human factors and usability—both fields with very strong ties to the world of software development. As a result, people often connect UX with technology (and user interface design). This isn't completely inaccurate, but it's only one part of the story. Increasingly, UX doesn't involve a technical product at all. Service designers, growth designers, systemic designers, and those people who are designing for an increasingly networked world are all working on the same basic problem:

How can they design useful, usable, meaningful user experiences that respect, engage, and empower real people—while simultaneously delivering value back to the businesses that fund these products and services?

So, does this shared mission mean that anyone can be a user experience team of one? Not necessarily. Certain backgrounds are better springboards for a career in user experience than others. You're a good candidate for UX work if you have past experience in one or more of these areas:

- **Web or software design and development.** This is a natural one. Many of the elder statesmen of the UX world started out as webmasters or web designers. And with part or all of just about every kind of service imaginable now delivered through a browser or an app, the core focus of their work may still be web-oriented. People with this background make good UX practitioners because they've usually seen firsthand how users make sense of and interact with unfamiliar designs. The fact that they know a bit about web and software technologies helps, too.

- **Editing, journalism, or copywriting.** This field is also a common pathway into user experience because it is fundamentally about how people consume and make sense of content. That's equally true whether the content in question is printed or on a screen. People with this background are naturals at thinking about a reader's needs and perspectives, which translates directly into a user's point of view. These folks also think a lot about how voice, tone, and structure influence a reader's perceptions and experiences with a medium. That's a core consideration for good product design and UX as well.

- **Graphic or visual design.** The user experience is impacted by decisions that are made at every level of the product. But when end users think of the product, they usually think of the parts that they can see and interact with—the visible, surface level. To most people, what they see *is* the system. Graphic and visual designers are trained to think about how people see and respond to layers of visual information. They have the ability to create designs that convey and reinforce practical information and guide people through it, while also evoking a desired emotional reaction. People with this skill know how to design for understanding, as well as meaning, which is a very user-centered ethos.

- **Industrial design.** Industrial designers are uniquely positioned to transition to UX. Emphasis on design decision-making to enable scalability and material reusability creates scalable design frameworks, which increase development efficiency and help ensure consistent, reliable use and user experiences. They're used to working with partners in other functional disciplines to ensure feasibility, desirability, and viability of products. In addition, one of the core drivers of good industrial design is affordance—designing the features of an object to prompt specific use or interaction—which just so happens to be a cornerstone of great user experience as well.

- **Research, sociology, anthropology, and psychology.** Understanding and empathizing with the user's perspective is a vital foundation for UX. People with this background know how to conduct studies or experiments to uncover what people *really* do—and more importantly, *why* they do it. That can be harder than it seems; it's very easy for the observer to unconsciously change the behavior of the observed. But sociologists and anthropologists have rigorous methods and techniques for getting at what people really do. They also have the ability to turn a dizzying array of observations and data points into broader themes and, ultimately, meaning. These themes and their significance become the foundation upon which user experience and product design decisions are made.

- **Engineering.** Engineers and developers write the code and build the systems that make the experience real. That moment when a flat concept on a page becomes a working, functioning, interactive thing is like making life. It's incredibly rewarding. It also enables them to see and understand how it will feel and function for the end user. And when it doesn't feel or function like they thought it would, they iterate and adjust. Engineers are skilled at jumping back and forth between the two mindsets that make this possible: the maker's mindset and the tester's mindset. This repeating cycle of making and adjusting (and making and adjusting and…) is the fundamental flow of UX and product design.

- **Product management and business analysis.** People in these roles are often the bridge between many different parties who contribute to product design. Consequently, they have one of the broadest views of the ins and outs of the product. That holistic perspective often enables them to envision where the weak points are—not just from the perspective of the project plan or the business goals, but also from the user's or customer's experience. Product management and UX prioritize understanding and meeting the needs of users. Business analysts, product managers, UX professionals, and product designers all share a common goal of creating products or services that provide value to users and customers, while addressing their pain points and measuring success via key performance indicators (KPIs) related to user engagement, conversion rates, user satisfaction, and other relevant metrics.

- **Marketing.** The job of marketers is, at its core, to understand and connect with customers. And while there are some differences in designing for customers vs. users, an overall customer-centric mindset aligns quite well with the user-centric approach of UX. In both cases, designing for the needs and preferences of the person using the product or service are job one. And similar to the way user experience professionals work to understand user needs, motivations, and behaviors, marketers often conduct market research, analyze customer behavior, and gather insights to inform their marketing strategies. Marketers run A/B tests and experiments to optimize marketing campaigns and improve conversion rates. In UX, that same approach is used to validate product design decisions and optimize user experiences. As different as these two professions may seem on the surface, they're a lot more closely related than most people think.

A UX TEAM OF ONE CAN COME FROM ANYWHERE

A UX team of one we know started out as a general contractor. Thinking about questions like how close to place the electrical outlet in relation to the sink naturally got her thinking about user-centered problem-solving more generally. Which led her straight to user experience design.

Another was a child actor, with a career in Bollywood movies and Indian TV shows since the age of 5. He always thought he'd be an actor but grew up to enjoy his profession less and less. His sister, however, was working as a product designer, and the more he learned about it, the more excited and interested he became—and eventually he transitioned into product design.

Another was a banker when her passion for UX was sparked. The bank mandated use of a new, complicated SAP-based system that was only tailored to one type of banker (advising private clients)—but did not take into account what corporate advisory bankers like her actually did all day. The last straw? A real-estate client with 500 accounts whose address had to be updated manually—one at a time, in every single account. "I thought, there must be a way to do that better," she said. "People build great online shops for customers who come by once a month. Why can't we build great systems for people who need to work with them eight hours a day?" So, she started studying business information systems...and the rest is history.

Another was working in Robotics Research & Development for an auto manufacturer. But after four-plus years, he realized that most of the products he and his team had built were not being used by people; most of them were just collecting dust. It began to dawn on him that the problem here was that they were designing and building solutions for themselves, instead of trying to solve user problems. He heard about a World Bank–sponsored program to train developers and entrepreneurs in product design and was accepted into the program. A year later, he began his career as a product designer.

Still another was running scoreboards for a minor league baseball team. She found that those skills transitioned easily into early web design, creating animated GIFs, and designing clickable user interface components. Her next job at a hospital found her working on grant-based work for its research institute—that experience taught her how to perform traditional research methodology to verify the team had met the needs of grants. Hello, UX research!

Another was working as a doctor in Nigeria for a few years and didn't really find it to be as fulfilling as he thought it would be—the regimen and routine of medicine sucked the life out of the work. Doctors are also underpaid in Nigeria; he was barely making ends meet. A difficult personal situation was the catalyst to explore UX. A friend who helped him at the time was a UX designer and suggested maybe it was time for a change. Once he discovered that he could create something people could use—combining his love for both science and art—he was hooked.

How about you? If you have one of the titles listed previously, you may already be doing user experience work, whether you realize it or not. Or maybe you started out in one of these fields and are now crossing over. Whatever your origin, you're here now, and you believe that user experience matters. You understand that it makes the difference between products and services that must be suffered through, and those that feel pleasant, effortless, and efficient.

So…how do you start working as a UX team of one? In the next chapter, we'll take a look and find out.

A Typical UX Team of One Job Description

If you happen to be in the job market, it can be helpful to know how to spot a UX team-of-one situation. Few UX jobs are advertised as a team-of-one gig, but there are usually telltale signs that give them away. Figure 1.11 shows a job description that is adapted from several real jobs posted to a popular UX job board.

This is, in many ways, a standard UX team-of-one job description. This employer shows a clear awareness that user experience is essential in creating a competitive product, but the focus is squarely on how the product looks, instead of whether the features, functionality, and UI design are appropriate for intended users and relevant to the work they need to do.

This job description shows an employer who is looking for someone who is an "advocate for our customers and internal users," but nowhere in the job description does it ever mention doing research with actual customers or internal users. And while they may actually want research capabilities, the focus of nearly every bullet is on visual design, which is expected to be based on the candidate's existing knowledge of "human-centered design and design-thinking principles, as well as best practices for software development methodologies" and "wider industry UX trends and relevant technology trends." Which means this is really just a UI design job where, at best, you'll be expected to guess what the right solution is.

We're looking for a passionate and talented UX Designer.
This role will work closely with product managers, engineers, and developers from initial concept and strategy through the execution. Your background in human-centered design will make you an advocate for our customers and internal users as you iterate and test your concepts in a highly collaborative team environment.

Responsibilities:

- Responsible for interacting with clients to gather requirements.
- Develop personas, journey maps, storyboards, wireframes, mockups, and design elements.
- Develop low- to high-fidelity mockups to present to the client.
- Work with developers to hand off design to ensure pixel-perfect delivery.
- As part of the above, the candidate will design applications utilizing human-centered design and design-thinking principles, as well as best practices for software development methodologies, ensuring their work is compliant, efficient, and effective.
- Design and deliver wireframes, user journeys, mockups, and prototypes optimized for a wide range of devices and interfaces per client requirements.
- Monitor and know wider industry UX trends and relevant technology trends.
- Create on-brand designs and follow a project's creative vision and business strategy while putting the user first.
- Collaborate with other groups like developers, engagement managers, and UX designers to deliver high-quality, creative designs for both internal and client-facing projects.

FIGURE 1.11
A potential UX job description.

People may not say it directly, but there's usually an expectation that having someone focused on UX will magically result in visual changes to the product that will immediately impress everyone. This can be a tricky expectation to manage, since design improvements often happen gradually, over time, based on research and testing. Chapter 7, "Testing and Validation Methods," will show you how to improve the quality of the product and bring people along with you in the process.

What you also see in this job description is a common challenge that UX teams of one face—employers are often confused about the relationship between visual design and user experience design. This may point to a lack of awareness about the processes and people involved in user experience work, or an unwillingness to do anything more than make things pretty. In these kinds of organizations, the strategic side of UX is often seen as a *nice to have*. And it can also mean that the idea of actually talking to users or customers scares the folks in charge, because they're worried about what problems that research may reveal.

We're not trying to scare you here; we just want you to be prepared for what you may have to deal with on the job.

Now, some user experience professionals *do* include graphic design in their arsenal of tools, but many do not. You can still be a UX or product designer even if you just stop at wireframes, but generalists—which most teams of one are—are often called upon to do a bit of visual design as well. To get a sense of what your colleagues do and don't know about user experience work, take them out to lunch and have a casual conversation. Consider a "Captive UX" campaign (see Chapter 8, "Evangelism Methods") to promote a broader understanding of the roles and functions of user experience.

More UX-mature employers expect UX practitioners to be able to back up their recommendations and show their work. These organizations may also expect practitioners to challenge and persuade others in the organization to adopt new approaches. All of which points to the reality that UX teams of one sometimes have to be diplomatic, informed, and well-meaning *meddlers*.

If You Only Do One Thing...

...remember the UX Value Loop! This chapter establishes some basic information about the field of user experience: what it is, where it comes from, and what skills it requires. We begin this way because understanding what user experience is and being able to explain its importance to other people is the first, and often the hardest, thing you need to do. As a UX team of one, you are pretty much guaranteed to find yourself in situations where you are asked to clarify what UX is and justify why it's important. Your first line of defense—and the most important thing you should take away from this chapter—is Joe's *UX Value Loop*.

The value loop drives all the *intentional* work described here that has to happen in so many related areas in order to deliver meaningful user experiences. Try to think about this in terms of examples— either the examples given in this chapter or one of your own. Examples are effective at triggering memory and imagination. A well-chosen example will help you illustrate the complexity of UX and what design elements must be executed well in order to create a useful, usable, valuable, and memorable user experience. And remember this as well:

UX happens whether or not there are any "UX people" on staff.

All created and delivered experiences are either *intentional* or *unintentional*. And when they're unintentional... they're usually bad.

CHAPTER 2

Getting Started

A s you read in the last chapter—and in Leah and Joe's stories in the Introduction—many people make their way to UX by crossing over from an adjacent field. What you may not realize, though, is that these crossovers are the people who are carrying the profession forward, taking it to new levels in new ways, in new kinds of organizations.

In this chapter, you'll find a basic framework for diving in and doing the same. And to be honest, *framework* may be overstating the case. It's really just five simple steps:

1. Get to know the UX improvement process.

2. Establish a point of view on what can be improved.

3. Get to know your users and customers.

4. Explore required information architecture.

5. Start designing.

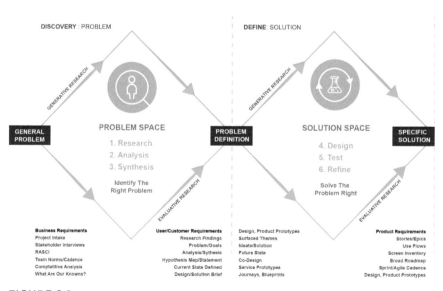

FIGURE 2.1

Thomas Ian Wilson's triple-diamond UX model.

Get to Know the UX Improvement Process

Countless models and diagrams have been created to illustrate the typical UX set of offerings and activities. They can be a great place to start in understanding the UX and product design process, and how it fits in with other business processes (see Figures 2.1–2.3). The rise (and, well, complete takeover) of Agile and Lean software development methods has led to entirely new approaches to how and when UX and product design work happen. Let's take a look at a few—but keep in mind that these models are only starting points, not ironclad recipes. All processes, methods, and techniques often have to flex, change, and adapt according to the context in which they exist: a company's culture, its existing processes, and interpersonal team and management dynamics all impact what happens, as well as *how* it happens.

Figure 2.1 shows a model created by Thomas Ian Wilson, which he refers to as the *triple diamond*. This is generally the model found in most UX-mature organizations. Activities are conducted in an iterative, user-centered design process where teams identify the right problem to solve (*discovery*), solve the problem appropriately (*define*), minimize risk by building iteratively (*develop*), release and test (*deliver*), and finally, analyze what worked and what didn't (*retrospective*).

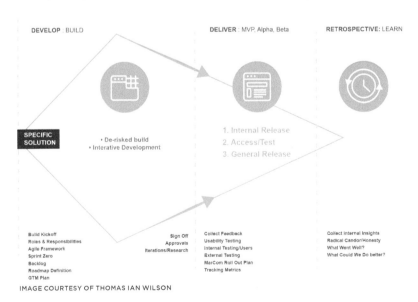

IMAGE COURTESY OF THOMAS IAN WILSON

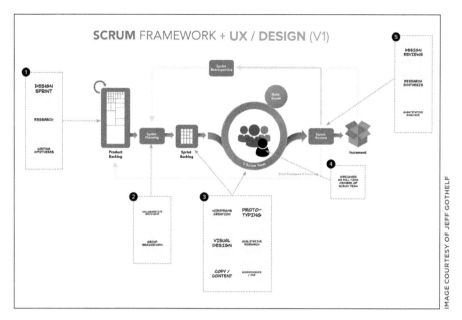

SCRUM FRAMEWORK + UX / DESIGN (V1)

IMAGE COURTESY OF JEFF GOTHELF

FIGURE 2.2

Jeff Gothelf's model for Scrum and UX Integration.

By contrast, the model in Figure 2.2 from Jeff Gothelf overlays UX and design activities on top of a well-founded model of Scrum, an Agile project management system commonly used in software development and other industries. Scrum prescribes that teams break up work into goals, to be completed within timeboxed iterations, called *sprints*. Each sprint typically lasts two weeks.

Figure 2.3 shows a model from Dave Landis, combining design thinking, Lean UX, and Agile product development. Here, design thinking seeks to figure out how to innovate and understand users; Lean UX helps the team validate that they're building the right thing and testing/measuring market fit; Agile UX is used to integrate activities and help people work together better and more closely. The idea is that combining these methods results in building the right thing, the right way.

As you can see from these examples, while there's no certified process that all UX practitioners follow, you'll find a relatively common set of activities and deliverables that they all use. A large UX team may have the luxury of conducting most of these activities on a given engagement. Teams of one use many of these methods, too, but quite often you're only doing small parts of the larger process, in less depth, without combining them all into a full-fledged work plan. That's largely because when you're the sole resource for UX—or a member of a small UX team—it's highly likely you won't have the time, resources, or budget that you need in order to pull it all off.

FIGURE 2.3

The "Better Together" model of design thinking, Lean UX and Agile, created by Dave Landis.

We need you to understand right now that this is OK! If you find yourself in these situations, remember that *something* is almost always better than *nothing*; any amount of research, for example, is always better than guessing. The bottom line: just do the best you can with what you have to work with.

That said, it's helpful to start with an understanding of the following options and activities, and then think about which ones seem most useful and relevant to the work you're doing. Think of this like having a huge collection of tools. You'll never likely use them *all* for any single job, but when different kinds of jobs come up requiring different tools than the last, you'll be glad you have them all.

In that spirit, what follows is a fairly exhaustive list detailing the kinds of work that may take place during UX and product design. Most of the methods described here are further explained in Part II of this book, "Practice." Where that's the case, you'll see a cross reference.

Discovery

All product design work starts with figuring out where you stand and what you need to do so you can design products that meet both user and business needs. In this initial phase of the product design process, researchers—and UX or product designers—collect information and insights about a project to better understand the problem to be solved, the people who will use it, and the context in which they'll do so. By the end of initial Discovery work, a UX team of one should have a solid understanding of the problem space, target users, and project requirements.

Discovery is the critical inch of UX and product design work because it lays the foundation for the entire UX design process. It also goes a long way in making sure that subsequent design and development decisions are based on a deep understanding of both the user's needs and the business's goals. Product managers, designers, developers, and programmers can use the work done here as a constant reference point as work progresses, to make sure that their decisions and their work supports the intended goals of the project.

- **Stakeholder Interviews.** Here, you spend time with key decision-makers to understand their expectations for the product, along with their concerns, insights, feedback, and perspectives on what constitutes success. It's important to note that this definition of success represents both their personal and political interests, as well as the broader goals and interests of the business. By design, every department and departmental leader has a slightly different perspective on what *success* means for them. Because of that, the *intent* behind their decisions and the work they do on the project differs as well. This can cause bumps in the road because what the VP of Sales wants may be very different from what the VP of Customer Support or the VP of Product wants. Including everyone's goals and intent helps everyone involved make informed decisions that increase the chances of project success.

- **Competitive Analysis.** Evaluate similar, competing products or services by conducting a SWOT (strengths, weaknesses, opportunities, threats) analysis, using various methods. First developed as a strategic planning tool, a number of UX techniques, such as competitive review, content audits, and heuristic or expert reviews, ultimately inform this analysis. It starts with identifying both direct and indirect competitors. Direct competitors offer similar products or services that serve the *same users* your product does, while indirect competitors typically provide alternative solutions that fulfill similar needs. A SWOT analysis compares features, design, quality, pricing, customer service, reviews, and any other factors that differentiate one competitor from another—and from your company and its product that you're working to improve. (See "Opportunity Workshop" in Chapter 4 for an inclusive technique that gathers SWOT information with the help of a team.)

- **Primary User Research.** This includes various methods for learning from users firsthand. Primary user research may include field research, diary studies, surveys, and other forms of guerilla research. This direct investigation can provide deep insights into the needs, behaviors, preferences, and pain points of users and customers. It usually means interacting with real users through interviews, observed use, usability testing, and field studies. The main goal of primary user research is to gather real, context-specific information to understand user motivations and challenges. Which, in turn, leads to more informed, empathetic design decisions. (See "Guerilla User Research" in Chapter 5, "Research Methods," for quick and dirty tips for conducting primary user research.)

- **Secondary User Research.** Here, you're gathering and analyzing existing data previously collected by other researchers or sources. For example, this could include publicly available research or research that's been conducted by other parts of the organization. (Marketing segmentation is one of the most useful forms of secondary user research, so if your organization has done segmentation work, definitely start there.) Unlike primary user research, which involves direct interaction with users, secondary research involves reviewing literature, market reports, academic papers, industry studies, and any publicly available data related to users, the product, or the industry. This is meant to supplement and help validate primary research findings, gain a broader understanding of user behaviors and trends, and leverage existing knowledge to inform design decisions. It also saves valuable time and resources, allowing you to build on existing insights while giving a deeper perspective on user needs and expectations.

- **Personas, Mental Models, and User Stories.** These are documents that synthesize what you've learned about users through primary and secondary research, and they distill the key points into a handful of memorable profiles, with supporting diagrams and stories for how the product should fit into their lives. They are essential elements that work together to inform and shape a user-centered design process. *Personas* are fictional representations of typical users, based on research data, and they help designers empathize with and understand their target audience. *Mental models* are the internal representations and beliefs that users have about a product or system, influencing their interactions and expectations. *User stories* are concise, user-focused narratives that capture specific user goals and scenarios, serving as the foundation for feature development.

  When combined, personas provide insight into user characteristics and needs, mental models reveal how users approach and perceive the product, and user stories articulate user requirements, ensuring that design decisions are aligned with real user behaviors and expectations, leading to more effective and meaningful user experiences. (See "User Archetypes" in Chapter 5 for more on personas. Indi Young's book, *Mental Models*, is also an excellent resource on mental models.)

- **User Journey Mapping.** A visual representation and storytelling technique that details the user's emotions, actions, motivations, and pain points from the time they consider interacting with a product or service to the time they finish using it and achieve an outcome. A user journey map includes all the different channels, devices, or platforms that the user engages with during their journey. It also hypothesizes the user's emotional state at different stages of that journey, which helps designers understand moments of delight, frustration, confusion, or satisfaction. This helps them figure out what enhancements might maximize positive emotions and minimize negative ones.

- **Requirements Generation.** The process of working with business decision-makers and others on the team to explore what features and functionality might be appropriate for the product—based on user needs and business goals—and, in some cases, how it might be implemented. Requirements serve as the foundation for project planning, design, development, and UX efforts, ensuring that what gets built fulfills stakeholder expectations and delivers value to the product's intended users or customers. (See "Strategy Workshop" in Chapter 4 for a method that uncovers explicit and implicit requirements.)

- **Scope of Work and Constraints.** Here's where you identify the constraints and limitations that impact what's possible in any given project, such as time, budget, and technical limitations. *Scope* defines what will be included and excluded from the project and the work to be done. In terms of UX, that usually means specific features, functionalities, and user interactions that the product or service will have. Defining scope clearly also helps prevent what's called *scope creep*, the gradual expansion of project requirements beyond the original plan, which delays progress and increases cost.

Strategy

While it conjures up visions of complexity and formality, all this official-sounding word really means is establishing a vision for the target user experience, so you can design products that are coherent and unified. *Strategy* is the result of multiple tasks, activities, and processes.

- **Design Principles.** A small handful of characteristics that collectively embody how the product design should be experienced by users. These typically include attributes such as simplicity, consistency, accuracy, efficiency, accessibility, inclusivity, clarity and feedback, error prevention and recovery, performance/speed, and more. The purpose of establishing these principles is to offer clear direction and purpose for design and UX. They serve as a compass, guiding and simplifying decision-making and design choices throughout the project. And perhaps most importantly, they serve as a shared "language" of sorts among all team members and stakeholders, enabling collaboration and making sure that everyone is working toward the same goals. (See "Design Brief" in Chapter 6, "Design Methods," for more information.)

- **Vision Artifacts.** Diagrams, schematics, storyboards, or vision movies convey the essence of the user experience and give a taste of how a person might experience a product that follows this strategy in the context of their normal lives. (See the tips for planning a "Strategy Workshop" in Chapter 4 to learn how to create low-fidelity vision artifacts with the help of your team.)

- **Minimum Viable Product (MVP).** An *MVP* is a test version of a product with just enough features to be usable by early customers, who can then provide feedback for future product design, development, and improvement. This term was coined in 2001 by CEO Frank Robinson for his consulting business SyncDev, and was later popularized by Eric Ries in his book, *The Lean Startup*. The key premise here is that you produce an actual product with a minimal feature set, offer it to customers, and observe their actual behavior using it, because seeing what people actually do is much more reliable than asking them what they would do. The sooner you can find out whether the product appeals to users and customers, the less effort and expense that's spent on designing and building features (or a product) no one wants.

It's worth noting, however, that this approach has some serious pitfalls. Many organizations and teams who use the term *MVP* don't fully understand its intended use. They mistakenly believe that an MVP is the smallest possible amount of functionality they can deliver. This approach omits the most important requirement of an MVP: including the core features in a way that they deliver an experience that is useful and valuable to intended users. Delivering something without considering whether it's the *right something* that satisfies user or customer needs is a product those users don't want, don't need, or can't use. In other words, teams often stress the *minimum* part of MVP but exclude the *viable* part. What's delivered is too low-quality to provide an accurate assessment of whether anyone will want to use it, much less pay for it. In addition, teams often deliver what's considered to be an MVP, but never make any further changes to that product, regardless of feedback they receive about it.

To combat this, Joe often suggests to clients that they replace the "V" in MVP with "valuable" instead of "viable." No matter how small the feature set may be, it has to be valuable enough to the users or customers you test it with for them to actually use it. Otherwise, you learn nothing about the true demand and need for that product—or the relevance, appropriateness, usefulness, and viability of what it provides to people.

- **Accessibility and Inclusivity Guidelines.** An effective UX strategy considers accessibility and inclusivity, ensuring that the product is usable and enjoyable by a diverse range of users, delivering inclusive and equal opportunities for all users, regardless of their abilities or characteristics. Guidelines may address the use of inclusive content, context, language, and terminology that respects and reflects diverse cultures, identities, and experiences. In addition, this up-front strategy work considers how the product or service will be compatible with various assistive technologies, such as screen readers, voice recognition software, and alternative input devices. As advocates for your fellow humans, it's your responsibility to make sure that you're designing equitable digital experiences for users—especially those who are all too often left out of the conversation.

- **Usability Testing Plan.** Incorporating a plan for usability testing into the UX strategy allows designers to create a framework for validating design decisions and identifying any usability issues before the product's launch. Typically, users are given specific tasks or scenarios to complete using the product and simulating real-world interactions. For example, the given task might be, "Imagine you are planning to buy a smartphone from (this website). Find a smartphone that meets your needs and fits your budget, add it to your shopping cart, and proceed to checkout." UX researchers or product designers observe how those users navigate the user interface in order to achieve this goal, noting where they have trouble finding information, or where they hesitate or become confused.

  Because the task simulates real-world behavior, it exposes the areas where the website's design fails to support the user's expectation and understanding of how to do something. (See Chapter 7, "Testing and Validation Methods.")

- **Consistency and Branding.** UX strategy includes considerations for maintaining consistency in design elements and aligning the user experience with the overall branding of the organization. Consistent design elements and branding create a sense of familiarity for users across different parts of a product or website—or across multiple systems inside an organization. An overarching strategy for creating and maintaining consistency in both UI design and interactive system behavior reduces cognitive load. For example, if things look and behave consistently from screen to screen or system to system, users don't have to relearn interactions or make sense of new design patterns. Eliminating the distraction and confusion of inconsistent or unfamiliar elements allows people to focus on the things they came to your site, app, or system to accomplish.

- **Measurement and Metrics.** Defining key performance indicators (KPIs) and metrics to measure the success of the user experience is an integral part of UX strategy. This data-driven approach helps assess the effectiveness of design decisions. While the choice of KPIs depends on the type of product or service, user goals, and specific project objectives, some examples of common KPIs include the following:
  - **Task Success Rate.** This measures the percentage of users who successfully complete specific tasks or actions within the product or website.
  - **Time on Task.** Time on task measures the average time taken by users to complete specific tasks; a lower time often indicates better usability or efficiency.
  - **Error Rate.** This is the percentage of user interactions that result in errors or mistakes; high error rates point to areas of content, design, or interaction in need of improvement or clarification.
  - **System Usability Scale (SUS) or Customer Satisfaction Score (CSAT).** The SUS is a set of ten questions that measure users' perceptions of the product's usability and overall satisfaction. The CSAT score is a customer experience metric that measures happiness with a product, service, or customer support interaction through a customer satisfaction survey, which typically asks some variation of "How satisfied were you with [product, service or company]?"
  - **Conversion Rate.** For e-commerce websites or apps with specific conversion goals (e.g., sign-ups, downloads, purchases), the conversion rate measures the percentage of users who complete the desired action.
  - **Retention Rate.** This measures the percentage of users who return to a product, website, app, or system over a specific period; high retention rates suggest a positive user experience and ongoing value to users.

Design

This is the job of imagining and defining how a user will encounter a product or service from moment to moment in the most intuitive, clear, and enjoyable way possible. And since we mentioned one of the most overused words in UX and design—*intuitive*—let's take a moment to clarify what it actually means: single-trial learning.

Intuitive doesn't mean that a user instantly recognizes what something is and magically knows exactly how to use it. Intuitive means that once that user runs through something, they've got enough of a handle on it to be able to do it again. This doesn't mean that people automatically remember everything the next time around, though. It simply means that the *first* time around, interaction design is clear, consistent, and visible enough that they'll easily be able to infer what to do first, second, third, etc. That first time is what we mean by *single-trial learning*. Here are the elements of design that enable this intuitiveness:

- **Information Architecture (IA).** IA refers to the process of organizing, structuring, and labeling information within a product, website, app, or system to support effective navigation and findability. IA defines how information is organized into categories, groups, or sections. It assigns clear, meaningful labels to content elements that accurately convey their purpose and context. It describes navigational structure—including menus, links, and navigation bars—to guide users through content and help them move between different sections or screens. Good IA is the key to making sure that information can be easily found through search. And a well-designed IA is what creates a logical, coherent, relevant journey for users as they move through different screens or tasks.

  The UX or product designer's job is to develop an IA that clearly communicates the relationships between different pieces of content, making it easier for users to find what they're looking for, as well as understand, use, or act on it when they do.

  If you're interested in learning more about IA (and we think you should be), *Information Architecture for the Web and Beyond* by Lou Rosenfeld, Peter Morville, and Jorge Arango is the most popular, comprehensive book on the subject.

- **Process and Task Diagrams.** These are models for how users will interact with the system step-by-step, and how the system will adapt or respond based on what the user does. These diagrams help UX and product designers, along with business stakeholders, figure out what the user's journey could be or should be; it's crucial exploration that often identifies potential pain points or opportunities for improvement. (See "Task Flows" in Chapter 6 for more information.) While there are many flavors of this work, the most common, helpful diagrams are these:

- **User Flow Diagram.** This is used to think through the step-by-step path a user takes to complete a specific task or achieve a particular goal with the product. UX and product designers explore and diagram the sequence of screens, interactions, and decision points that a user might encounter along the way. For example, a user flow diagram for an e-commerce website might depict the steps a user goes through to browse products, add items to the cart, proceed to checkout, and complete the purchase.

- **System Flow Diagram.** Created in collaboration with developers and programmers (who are the experts here), a system flow diagram provides a high-level overview of how different components of the system connect and work together to support the user's journey. It details how data and information are created, updated, and served in the user interface; how users can access and act on it; and how and where that data is sent, shared, and stored in databases or other data repositories. If the system interacts with external services or APIs, the diagram represents these interactions, indicating the data exchange between the system and external sources.

While this may not seem to be explicit UX work, the relationships detailed have a profound effect on the quality of the user experience. In a mobile app, for example, appropriate interactive and UI design hinges on understanding how user interactions trigger API calls to retrieve real-time data from external services, like weather information or location-based data. If the product is a social media platform, the designer needs to understand how user-generated content is stored and displayed in a feed using a combination of databases and caching mechanisms. Those constraints dictate how content shows up in the UI, along with what's possible in terms of interactions that allow users to create and edit that content.

- **Task Analysis Diagram.** A task analysis diagram breaks down a complex task into smaller subtasks or actions, highlighting the dependencies and relationships between each step. It helps designers identify potential points of confusion or inefficiency. For example, a task analysis diagram for setting up a new user account might outline subtasks like choosing a username, setting a password, and entering basic personal information like name and email.

- **Low-Fidelity Prototypes.** These are essentially schematic dia-grams of each screen or state in the UI of the site, app, or system. They're simplified representations of a product's interface, focusing on layout, content placement, and basic interactions without detailing specific visual elements like colors, images, and fonts. They're used to quickly explore, iterate, and test ideas before investing significant time and resources into high-fidelity design and development. By emphasizing functionality over aesthetics, everyone involved in product design and development can concentrate on getting the user experience right without being distracted by visual details. Low-fidelity prototypes are invaluable for getting early feedback from stakeholders, and they can be tested and validated with users to identify usability issues and refine the design. Changing direction in low-fidelity, before code is written, is much less time-consuming and resource-intensive compared to high-fidelity designs or full-fledged development. This saves costs during the initial stages of a project. (See "Interactive Prototypes" in Chapter 7.)

- **UI Design and Specification.** UI design software like Figma has helped evolve traditional design comps, working hand-in-hand with developers and product managers to deliver detailed product specifications. Figma allows multiple designers to collaborate with other designers and developers in real time on the same design file, enabling teams to work together, provide feedback, and make changes collaboratively, reducing the need for back-and-forth com-munication. In addition, interactive prototypes are built directly within Figma. These prototypes can help smooth the transition from design comps and their implied requirements into code, with a much more accurate, dynamic view of the product's UI compo-nents, interactive behavior, and user/screen flows.

  However, Figma isn't the only game in town. Several types of prototyping software, most notably Axure RP, generate design specifications automatically, eliminating the need for design-ers to manually annotate design elements or create separate specification documents. Detailed specifications include things like how the product adapts in response to user interactions like clicks, taps, or swipes; how it handles errors; and how the system adapts and evolves in response to various system and user states (for example, signed-in vs. signed-out, first-time visiting vs. repeat visits, and so on).

In these cases, developers can also access detailed UI information about colors, typography, spacing, and layout directly within the prototype files. They can inspect design elements, export assets, and copy CSS properties directly from the shared files, saving an extraordinary amount of time and ensuring accurate implementation of the design.

- **Design and Pattern Libraries (and Design Systems).** Since we're on the subject of prototyping software, many have features (built-in or via third-party plug-ins) that enable designers to create reusable design elements, such as buttons, icons, and navigation bars. These components can be stored in libraries and shared across projects, ensuring consistency, and reducing the risk of inconsistencies during handoff. In addition, these components can serve as a springboard for larger, enterprise-wide design systems.

  A *design system* is a comprehensive set of reusable design components, guidelines, and standards that ensure consistency and cohesiveness across all products and experiences within an organization. It serves as a single source of truth for design decisions, allowing designers and developers to work collaboratively and efficiently. Design systems are created through a combination of design principles, UI components, patterns, and documentation, reflecting the organization's brand and user experience goals. They are used to streamline design and development processes, foster a unified visual language, and provide a consistent user experience across different platforms and products.

Implementation

Implementation is where everything becomes real. It encompasses all the processes and procedures needed to take a product from planning, design, and initial development into full production. It's worth mentioning, though, that product implementation, like design, is iterative—and it doesn't end once a site, app, or system "goes live." It also includes critically important work to address issues of user adoption, education, and training, as well as future improvements, upgrades, and releases. Here are some of the core activities that make up implementation work.

- **Front-End Development.** Front-end development (CSS, HTML, JavaScript) has become an increasingly expected part of the job for many UX and product designers. In recent years, the roles of designers and developers have started to overlap, leading to the emergence of job titles like *Designer-Developer*, *UX Developer*, and *UX Engineer*. Front-end development refers to the process of creating and implementing the user interface and user experience of a digital product. This front-end work is focused on the visual and interactive elements that users see and interact with using their web browsers or other user interfaces. This works in conjunction with back-end development, which involves server-side programming and managing databases. Together, front-end and back-end development form a complete web development process, delivering a functional and user-friendly digital product.

- **Implementation Collaboration and Assistance.** While the lion's share of the work eventually shifts from design to development, your job isn't over. UX and product designers should work closely with developers to clarify design intent, provide additional designs or components to address necessary changes or improvements revealed in testing, and answer any questions that arise during development. For example, designers ensure that design system components and guidelines are appropriately integrated into the development process, creating consistency and enabling scalability across the product.

  What's more, software development of any kind always includes unforeseen challenges and technical constraints that aren't obvious until programming starts in earnest. When this happens, active collaboration with engineers, programmers, and developers ensures that the end product still delivers on established UX principles.

- **Usability Testing.** Usability happens throughout the project lifecycle, and it's most critical during implementation, as the window of opportunity to make significant improvements narrows. As discussed previously, these are various methods for assessing whether and how easily people can use the design to accomplish anticipated tasks. (Chapter 7 includes a range of testing and validation methods.)

- **Metrics and Analytics Tracking.** While this is often the role of a business owner or product manager, UX and product designers may also work with engineers and developers to make sure that user interactions and events are appropriately tracked to gather relevant data via analytics tools and tracking mechanisms in the finished product. They also analyze data collected from these tools to gain insights into user behavior, use patterns, and pain points. This can help identify opportunities for future UX improvement or enhancement. Even if someone else handles this work, it's wise for you to immerse yourself in understanding how it happens, what's measured, and why.

NOTE THE UX STARTER LIBRARY

If you're interested in reading more about the core principles of UX and how UX work actually happens, there are a number of established classics that get the job done. (Google "UX books," and you'll see that list across just about every result.) And don't get us wrong, you *should* read those books. But times have changed a great deal since they were written, so we'd like to suggest this batch of newer titles (and one timeless title) that do an excellent job of covering how design and UX manifest all around us, why the core principles matter so very much, and, of course, how to practice user-centered design in a rapidly changing technological, cultural, and global landscape (see Figure 2.4).

Build Better Products : A Modern Approach to Building Successful User-Centered Products, Laura Klein

Laws of UX: Using Psychology to Design Better Products & Services, Jon Yablonski

Just Enough Research, Erika Hall

This Is Service Design Doing: Applying Service Design Thinking in the Real World, Marc Stickdorn, Adam Lawrence, Markus Hormess, and Jakob Schneider

Inclusive Design for a Digital World: Designing with Accessibility in Mind, Regine M. Gilbert

The Pocket Universal Principles of Design: 150 Essential Tools for Architects, Artists, Designers, Developers, Engineers, Inventors, and Makers, William Lidwell, Kritina Holden, and Jill Butler

FIGURE 2.4
A user experience starter library.

Establish a Point of View on What Can Be Improved

Before you get started, it's a good idea to have a clear picture of what work needs to be done to improve the product and how you can best contribute to it. The good news is that you don't really need permission to be a UX team of one. You might think that if you want to transition to UX, you should start by changing your title and your role. But asking for a wholesale role change before you've gotten people to understand and see the value in UX might be a long shot. You'll have better luck if you simply start doing UX-related activities in smaller, under-the-radar ways, in the work you're currently doing. From there, you'll be able to build momentum from the positive support resulting from your work.

Here are a few approaches we recommend as a foundation for any crossover. They're not UX activities per se, but they pave the way for those activities:

- **Find the low-hanging fruit.** Find the parts of the product that everyone knows need improvement and entice your colleagues with a vision of what could be. Plan your attack from there, making sure that you address the outcomes of those improvements from a business perspective. Remember the value loop? Any time you suggest design or UX improvement, you've got to connect it—along with the benefits to users and customers—to the things the business folks you work with already want. The outcomes they are responsible for in their day-to-day jobs. Which, truth be told, is usually money made or money saved. That said, it's key to do it in a way that is positive and respectful. Use a "Black Hat Session" (Chapter 7) to get people thinking about where and how your product might be improved, or a quick "Heuristic Markup" (Chapter 5) to do the legwork on your own.

- **Make a plan.** If you want to get people to buy into the concept of UX, you've got to be offering them something of value. How do you do it? Sit down and sketch out how you'd like to approach a UX project. Think about what activities you'd propose—when and why—from research to design iteration to prototyping and testing. Think about what big questions you believe need to be answered, and work your way backward, thinking through how you'd find those answers. Write a UX project plan (Chapter 4) to make it clear in your own mind. And then, ask yourself, "Do I need permission or support to do this, or can I just do it now, myself?" You may find that the answer is that you can just get started.

And in situations where your managers or executives don't really get the importance of UX or design, asking for permission is asking to be told no.

METHOD CARDS

Method cards are a great tool for identifying quick activities that you can do in the course of a normal workday to infuse a user-oriented perspective in your work (see Figure 2.5). Here are some of the best we've seen:

- **Laws of UX Card Deck (lawsofux.com).** Author Jon Yablonski's "Laws of UX" card deck covers 54 psychological principles and UX methods that help you design and justify your user interfaces, get buy-in from stakeholders and clients, and infuse your design work with psychology principles.
- **UXD Cards (uxdcards.com).** This set contains 75 informative UX method cards to help you, your clients, and your team understand design, build a common language, and work toward better project and product outcomes.
- **Pip Decks (pipdecks.com).** Pip Decks are "business recipe cards" invented by designer Charles Burdett. Like a traditional recipe card, they show you what the recipe is for (and why you should use it) on the front. And on the back, the exact steps to make it. The beauty of the Pip Decks format is that it can be applied to any practical activity, from running workshops to crafting presentations to developing innovative product and design ideas.

PHOTO COURTESY OF JON YABLONSKI

FIGURE 2.5
Jon Yablonski's excellent "Laws of UX" method cards.

TIP BYPASSING OBJECTIONS

If you encounter objections and you need permission, the following tip might be helpful. In the days where department stores had salespeople walking the floor, they used a clever technique called the *alternative close* to encourage people to buy whatever product they had in hand. Instead of asking "Are you ready to check out?" they would ask, "Will that be cash or charge?" Instead of asking permission to close the deal (or, in this case, to do the work), they provided two alternatives for how to go about it. In UX, the equivalent would be *not* "Can we do some research?" but rather "We could do a research study, or a small informal evaluation, to get some quick feedback." This changes the negotiation to *how* you'll do the work instead of *if* you'll do the work.

In a similar fashion, UX and product designers are often given specific direction as to how to design something by well-intentioned product managers. And when that manager won't budge from what they think should happen—and you're sure there's a better way—you give them two solutions. The first is exactly what they asked for. The second is your solution, along with a rationale for why it's more likely to achieve the outcome they're after: "I worked up this first option based on the direction you gave. But I also worked up a second option that I think is actually going to get you what you want here, because (give your reasoning)…"

If you ignore orders and do your thing, feathers will be ruffled. If you do both theirs *and* yours, you're communicating respect for their opinion while trying to do the right thing.

Get to Know Your Users and Customers

Once you've identified some opportunities and developed a rough plan, your next priority should be to get firsthand experience with users and customers, talking with them and learning about their needs. These people are at the core of user experience. Simply put, they are the people who use (and buy) the products you help create. So, it's obviously pretty important to keep them in mind when designing products, because they're the ones who will endure the consequences of all design decisions.

Good products eventually become somewhat invisible, sinking into the background as users achieve a kind of flow, where they're actively, fluidly doing whatever the product is supposed to make possible. Not *tapping the Like icon* but expressing support for an idea. Not *formatting a Google document* but writing. Not *entering text in a field and submitting* but posting to LinkedIn. If you're a product maker, this is nirvana...but it's also pretty damn hard to accomplish. In fact, you're virtually guaranteed to get some of it wrong, especially at first. This is why the field of UX places so much emphasis on understanding user needs and testing product designs with them.

Connecting with people is so essential that it's one of the core tenets of user experience: design products *for* and *with* users.

Now personally, we dislike the word *user*. We much prefer to call them, simply, *people*. That helps us remember that it's the people all around us that we're designing for. But to design appropriately for people, you have to *know* something about them. That starts with resisting the tendency to treat them as flat statistics derived from market segmentation and striving to understand them as the complex, erratic animals that they all are. Eric Ries of the Lean Startup movement has a great one-liner that sums it up perfectly: "Data are people, too." This requires you to suspend what you think you know and adopt someone else's perspective—long enough to feel their pain and envision better alternatives (see Figure 2.6). That's harder than it sounds, which is why it's essential that you take time to actually get to know real users and customers.

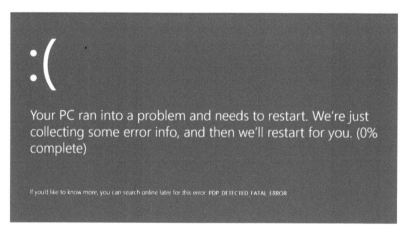

Your PC ran into a problem and needs to restart. We're just collecting some error info, and then we'll restart for you. (0% complete)

If you'd like to know more, you can search online later for this error. PDP_DETECTED_FATAL_ERROR

FIGURE 2.6
A well-designed product enables a user to accomplish their goal efficiently and without confusion or disruption. When a user encounters a breakdown in the system, like Microsoft's infamous "Blue Screen of Death," the lack of clear communication design really shows.

At the same time, there are many situations in which UX and product designers have no access to actual users or customers. Sometimes that's because managers and executives are afraid of what actual direct user or customer research would reveal, which is confirmation of the problems they already know exist (but have been avoiding doing anything about). Sometimes it's because another department owns access to customers and simply won't play nice and share the wealth. And to be honest, in many cases, there's just no time for user research because UX and design folks have to meet deadlines and project schedules they had no say in creating.

All of this happens more frequently, by the way, than anything you read online would have you believe.

By the same token, there are those out there who never take the time to talk to users or customers, even though they have the time, authority, and ability to do so. But whether you do or don't have control in these situations, the bottom line is that the most successful UX teams of one are those who truly understand the people they're designing for. Not just users in the abstract, but the people who *really* use their products. Direct contact with users pays off—so when you can, you *should*.

Jared Spool of User Interface Engineering has done research that shows that the amount of face time a team has with end users directly impacts the quality of the product. You can read more about the optimal number of user "exposure hours" here: https://articles.uie.com/user_exposure_hours/.

So, it's very important to start reaching out and talking to your actual users. Here's how to do it:

- **Figure out what you know (and what you don't know).** Start with what's happening now: where and what are the gaps between what people expect and what they actually get? Between what they need and what is provided? And are those expectations and needs actually defined? Do you know what they are? If not, why not? From there, you can define objectives. Identify what you want to learn through research and connect it to business goals: how will what you learn contribute to the overall success of the product? Explore the questions you want to answer, along with the problems or deficiencies you're aware of that you need to understand better. Existing data on use of the product, complaints users have, or recurring technical issues can help you figure some of this out. This may come in the form of anything from analytics data to reporting on sales, marketing, or customer support issues. (See Chapter 5.)

- **Figure out who you need to talk to.** Who are the specific user groups or personas you want to engage with? What characteristics, demographics, job roles, and behaviors are characteristic of them? Who do you have access to, and how will you get that access if you don't already have it? How will the information, insights, and feedback you collect from them be used, and how will you ensure their privacy is respected? These questions are all good places to start in determining who can and should participate in your research.

- **Choose the appropriate research method.** Common methods include interviews, surveys, usability testing, focus groups, and direct observation. These are only some of the ways to conduct user research, and choosing the most appropriate method depends a great deal on the context of your situation: your research objectives, who your users or customers are, your access to them, the time you have available to do the research, and their comfort level and psychological safety in giving you their time and opinion or allowing you to observe them.

Of course, there's a lot more to user research than this. But don't worry, we'll dig into the details of these methods (and what to use when) in Chapter 5. For now, it's enough to start thinking about how you'd answer the previous questions.

Explore Required Information Architecture

Lou Rosenfeld, Peter Morville, and Jorge Arango, three fine human beings who quite literally wrote the book on information architecture (IA), posit that the vast majority of our problems with websites, apps, and systems are *information problems*. Specifically, at any given time, we either have too much information, not enough information, not the right information, or a combination of the three. The job of IA, and our job as designers, is to solve those problems, by arranging that information to make it searchable, findable, and understandable. Which, in turn, helps users make sense of the digital environments they use every day on a wide variety of devices—from smartphones to cars to home appliances.

This is why the very next thing you turn your attention to after research is the task of consciously organizing, prioritizing, and labeling the content in a website, an app, or a system. It also means organizing the flow of that content: the flow of information, the flow of data, and the flow of everything that appears onscreen.

That organization has to be meaningful to the people interacting with it, so it has to be based on what you know about the people using the product—on everything you've learned about their needs, behaviors, preconceptions, and expectations. On what they think they're going to find and what they expect it to be called. On what's important, relevant, appropriate, and necessary for them.

Information architecture sits at the intersection of three things: *users*, the people who are using the thing in the first place, the *content* itself, and the *context* in which they're using that information (Figure 2.7). Of the three, *context* is possibly the most important, partly because it's often overlooked in design work. While the diagram specifically describes context as business goals, funding, politics, culture, technology, resources, and constraints, it's worth mentioning that context actually extends even further in terms of its impact on how someone understands IA.

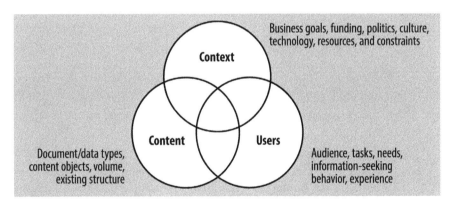

FIGURE 2.7

A Venn diagram from *Information Architecture for the Web and Beyond* by Louis Rosenfeld, Peter Morville, and Jorge Arango.

The user's environment, the type of device they're using, their cultural presuppositions and beliefs, their emotions, and even their physical state or characteristics all affect how they make sense of what they see (or hear). This context helps determine how content will be organized and what content will be called. What (and how much) people expect to find; how and where they expect to find it; how they expect to be able to navigate to it and through it; and how they expect to be able to view, enter, download, manipulate, or otherwise interact with it.

The only reason Spotify or Apple Music or TIDAL is valuable or useful or easy to use for you is because how you listen to and curate your music—how you manipulate things, play songs, create playlists, find artists, whatever it is—makes *sense* to you. It meets your expectations. You *get it.*

So, part of your job as a UX or design professional is to help users *get it*—help them understand where they are, where the information or interaction they want is, and how to get to it from where they are now. When a UX writer or content strategist works to organize, categorize, and prioritize content, they're doing IA work. When you design a global navigation menu or jump links on a screen, or a system of saved, categorized lists, or bookmarks, you're doing IA work.

But no matter what the larger project may be, or what kind of product you're designing, the basic questions that have to be asked and answered remain the same:

- **What do users need to be able to do?** In the world of digital products, content exists to enable interaction. So, what do your users or customers need to know—and what do they need to be able to do? That has to be clear to you in order to present that information accordingly. It has to be clear to them so that they don't get frustrated, give up, and go somewhere else.

- **What does the organization want or need them to be able to do?** Are those information and interaction needs related to their jobs? If this is a consumer-facing app or website, what do you need to provide to educate, inform, and enable enough trust for them to try or buy? In either case, what's the consequence of not finding something?

- **Where do users expect to find information, and what do they expect it to be called?** Understanding the mental models that users have—their expectations for what things are called and how the site or app should present them, based on beliefs and past experiences—is the first step in answering this question.

The labels in navigation menus, for example, should use words that either follow established conventions (e.g., about) or clearly explain what to do (e.g., sign up, log in, etc.).

- **How do they expect information to be categorized, organized, and prioritized?** There are expectations to be met here as well; a quick walk through any grocery store will show you just how important categories are in a browsing or buying experience. The more content or data or interaction opportunities your product offers, the more important it is that you place it in categories (and subcategories) that people will easily recognize.

Once you have a sense of this, you develop a draft IA model. And while there are all sorts of flavors of this, a UX-centric diagram like the one shown in Figure 2.8 can be useful to help you think through what a user needs, wants, and expects to do with an app or site or system. What information are they looking for? To answer what need or question? Using this as a starting point helps you explore possible paths to information, as well as actions they can take (and what order to take them in).

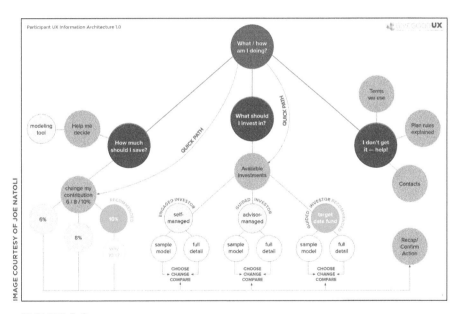

FIGURE 2.8

An IA diagram exploring a user's possible paths to changing contribution amounts to an employer-sponsored retirement plan, based on questions they commonly ask themselves.

The purpose of this diagram is first to help you, your team, and your stakeholders think through what information your product needs to provide—and how. And second, it gives you something to test with actual users to see just how appropriate and relevant to them this proposed information structure really is.

Once you've got your draft IA, it's time to test it with potential users in order to determine:

- Will users be able to find specific items easily?
- Can they find those items directly, without having to backtrack?
- Can they choose between topics quickly at every level, without having to think too much?
- Which parts of the IA work well, and which need improvement?

In our opinion, the quickest way to do this, and walk away with solid evidence to base your decisions on, is by doing something called *tree testing*. Donna Spencer, a pioneer in IA from Australia, introduced this method. You may have heard of card sorting, which is similar. In card sorting, the user is provided with predefined category "buckets" and asked to sort a pile of content cards into those buckets. The idea is that if there's general agreement about which cards go in which buckets, then those buckets (the categories) should perform well in the IA.

People start every experience of use with a *task*—a contextual need to do or find something. Tree testing addresses this directly because it closely simulates how people browse sites when looking for something specific. Tree tests tell you how easily people can find stuff on a website, an app, or a system, and they also tell you exactly where they get lost. Tree testing can indicate whether language and labels make sense to people. The results can tell you if your content is organized and grouped in a way where people can find the information they want easily and quickly. And when they can't, tree testing can also help you identify what's stopping them.

For more detailed instruction, check out Optimal Workshop's incredible library of how-to articles and videos (optimalworkshop.com/learn/tree-testing-101-tree-testing-overview/).

Start Designing

It's a funny fact of user experience work that people expect that you're going to produce designs that are just undeniably lovelier. Simpler. More intuitive. You know, *better.* And you certainly don't want to disappoint them. The challenge is that many of us come to this field by other routes, and don't have formal design backgrounds. As a result, it's not uncommon for teams of one to find themselves in a position of defending a design, without necessarily believing or knowing with 100 percent conviction that it is, in fact, a *better* design. As such, the challenge for UX professionals is to understand user needs well enough to be able to look past the prosaic solutions—to discover the elegant ones (see Figure 2.9).

FIGURE 2.9

Sometimes the right user experience solution can be deceptive. While this giant remote may solve one problem (visibility and motor control when using a TV remote), it may also introduce other ones (the awkwardness of handling a remote the size of a TV dinner tray, perhaps).

For many of us, our first taste of design is through a software tool that makes laying out a screen easy but doesn't necessarily teach us anything about how people encounter and make sense of what they see. It doesn't help us to understand why certain features and information, in an interactive medium, are useful, usable, or valuable to those users. While it's tempting to throw yourself into the software and get lost in the satisfying process of designing elements on a screen, that's not the best way to ensure that your designs are appropriate: that they successfully balance user, business, and team expectations.

This is where many of the tools of classically trained designers can be lifesavers for UX folks—in particular, sketching, critique, iterative improvement, and seeking inspiration from the world around you. Here's how you can start bringing these techniques into your work as a team of one:

- **Sketch your ideas.** The simplest and most beautiful designs are seldom born that way (see Figure 2.10). It actually takes a *lot* of work to make something simple. That process often starts with sketches and back-of-the-napkin inspiration, and evolves over time as you iterate, refine, and mold your ideas into increasingly higher fidelity. The goal here is quantity, not quality—creating, not editing. Quite often, the first ideas you come up with will be things you've already seen or things you personally happen to like, neither of which is what the job calls for. Getting all that stuff out of your head and down on paper or a whiteboard helps you move past it to more informed, meaningful, and objective solutions appropriate for your product, your users, and the business. Chapter 6 provides a range of methods that you can use to guide yourself and your team through the sketching process.

FIGURE 2.10

Paradoxically, beautiful designs often start in an unattractive place, as mere sketches on paper or scribbles on a whiteboard.

- **Enlist colleagues to generate design ideas.** Host activities that invite others to participate in the design process and share their unique points of view. See Chapter 6 for a variety of techniques for planning and hosting such sessions—especially sketches, which are tailor-made for this purpose. Figure 2.11 shows what a successful, cross-functional collaboration between a UX team of one and her team should look like: lots of sketches and visual artifacts, and lots of notes as a record of the conversation.

FIGURE 2.11

An example of a completed sketchboard, made up of sketches from multiple team members to think through an interaction sequence.

- **Learn from other successful products.** Create inspiration libraries of UX, design, and interaction patterns from other apps, sites, or systems, to keep abreast of current standards and have a place to turn for ideas when working on a new problem (see Figure 2.12). Keep in mind, though, that what you're seeing is someone else's solution to someone else's problem, which means not everything you see will be applicable to what you're designing, or the problems you're working to solve. Which means you need to question things. Spend time asking yourself "What makes this particular design work?" When something doesn't work, see if you can pinpoint why.

FIGURE 2.12

An inspiration library can be as simple as a collection of reference sketches of UI designs you've encountered that are notable, either for being good or bad.

You might even go so far as to practice verbalizing these thoughts (either to a friend, or to your mirror, if you'd prefer). Being confident in the language of critique is one hallmark of a strong designer, and it helps nondesigners objectively understand what works and what doesn't—in an otherwise subjective medium.

If You Only Do One Thing …

…get started with user research! This chapter covers the building blocks of UX work of any kind. First, establish a point of view on where to start. Then figure out a sensible process with an appropriate balance between user research, information architecture, and design. However, the most important concept here—and indeed, the most important concept in the whole field—is to actually talk to or directly observe users.

So, if you only have time to do one thing from this chapter, focus on getting started with user research. Usually, even a little bit of time spent investigating the needs and realities of users will lead to *ah-ha* moments so important (and so obvious) that they'll create their own momentum to get you started.

PHOTO COURTESY OF
MARLENE LEPPÄNEN

CHAPTER 3

Building Support for Your Work

Dedicated as you are, it can still be difficult to get others to stand behind the UX approach, particularly when it clashes with executive directives or the very real constraints of time and budget. It's not that people are hostile or unsupportive of the idea of a well-designed product that meets users' needs. It's that sometimes UX just doesn't have enough muscle in the face of other challenges, like an unhappy VP, or a constrained project schedule. The commitment of organizations new to UX ebbs and flows—sometimes teams of one get more support …and sometimes less. And a lot of that comes from differences of intent across departments and job roles: people are literally incentivized and rewarded for business outcomes that are often in conflict with those of other people and departments. This isn't malice or politics; it's how corporate entities, unfortunately, are designed.

The constant push and pull of trying to help others understand or care about user experience often creates confrontations and conversations that feel like battles (and at worst, losing battles). But it doesn't have to be that way—if you're willing to be creative and strategic about turning that combat into collaboration. You do this by learning more about what outcomes those folks outside your discipline want and need, and why they want and need those things. You do this by building trust and showing them that what they want is what you want, too—by setting expectations and then showing progress against them.

This chapter tackles the squishier side of life as a team of one: how to deal with the inevitable people and organizational issues that influence—and often determine—how successful your work ultimately is.

Principles over Process

We often hear different flavors of this common refrain from teams of one: "We don't have the process in place that we need. In the next year, I'm going to push for that." But while this belief that more processes will solve the issues at hand is common, the truth is that it rarely works. For starters, too much emphasis on process can be a distraction that takes your energy and attention away from relationships, which are much more important. This is especially true when UX is new and still trying to establish itself inside an organization. You can have all the processes in the world on paper, but if people see them as something that just gives them more work to do, they'll never be implemented. If you can't get people outside UX or product design to see how a more UX-focused approach benefits them, they won't support that approach—much less participate in it.

For these reasons and more, in our experience, you're better off focusing on principles instead of processes. Why? Because principles are what keep the work anchored.

Principles are deceptively simple: they're really just statements. They're a way for you to communicate the *why* behind the *what*, to articulate what's actually worth doing. To make a case for why those user-centered activities will get executives, stakeholders, developers, and the product team as a whole what they already want. And, of course, why and how those things benefit users and customers. But make no mistake: to build trust and encourage collaboration, all of your compatriots inside the company need to clearly see how what you're proposing helps them and the work they're doing. Principles, then, apply not only to what you make, but also to how you work.

In that spirit, we offer the following principles as core tenets for how to work (and succeed) as a team of one. With startling consistency, the most happy and successful teams of one explain that it's their mindset, not just their methods, that keep them going. This mindset is embodied by the following principles of engagement.

1. Invite People In

Overworked teams of one can sometimes spend more time at their desks than in conversations with colleagues. You think you're getting lots of work done and surely people will recognize and applaud your efforts, but it can have the unintended effect of making you seem inaccessible and unfriendly. In bringing people over to your cause, openness and friendliness can go a long way.

Every day is an opportunity to invite your non-UX colleagues into the world of UX (see Figure 3.1). In fact, your coworkers may already think of themselves as savvy UX supporters. Even though you may see missed opportunities or inconsistent support, you can still cultivate advocates for UX. Invite them into the conversation and the community; treat them as partners in the ongoing project of making products as user-friendly as possible. Here are three ways you can make that happen:

- **See them as people, not job titles.** Think about those other people in other roles in other departments who have strategic influence on product decisions. Look outside their departmental goals, the business mandates or milestones, or KPIs they're on the hook for. What do they want, personally? What are they struggling with? What outcomes or consequences are they afraid of? What pressure is on them personally? Are those issues persistent? How would solving these problems or getting those outcomes make them (and you) look like heroes?

- **Focus conversations on *outcomes*, not on good design or UX.** When proposals to improve UX are shot down, the reason is frequently a failure to communicate. Quite often, the problem isn't the improvements the UX team of one was proposing—it was the complete failure to explain how that work solved the pressing problem on that manager's mind. The failure is the result of not leading with that information *first*, before anything else. As Joe is fond of saying, no one outside you and your UX colleagues cares about better UX or better product design. They care about what those things are going to *achieve* for them (and for the business). How that work is going to help them hit their numbers. How it's going to solve their problem or capitalize on an opportunity. So, you lead with that. Every single time.

- **Speak their language, not yours.** We're talking about the UX- or design-specific terminology and jargon and acronyms you use in your conversations with non-UX or design people inside your organization. Many of us do this because, well, it's what we know best. It's second nature and, in all honesty, some of us do it because we're trying really hard to impress people—because we're worried they don't respect what we do. It's a bid for legitimacy.

But no matter the motivation, you must remember this: jargon isn't communication. In many cases, the people you're speaking to don't understand those words. And even if you're getting head nods, it's often because they've heard some of this before, or they're pretending to know what you're talking about—and they're too embarrassed to say otherwise. That mystery doesn't increase your credibility; it only builds a higher wall. So always strive to be clear, using the simplest language possible.

FIGURE 3.1
The more you can facilitate a cross-functional team, the more you empower others to feel ownership and involvement in the process.

2. Make Things Together

User experience work (and who are we kidding—work in general) can often be adversarial. Even though everyone on the team is presumably working toward the same goal, the topic of how to accomplish that goal can become a battlefield of differing opinions. Which, inside an organization, is quite natural: each person's position is informed by their professional experience, their expertise, and the very specific (and often differing) business outcomes they are responsible for getting.

Meetings bring all this to bear, as do unstructured conversations. The two in conjunction create fertile soil for endless back-and-forth discussions, mired in all the bad habits of interpersonal communication. But you don't want that, and odds are pretty good that your colleagues don't want it either. Fortunately, you have a very important (and powerful) tool at your disposal: the ability to make abstract ideas tangible—and to then use that tangibility as a tool to discuss and refine those ideas. Simply put, if you can quickly make visual examples of what you and your colleagues are talking about (even the sketchiest, most rudimentary examples), you can break that dysfunctional conversational cycle. And you can help foster the constructive evolution of a shared vision instead.

The best way we know to do this is to use a tool that's likely either already in the room or accessible through your screen: a whiteboard. Whether we're talking about a traditional whiteboard or collaborative apps like Miro, Mural, or FigJam, quick low-fidelity approximations of screens or workflows change the level of attention and shared understanding in the room almost immediately. People go from expending a lot of cognitive effort to imagine what you're talking about (or what they're thinking about)—to being able to reference a visual model right in front of them. This approach frees up their mental energy to really listen and consider what's being discussed. The visual representation helps everyone get to clarity much quicker than if they had to imagine it in their heads. It also gives the entire team the ability to confirm and correct as they go, by asking questions about what's on the board: "Does it work like this?"

So, get in the habit of sketching and whiteboarding, whether virtual or in person. Embrace an in-the-moment willingness to say "can we draw that out?" We promise you'll see a very big difference in the level of shared understanding and productive conversation in the room. Figure 3.2 is a great example of what these sessions look like in person with a team.

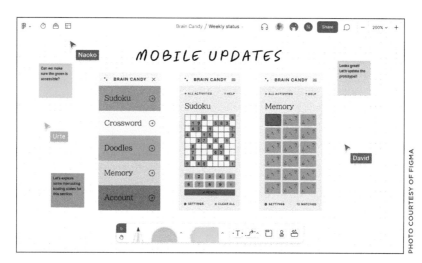

PHOTO COURTESY OF FIGMA

FIGURE 3.2
FigJam allows cross-functional remote team members to participate in collaborative brainstorming design exercises, which are great for loosening people up and getting ideas rolling.

3. Truly Engage and Actively Listen

Closely related to the previous principle, happy teams of one have learned to see themselves as facilitators and conduits of ideas held by an *entire* cross-functional team. Their job, once all the information and viewpoints are understood, is to create a design solution that cleverly reconciles those tensions and produces a satisfying experience—both for users and business stakeholders. But to play this role of facilitator, you have to be truly interested in other people's viewpoints. You need to be actively engaged to understand where they're coming from, question what you believe must be questioned, and make a good faith commitment toward achieving the right balance in the end (see Figure 3.3).

FIGURE 3.3

Collaborative discussion while iterating ideas together on a whiteboard works wonders—strengthening both the work itself and the relationships among the team.

Here are some tips for doing just that.

- **Say *we* instead of *I*.** Instead of responding with *"I think,"* get in the habit of saying "Maybe *we* could consider …." That subtle change implies shared ownership of problems and solutions— and goes a long way in communicating that you see this as collaboration, not competition.

- **Share the *why* behind your questions.** When you ask a question, follow it with "Here's why I'm asking," and then explain why you're curious. This defuses defensiveness by communicating that your curiosity is not a challenge or contradiction; it's an honest desire to know more. This adds context and helps others see the relevance of your question.

- **Mirror others' vocabulary.** We're not suggesting you parrot what other people say, of course. But adopting some of the same language your teammates use creates a sense of rapport and understanding. It shows that you're tuned in to their way of thinking—and that you're truly listening and absorbing the things they say.

- **Repeat and connect ideas.** When someone shares a thought, reiterate its value and connect it to the ongoing conversation, either now or later in the discussion. This reinforces that you *were* listening, and that the idea has merit: "Just like Eva said a few minutes ago, it might be wise to…" This highlights their contribution and keeps the dialogue flowing.

- **Validate before responding.** Before you suggest your own idea or solution, validate the speaker's feelings or concerns: "Yeah, I can certainly see why you're worried about that. I honestly wouldn't have thought about it, but you're right. We need to tread carefully here." That clear display of understanding and empathy opens the door to more respectful, receptive communication.

- **Communicate that you're listening intently with body language.** Subtle nods, smiles, and expressions of agreement show you're engaged—even if you're not the one speaking. Following this principle often means letting the other person do more of the talking and asking "why" whenever the opportunity presents itself.

4. Know When It's Good Enough

Finishing a UX project is like sweeping a floor. You get the big pile fairly easily, but those last few specks of dust are impossible to ever really clean up. You just keep cutting the dirt pile in half until finally you're left with an acceptable amount of grime to put the broom away and get on with the next thing. Suffice it to say, the work is never really done. Having an ongoing conversation with your non-UX colleagues about what's most important to get right—and taking a "let's show the sausage being made" attitude—can turn that problem into a compelling way to get others involved. By committing to the idea that it will be imperfect and that others will have good ideas for how to improve it, you start to get a feel for what *good enough* looks like—good enough to convey the basic idea, good enough to have a conversation about, good enough to get started writing code.

And all of that starts with understanding what the most critical, core project goals are—and when they're met. Think about it like this: on any given list of project objectives, there are really only one to three items that are truly of critical importance. We define them as critical because if they aren't met, nothing else on the list really matters much. We liken it to an episode of "The Walking Dead." While there are always multiple problems people have to solve in every episode, the most critical problem to solve is always the same: how to avoid getting bitten (or eaten) by zombies. Because if that happens ...all those other problems cease to matter.

In the same way, let's say the new shared document editing system you're working on has multiple goals, but the two most important on the list are 1) implementing shared, tracked editing by multiple people and 2) allowing both search and browse by category functionality. Once these two key objectives are met, it's good enough for launch.

Here are some tips to help you determine what "good enough" looks like:

- **Positive usability test results.** When usability tests consistently reveal positive feedback, this suggests the solution is effectively addressing user or customer pain points. Let's say we conduct several rounds of usability testing. If users can navigate through a redesigned checkout process more smoothly, in half the time of the previous version—even if the UI could be a lot better—the current version is likely good enough for implementation.

- **Minimal bounce rate.** If analytics are showing a low bounce rate on a landing page or specific app feature, it often means that users are finding value, and that they're generally satisfied with the effectiveness of the solution. For example, if the bounce rate for a new product recommendation feature is significantly lower than before, it's performing well enough to retain user interest. While it may not be the best it can possibly be, it's good enough to be left alone for now, so the team can turn its attention to other pressing problems.

- **Improvement effort outweighs potential reward.** If the effort and resources required for additional improvements to the design outweigh the potential benefits of doing so, it's usually wise to call it good enough and move on to the next thing. For example, if you've got a launch deadline for a product demo in five days, and no clear, solid evidence that additional design options are going to increase the number of sign-ups, you call it and start QA testing for launch. In these situations, *done* is typically better than *perfect*.

- **Feedback stops (or repeats).** When feedback from multiple sources stops coming in after rounds of iteration—or is essentially just repeating the same similar suggestions and concerns—it's likely that any further iteration won't really improve anything. For example, if after multiple design iterations and input from various team members, the only feedback you get is nitpicky or subjective ("I'm just not sure about that color"), the design is likely good enough to build.

- **Critical risk is addressed.** When your solution mitigates or resolves significant risks or issues identified in design, the current iteration is likely good enough to proceed. If you're working on a cybersecurity app, for example, and it fixes the most critical and common vulnerabilities, or significantly reduces the chance of security breaches, it's solid enough to implement and test.

These are all examples of situations and scenarios that can help you determine when what's in front of you is stable enough to call it done—for *now*, anyway (see Figure 3.4).

You'll see all four of these principles in action in the two main challenges we'll tackle next: dealing with *people issues* and *organizational issues.* And it's worth mentioning that both of these are often directly responsible for the UX defects or bugs that surface in a product;

it's rarely the result of UXers, designers, or developers not knowing how to do their jobs correctly (or not wanting to).

With that in mind, let's turn our attention to common objections and questions you might expect to encounter, and some ways to respond to them.

FIGURE 3.4
Wise words.

Dealing with People Issues

Relationships are one of the most important means by which you can establish a foundation for (and build trust in) UX. But in a complex corporate organization, it's often very difficult to engage without getting sucked into interpersonal politics. The people we've known to be most successful in this area seem to make themselves ever-present and available, while managing to remain impartial and without soiling their reputations. Both of which are no small feat. They have the ability to assume that everyone has good intentions until proven otherwise, and they actively work to see the situation from other people's perspectives, rather than just their own. That may sound all warm and squishy, but it speaks to one of the supreme paradoxes of our work: it's frustrating when our efforts are impeded by others, but it's only by working with those people that we build unofficial and official support for UX. Here are some techniques that will help.

- **Abandon the idea that you're here to "educate" people.** Gaining support and trust starts with abandoning this idea that you're going to educate your product owners, product or project managers, developers, executives, marketing or salespeople, etc. Why? Because the minute you decide it is your job to educate someone, you put yourself up on a pedestal. You're up here because you know it all, and they're down there because they know nothing. No matter how well-intended you may be, this is how it will land. No one in that room wants or is asking to be educated. This is not a class, and you're not here to teach, lecture, perform, or impress. You're here to prove to these people, through your words and actions, that you care about what they care about. That the outcomes *they* want are what *you* want, too. That's what will get them to pick up the oars and start rowing in the same direction you are. In order to truly welcome and invite people into your world, you must take off your UX badge.

- **Ask the team and people in other departments how they want to engage with UX.** One thing we've both learned in consulting is that you must work with the resources that are available. People are resources, too. You start with what *is*, not what *should be*.

- **Build an informal UX network.** In larger organizations, the number of people who also think of themselves as user-savvy advocates is often much larger than you think. Develop communities of practice, or a lunchtime sharing session, where you feed people and share what you're up to. This helps to pull these UX enthusiasts out of the woodwork and promote broader UX maturity within the company. Create a peer-to-peer learning community (see Chapter 8, "Evangelism Methods") to create an informal community of support for UX and to share what your efforts are accomplishing and enabling. This is important, because your non-UX counterparts often don't realize that they can get a lot more from you than just making things look better. They're often unaware of how what's between your ears can deliver real, strategic, bottom-line value that can make them look like heroes. So, make it a point to show and tell them.

- **Ask others to participate in your work.** This idea ruffles feathers among design and UX folks, but reality is that improving a product is a collaborative team effort. You can't do it alone, and you shouldn't. Invite managers and colleagues into your process—and yourself into theirs—so they get a better sense of what UX means and what value it provides, and you get a better sense of their responsibilities and pressures. When conducting user research, invite your non-UX colleagues to come along. Offer to facilitate a strategy workshop (Chapter 4), where a cross-functional team can openly discuss opportunities to improve the user experience of your products. Also, hone your sketching skills so you can turn any meeting into a design session (see Chapter 6, "Design Methods") and invite your colleagues to sketch as well. People love it when ideas start to become tangible, and it's a way for you to demonstrate your leadership and help guide a conversation if it seems to be spinning. Host sketching ("sketchboard") sessions (Chapter 6). These are generative design workshops that allow your nondesigner colleagues to contribute to the design process.

- **Arrange pre-meetings to avoid the "big reveal."** Leah was on a project once with a manager who set up pre-meetings with all of her senior executives prior to a formal share-out of proposed designs. At the time, it seemed like a lot of unnecessary conversations, but it had a magical effect on the big meeting. When the UX team pulled out the designs and started explaining their logic, the senior execs smiled knowingly and nodded their heads in the affirmative. There were none of the puzzled "I'm thinking about it" expressions that are all too common in such presentations. Pre-meetings like this help you get people to commit their support for your approach prior to going in for the big reveal, and they give your colleagues a very important gift: the time and space to really think about proposed designs and establish their own point of view. Put another way, the longer the wait is between the time you discuss an approach with a stakeholder and the time they actually see something, the more likely you are to hear "This isn't what I thought we were doing/what I expected."

- **Use relatable language.** UX is rife with jargon that can be off-putting to people from other fields, and it makes effective communication across internationally distributed teams extremely difficult. Terminology, jargon, and acronyms obscure meaning. So, if you're feeling like people aren't listening to you, or aren't giving your words and work the attention or respect it deserves, this may be why. Quite often, people outside UX and design don't understand those words you use, and they're too embarrassed to admit that. So, when you speak or write, strive for clarity and simplicity. Break language down to its basic, common elements so that every single person in the room—no matter their experiences, education, understanding, or language skills—can easily understand your meaning.

Dealing with Organizational Issues

User experience practitioners, due to their focus on both user and business needs, can provide a holistic view that's often rare within an organization, even now. That's particularly true if your business is siloed or heavily segmented by department. If you find that your vantage point is restricting you from looking beyond *one single piece* of an enterprise system, for example, then you're ultimately hampered in your ability to improve the overall UX of using that system. Which means you may need to find novel ways to gain access and visibility across departments, deal with conflicting priorities, and make the most of insufficient or unclear resources. Here are some ideas.

- **Invite yourself to strategy sessions and offer to visualize requirements.** Early in the process, offer to be the design hands to help others visually convey what they have in mind and help surface their ideas. If you know that preliminary product strategy conversations are taking place, or that use cases and requirements are being written prior to UX involvement, this is the perfect moment to offer your services and suggest in a friendly fashion that your involvement in these early stages ensures that your work will support their overarching goals and achieve the outcomes they're after. How you frame this matters a great deal: attempting to lecture your non-UX counterparts on why UX must be involved early is usually a losing battle. So, instead, make your pitch about helping them get what they want. By getting a seat at those conversation tables and offering yourself in the capacity of early-stage visualizer and prototyper, you'll be in a position to ask important questions, offer possible solutions, and demonstrate why what you do matters—simply by participating.

- **Help others see how UX makes their lives easier.** Make it clear how your involvement can actually save time, effort, and headaches. For example, one of the banes of every product team everywhere is rework. For example, it might be wasted effort changing things again and again because requirements were unclear or not fully thought through, or because stakeholders keep changing their minds about what they want. Everything is designed, the deadline is looming, and new requests keep coming in. Everyone involved is deeply frustrated and wondering why no one thought about any of this earlier. But this isn't about teaching anyone the error of their ways. What you're really after here are opportunities to ask better questions, much earlier in the process, and demonstrate how early UX research and side-by-side iteration and testing with developers *eliminates* any number of possible development paths that don't need to be taken.

  Sharing a UX project plan (see Chapter 4) demonstrates how this will happen, along with why it won't slow down any other project efforts. To address these concerns, create one version that shows the project timeline with UX, and one that shows it without. This also gives you a tangible way to talk about trade-offs and compromises—where you could shorten your process, where there are dependencies, and what the team will be losing if UX isn't involved.

- **Play nicely with vendors and outside consultants or agencies.** You may find yourself having to work with these folks, brought in without your input or consent, from time to time. Their focus may be analytics, marketing, development, or even UX and design. And let's be honest, when it's UX or design, that hurts a little. If you've been struggling to establish a robust UX practice, fighting for respect and a seat at the table, so to speak, this can be more than a little frustrating. Someone from outside the organization comes in and magically has the freedom and the support to do all the most interesting work! But, in reality, this is actually a great opportunity for you—don't waste it sulking or being bitter. Here are a few tips to use the situation to your advantage:

  - **Get invited to their meetings or invite yourself.** Position yourself as someone who can help support their work and can share internal knowledge. Communicate to your managers and stakeholders that you can bring the work those consultants generate back in-house.

- **See it as an opportunity to learn and improve.** Watch them work. See how they talk to managers, stakeholders, and executives. Pay attention to what works and what gets approved with little or no argument. They might have some tricks and techniques you can add to your own arsenal.

- **Work *with* them rather than *against* them.** In many cases, what they want is what you want, and you're definitely stronger together. Not to mention that a positive attitude will reflect well on you, and it shows maturity and understanding of the organization.

- **Know that outside vendors never really do all the work.** True, they're often the ones who set a direction. But due to a limited statement of work, the nuts-and-bolts work that happens to extend that vision through the product will be done by you and the product team. Stay actively involved to improve your chances of owning and directing how that work gets executed.

A UX TEAM OF ONE SUCCESS STORY

Vic Costic is a UX team of one who's worked for several startups. Vic shared this story to illustrate why they've been successful despite being outnumbered by developers and thrown into the deep end, so to speak, especially early in their career.

I always take things from the perspective of, if I'm asking "What can you do for me?" then I also need to be asking "What can I do for *you*?" Developers, for example, are obviously very strapped for time. They've got to hit their marks over a sprint. So, they're far more likely to be able to give me their time if I'm very specific about how much time, what exactly we'll do, and most importantly, what they'll get out of it.

So, I say "I need an hour of your time to review these specific things— but if you have any written resources that I can refer to, that works too. I'm trying to optimize your time as much as possible. You benefit because I'll be able to get you designs that actually consider the technical limitations and respect your time a lot better than they would without your input. That's gonna save your sanity in the long run, and it also means that anything we show to leadership is something that can actually be done."

- **Turn the rubber stamp into an opportunity.** One common problem for teams of one is getting called in only near the end of development to do a quick usability review—in other words, to rubber-stamp a product. This can be frustrating and makes it very hard to suggest anything beyond simple, surface-level UI changes. But you can treat this scenario as an opportunity to expose others to what user-centered design can improve, what rework it can eliminate, and how it can make the bets that management is placing a lot more likely to pay off. One way to do this is with guerilla user research (see Chapter 5, "Research Methods") to quickly surface what needs to be improved, based on first-hand observation.

- **Develop case studies.** Often, people don't really know what you do, even after you've done it. People love stories, so wrap up past projects into a clear, succinct, outcome-focused story. Instead of talking about the deliverables that you produce or UX concepts

The best piece of advice I heard very early in my career was when you start a new job, ask everyone you talk to two things: "What keeps you up at night, and what might I do to make your life easier?" That's a little empathy hack; you could work with someone for six months and maybe guess at what their stressors are. But if you just point blank ask them, you know what they need in return from you to invest in giving you their time. You know how to step in their shoes, cultivate empathy for their perspective, and reflect on their pain points. Just like your job as a UX designer is to focus on the pain points of your users, you can also focus on the pain points of your colleagues.

That helps you deal with a no answer more constructively. Ask questions. If you're hearing a no, don't just shut down and get frustrated—listen. And then, ask what's behind it. That's how you understand and learn how to compromise around the no. It's how you turn that no into a maybe—or a yes for something that isn't exactly what you wanted. But even if it's not what you think is the ideal state for the user, that compromise is still better for them than if you shut down completely—or argue and get nothing.

in the abstract, case studies and stories give people a memorable narrative that they can envision themselves in. And when you write that story, lead with the outcome of the work: what changed or improved? What risk was reduced? What money was made or saved? And you can also use those same case studies in your portfolio, so create them as you go, at the end of every project. That way you'll never be faced with the daunting task of trying to remember everything you've ever done over the past several years! Develop a collection of "Mini Case Studies" (Chapter 8) that you can call on or conjure up whenever you need.

- **Break bread.** Turn lunch into relationship-building time. Shared experiences (even minor ones) build trust and can turn coworkers into allies. Getting out of the office and trying to relate on a personal level can change the dynamics of your relationship for the better. There's no agenda here: just open, honest communication.

Responses to Common Objections

Talking about UX often leads to questions, and in some cases, objections. But any seasoned salesperson will tell you that objections are an opportunity, not a threat. Think of an objection as an invitation to a more direct, honest conversation, where you can really probe about what's driving someone else's point of view. The following is a cheat sheet of the most common questions you'll face, and some good ways to answer them.

Objection: *"Just make the UI look better."*

Answer: Limiting the scope of responsibility and involvement that the UX designer has to the interface level limits the potential impact and effectiveness of their work. The degree to which user needs are researched impacts the product at many levels: which features and functions should be included (and which should not); how data, content, language, and labeling should be written and presented; how support should work; and how well it needs to integrate with other touch points like mobile, desktop, and print. As such, many UX and product designers never even touch the UI. Product design and UX are roles that should span product development from start to finish, contributing to and impacting all major product decisions.

Objection: *"But we already do market research."*

Answer: User-centered research is fundamentally design research. Design research differs from market research in approach and intent. They are complementary but different. Market research is about identifying *what* people want; design research is about understanding *why* they want it. Design research is about identifying how best to serve that underlying motivation in a way those users recognize as valuable. Market research is often centered around demographics, but knowing someone's gender, age and income doesn't tell you anything about what motivates them emotionally—and all buying decisions are emotional (Google it).

In design research, you look for evidence of habits, biases, needs, and native worldviews. The goal is to develop empathy and insight into why people do what they do and to spark inspiring ideas for how products can serve unmet needs and enhance their lives. What you learn through this research can help you develop tools like user archetypes (see Chapter 5) that help focus everyone's efforts on delivering value to users—so that value comes back to the business as well.

> **NOTE NO RESEARCH CAN MEAN NO CUSTOMERS**
>
> In 2013, Google introduced Google Glass, a wearable technology that aimed to provide a hands-free, augmented reality experience. But as brilliantly innovative as the concept was, it failed. Why? Because Google never really identified its users. Glass was initially marketed as a revolutionary product with a wide range of potential uses, from professional applications to everyday consumer interactions. But because Google didn't clearly define specific user personas and related needs, the product lacked a clear focus on who its primary users would be—and how it would fit into their lives.
>
> As a result, potential users couldn't identify the real value the product offered. They couldn't see how Google Glass would be useful to them.

Had Google taken the time to do user research and develop sound user personas, they likely would have uncovered the massive privacy and social acceptance concerns that arose like wildfire after the Google Glass debut. Users were extremely uncomfortable with the idea of being recorded without their knowledge, which led to privacy concerns and social backlash. If Google had conducted thorough user research to develop user personas, they might have realized:

- The product was really only appropriate for specific target audiences, such as professionals in fields like healthcare or manufacturing, who could benefit from hands-free information access.
- There were massive concerns around privacy and social acceptability, leading to the development of features that respected privacy and allowed users to control recording more effectively.
- There was a need for clear use cases and scenarios that illustrated the product's value in everyday life.

With even a little user research and well-defined user personas, Google could have tailored the product's features, marketing, and messaging to specific user needs and expectations. This could have addressed concerns, clarified its value proposition, and improved its chances of success in the market.

Objection: *"User experience work is too expensive."*

THAT SOUNDS EXPENSIVE.

Answer: It's always less expensive to fix or improve the plan for a product before it's built, instead of after. For example, let's say the latest iteration of a product launches with no UX research or testing. Everyone learns pretty fast that it now takes users twice as long to do their daily work, so productivity slows across the company. Now the team has to rush to figure out what's wrong and fix it. In our experience, at the very least, it's going to take the team two sprints (four weeks) to find and fix whatever's wrong, and without research, they'll still be guessing. Which means they may get it wrong again.

Let's assume the internal cost of a sprint is $100,000. That means the company just lost $200,000 because they were unwilling to spend a fraction of that—just a couple days—doing simple research and testing.

UX, as you can see, is a preventative investment to keep the costs of your product from getting out of control down the road. Ultimately, user experience work can be as expensive or as affordable as everyone is prepared to make it. But, in truth, it only takes a quick chat with a real user, or showing a proposed design to a few people, to quickly uncover major misalignments between how the product is framed and how people are likely to use it.

Objection: *"It takes too much time."*

UX TAKES TOO MUCH TIME.

Answer: UX work doesn't have to add weeks or months to a project schedule. As Joe is fond of telling his clients, "If UX slows down development, you're doing it wrong." In fact, one benefit that UX can bring to your process is the ability to *rapidly* prototype, test with users, and evolve product design in the space of a single two-week sprint. As you read a minute ago, the time you put in up front isn't an expense; it's an *investment* that defrays other, more burdensome, costs down the road. And whether your organization realizes it or not, UX already exists in your products and processes, in some surprising forms. It currently shows up in places like time in the call center providing support, or extended sales cycles, or time in QA testing, or time in maintenance and bug fixes. Ultimately, formalized UX can save you time by addressing usability and experience issues quickly and inexpensively in the early stages of the project—because they usually become a lot costlier to fix once built.

In general, it's a lot cheaper to fix UX defects early in the development process. And as multiple reports throughout the last decade have shown consistently, that cost increases by a factor of 10 as a project progresses. By way of example:

- Fixing UX defects during the *requirements/discovery* portion of the work costs **$10**.
- Fixing it during *design* costs **$100**.
- Fixing it during *production* coding costs **$1,000**.
- Fixing it during *testing* costs **$10,000**.
- Fixing it after it's already launched costs **$100,000**.

While the numbers change inside organizations, the reality of that 10X increase remains the same. If a company has missed the mark with features and functionality, the time to learn that is obviously at the start of the project, not after launch. Without design research, this isn't possible.

Objection: *"But UX research isn't statistically significant."*

IS UX STATISTICALLY SIGNIFICANT?

Answer: *Statistically significant* means that a given result is unlikely to have occurred by chance. It means we know this because statistical research methods *tell us so.* This creates confidence about the linkage between cause and effect. With quantitative research—conducted with large numbers of people—it's easier to *prove* statistical significance, which is why most business folks are so attached to it. With qualitative research—focused on gathering in-depth understanding of behavior, but often based on relatively small sample sizes—statistical significance is pretty hard to prove. This discrepancy is what creates the skepticism that causes the objection to UX research. User-centered research typically errs on the side of the qualitative: small sample sizes, usually between six and twelve people. This allows us to spend a *lot* more time with each participant one-on-one. It also makes a larger sample prohibitive in terms of time and cost.

Here's the thing about quantitative research lots of people think to themselves, but never say out loud: *you don't really need to do it.* A small sample size is usually enough to give you a sense of bigger trends. Sometimes, seeing just one or two users experience the same problem can clue you into a major opportunity for improvement. You can also get some pretty fascinating and rich detail, which, ultimately, is the main goal of design research.

That said, rich contextual research probably should *not* be used to influence major business decisions, because it isn't necessarily representative of market averages. But it's perfect for triggering empathetic thinking about the context and mindset that people will have when interacting with your product, which enables you to think creatively about how to help your customers. It absolutely can provide valuable clues for what people have trouble with, why that's happening, and what to do about it. It's also possible to combine quantitatively valid research, such as A/B or multivariate testing, with qualitative user research, to create a complete picture of what people do (quantitative) along with *why* they do it (qualitative).

NOTE A MAGIC NUMBER FOR USER RESEARCH

Usability experts Jakob Nielsen and Tom Landauer conducted research in the early 1990s that showed that *by testing with just five users, you can uncover 85% of the usability issues with a product.* The more users you add, says Nielsen, the less you learn—because you keep seeing the same issues over and over.

In 2012, Nielsen revisited this question to see if the magic number five still held true. By analyzing the number of usability findings relative to the number of users across 83 different research studies, Nielsen concluded that *"testing more users didn't result in appreciably more insights."* So, the optimal number of users to test in a qualitative study is still five—just five.

Conversely, warns Nielsen, *"Zero users give zero insights."* By taking the time to conduct research with just a few users, you gain significantly more insights than you'd have with no research at all. (See **www.nngroup.com/articles/how-many-test-users/** for more.) And if you're thinking to yourself *"Yeah, but that was more than a decade ago,"* Joe would like you to know that the five-is-enough-rule is one he still follows to this very day with his clients—who happen to be some of the largest, most highly visible and design-centric companies in the world.

Objection: *"But we already know what needs to be done."*

WE ALREADY KNOW WHAT NEEDS TO BE DONE.

Answer: Let's be honest here. If executives and managers truly knew what users wanted, those users would *have it already*. If they knew what needed to be done, they'd have done it already, and you wouldn't be having this conversation. Here's what you need to understand: when managers or executive leaders are opposed to doing user research, it's partly because they're really, *really* scared of what that research might show them. They're afraid it will confirm the fears they already have, confirm the mistakes that they already know are being made, and confirm that customers have reached the apex of fed-up and are done waiting for the company to do the right thing. All of which may, unfortunately, require that they *do something* about it.

Be that as it may, there are business results they still care about. UX research tells you how to get those results; it tells you not just what's wrong, but also why and how to fix it. It also gives you an opportunity to validate that you got it right. Sometimes, things that seem pretty straightforward or that users may even have asked for explicitly really come from a deeper need. And the only way you'll discover it is by getting out of the office and into people's lives. In the long run, observing real people using your products (or their preferred alternatives) may teach the team some things they didn't know before.

Objection: *"That's marketing's/engineering's/ product management's job."*

THAT'S SOMEONE ELSE'S JOB.

Answer: Actually, it's *everyone's* job. In product development, there are a lot of people who are thinking about the product from various angles. Engineers think about how to write code that's efficient and reliable. Marketers think about how to connect to and engage the target market for the product. Quality assurance folks think about whether people can use the product to complete the intended use cases. All of that directly impacts the quality of the user experience. And UX is, in some respects, the *glue* that binds all these considerations together, ensuring that the actual experience of using the product is, from moment to moment, clear, relevant, appropriate, fluid, and even a little bit delightful. And not incidentally, UX is also the critical inch that ensures the final product is productive, efficient, cost-effective, and profitable. But the bottom line here is that we all need each other to make that happen—*every* person in *every* role.

NOTE THE ROLE OF USER EXPERIENCE

A 2005 article from IEEE called "Why Software Fails" listed the top 12 reasons why software projects are unsuccessful. Of the 12, three were directly connected to issues that user experience practitioners can help with:

1. Badly defined system requirements
2. Poor communication among customers, developers, and users
3. Stakeholder politics

Surprisingly enough, those same three issues are still very much a reality in software development today—possibly even more so due to the rise in both software complexity and an exponentially increased rush to market.

Experience Dynamics made a strong case for UX involvement back in 2014, when they revealed that the input of a UX designer reduces the amount of time developers have to rework a product by up to 50%—and reduces development time overall by between 33% and 50%—by improving decision-making and helping to prioritize development tasks.

While UX isn't a silver bullet for all the complexities of product development, much of a user experience practitioner's work is about making sure that what is being built is relevant to both customers' goals and business goals. A UX practitioner can help the larger product team ensure that system requirements and product designs are aligned with what users expect, need, and are willing to use.

If You Only Do One Thing...

...follow the principles at the start of this chapter! Invite non-UX people into your process. Listen with genuine curiosity. Make ideas tangible. And, above all else, be patient with yourself and others, remembering that design is an iterative process that takes a cooperative, collaborative team effort to get right.

In UX, designing great products is only half the work. The other half is handling all the *people stuff* that goes along with it: building support, ferreting out lingering objections and concerns, untangling a knot of competing agendas, and rallying your colleagues around a new direction. This chapter encourages you to address those challenges and objections head-on. Having the right attitude matters: be vigilant against feelings of defensiveness or combativeness in yourself—and instead, work to cultivate a collaborative, curious, and respectful mindset.

Practice

Up to this point, we've focused on the UX team of one philosophy—why you do it, how you build support, how you can identify and handle common challenges, and how to keep growing. Now, let's turn our attention to the nuts and bolts of tactical user experience work. These are the practices and methods that make this philosophy a reality.

While passion and vision are what bring many people to UX in the first place, it's the successful practice of the craft—outcomes that serve both users and businesses—that keeps them here. At the same time, UX teams of one have to navigate the precarious balancing act of continuously learning their craft, involving others, and improving products and services, all at the same time.

Part II, "Practice," gives you tangible tools for managing this balancing act.

Before we get rolling, a quick caveat to all of this. In order to truly take this no-stone-unturned approach we're advocating in Part II, you need to be working in a company with a high level of UX maturity. One where urgency doesn't trump importance, and where you're given the time, space, resources, and autonomy to step back and really dig into what's needed and why. Those places certainly do exist, and we're happy to report that overall UX maturity across corporations has grown greatly since the first edition of this book. Many UX and product design professionals work in environments where collaboration and respect for these disciplines is high.

However, there are just as many people who work in companies where everyone has far too much to do and far too little time to do it in. And that usually walks hand-in-hand with the reality that no one really understands what UX is or why it matters or *just how much work is really required* to improve a product and see some measurable business outcome. When this is the case, all of the methods we're about to discuss are still infinitely valuable to you—but don't count on being able to do it all up front, *before* developers start building stuff. Don't expect stakeholders or subject matter experts to block out dedicated time to answer your questions or do these workshops.

In these environments, things like a UX questionnaire or UX project plan are for *your use only*, to help you think through things—because it's likely no one else will have the time or inclination to look at them. In these situations, all you can do is your best: ask the questions that need to be asked anyway and think through what you can, when you can. Don't take the lack of time or interest personally (because in most cases, it has nothing to do with you). Focus on the work, on making it the best it can be. Commit to learning and trying to work in small, incremental improvements on the fly for the duration of the project, instead of trying to answer and plan everything up front.

The point: be flexible. Be patient. Remember that there is no one right way to do anything, no magical prescription for good UX and design that you must adhere to. What follows are suggestions—possibilities you should explore, adapt, and change as necessary. Use the parts that work for you in your situation and ignore the rest. And above all else, remember that something is always better than nothing.

MOSCOW

Should Have | Could Have | Want to Have

Customer Journey.

Today
Frustrated
Not enough options
No time

OPT-out
Choose complete Survey/F

CHAPTER 4

Planning and Discovery Methods

N o matter what kind of product you're designing, all work begins with planning and discovery. Planning and discovery methods focus and guide your efforts, and, in the end, set you up for long-term success. This is the point in the process where you get focused, get organized, and get agreement with everyone else involved—especially stakeholders from other departments—on priorities and goals before jumping in and overhauling the product. Not only do all of those things give you more confidence as you work, but they also give others confidence that there's rigor, practicality, and predictability in this practice. In other words, that it's good business.

The practices and methods in this chapter will help you ask and get answers to these questions:

- What do you plan to fix or improve—and *why* does it need fixing or improving?
- What's the expected outcome of that work for users or customers?
- What problems are you solving—and are they worth the time, effort, and expense of solving them?
- What will that work do for the business's bottom-line goals?
- How likely is it, given the market and your organization's own standards, that you'll be able to achieve a quality outcome?
- What specific tactical activities make up the work you'll be doing?
- What's the plan? How will UX work integrate with the other parts of the product development effort?

Any time any one of those questions goes unanswered at the start of a project, it's very likely that trouble of some kind is on the way. So, in this chapter, we'll cover multiple methods you can use to get answers, leaving no stone unturned. In our experience, the following methods, and the questions they provoke are the best ways to do just that:

- **Method 1: UX Questionnaire.** What do you know about your product and the user experience that it's intended to provide, and what do you need to know?
- **Method 2: UX Project Plan.** What UX practices will you employ to design a great user experience?
- **Method 3: Stakeholder Interviews.** What are the team's priorities, and how much awareness and support for UX currently exists?
- **Method 4: Opportunity Workshop.** What areas of the product are most in need of improvement from a UX perspective?

- **Method 5: Project Brief.** What are the expected outcomes for this user-centered design project?
- **Method 6: Strategy Workshop.** What is your team's vision for the ideal user experience, and what do you need to focus on to bring that unique experience to life?

METHOD 1

UX Questionnaire

How much do you know about your product and the user experience that it's intended to provide? What else do you need to know?

A user experience questionnaire is deceptively simple: it's just a standard list of questions for you to ask yourself about a product and its ideal user experience at the start of any engagement. But we hear you asking, why not just start working on improving the user experience and see where things go? After all, if a product has a clear purpose and a specific audience, and you have some good ideas for how to improve the user experience, then you're all set, right?

Not exactly.

Reality is that product design can—and most certainly *will*—go off track any number of times, for any number of reasons. UX work is often positioned as a silver bullet to solve what can be a dizzying set of challenges, ranging from a lack of product strategy to issues with the organizational structure. The user interface is often where these problems become visible, but the cause is usually much deeper than surface level. And, in some cases, it has nothing to do with the product itself. People, politics, and power struggles inside organizations can often play a very large role in pushing through an unfinished product riddled with significant UX defects.

A good UX questionnaire can help you spot these issues early on, which puts you in a better position to point out all those red flags and prevent them from putting the product's design and UX at risk. On a more practical level, the answers to these questions can also help you make sure that the goals are clear—that you know *what* you're designing as well as *why*. A good UX questionnaire will also get you thinking about what work still needs to be done, when that should happen, and how you might want to proceed. This then feeds into the UX project plan described later in this chapter.

You can create a template like the one shown in Figure 4.1 to make it an easily repeatable process. As you can see, the final document doesn't have to be polished. This is essentially a scratch pad for you to help yourself think through specific questions.

Average Time

1–2 hours total

- 1 hour to put together
- (Optional) 1 hour for follow-up questions with colleagues

Use When

- You're about to start work on a new project and have questions about whether you're set up for a successful engagement. You wonder if there is more planning, positioning, or strategic thinking that needs to be done before overall UX or UI design can be improved.
- At any point to help you assess your own understanding of the product.

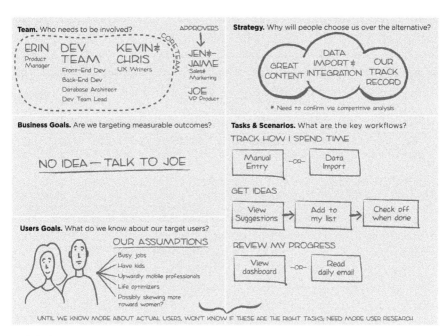

FIGURE 4.1

A sample UX questionnaire.

Try It Out

1. **Ask yourself some key questions.**

   Set aside an hour at the start of a project to answer the following questions.

   - **Project Goals.** What are the project goals? Ideally, you can summarize this as a short list of things you, the business, and its stakeholders aim to achieve with this project. If you have 3–5 items on this list, you're probably in good shape. If the project has dozens of goals, expectations are likely overly broad or ambitious, which means the project scope is too large. Ask around to figure out which goals are top priority, and which are less critical, if push comes to shove.

   - **Users.** Who are the target users? Describe the main categories of users who will use the product in as much detail as possible. Are they commercial consumers? Business customers? Internal employee users? Why do they use the product? What are their primary motivators, problems, pain points, and goals? What are the biggest problems, obstacles, or inefficiencies they currently deal with? If the answer is "Our users are everybody," that's a red flag; there's no such thing. Talk to colleagues to try to define your target users with more specificity.

   - **Strategy.** What's the value proposition of the product? Why do people use it? What does using it help them do, be, or have? Why do they choose to use it over competitors' products? If a significant portion currently does use a competing product, what would it take to get them to switch to this one? What level of feature and functionality does this product need to achieve—and exceed—perceived parity with direct and indirect competitors?

   - **Tasks, technology, and scenarios.** What are the primary tasks and scenarios that the design should support? How do users undertake those tasks now? What do they use to do that, and what other products do they use before and after doing that work? What technology is in place now, and what related technology decisions have already been made? Where would (or do) people typically use this product, in what environment? On what device(s)? Platforms? Operating systems?

   - **Success measures.** How does the product make money? Which levers influence whether the product is profitable or not? What user or customer behaviors translate directly to

- **Feed into the project brief.** If you fill out a user experience questionnaire in relation to a specific project or initiative, the answers you provide here can become the foundation of your project brief (described later in this chapter).

- **If you work remotely:** It's even more important to ask yourself these kinds of questions, to ensure that being at a distance isn't creating any blind spots for you. Using a template like the one shown in Figure 4.1 can help you identify any areas that you may be overlooking.

profit? What key performance indicators are tracked and how? Are there any other numbers that people track to determine if the product is performing well or poorly?

- **Key dates and milestones.** Are there any significant deadlines that you should be aware of, either related to one-off projects or regular production or milestones? What's driving those dates, and how flexible (or inflexible) are they?

- **Risks.** Are there any significant red flags that you see up front? Are there obstacles to success, or external factors that may prevent progress, implementation, or user/customer adoption? Are there legal compliance or security risks that must be addressed by UX and design?

2. **If you don't know, ask.**

   If you encounter a question you don't know the answer to, ask a coworker—ideally, a few of them. Different people may give you different perspectives on the situation.

UX Project Plan

What UX practices will you employ to design a great user experience?

A UX project plan shouldn't be confused with the overall project plan, which is usually owned by a project manager and includes such things as engineering and quality assurance. The UX project plan may help you think about how UX work will integrate with the broader project timeline, but it is primarily your plan for how you're going to conduct UX activities. Sometimes, the work you are asked to do as a UX team of one doesn't warrant a full-blown plan. Fix a form on a particular screen. Do a heuristic assessment. Such activities may just take a day or two. However, if your involvement is likely to span more than a few weeks, a plan is important. Mainly, a UX project plan forces you to be honest with yourself about how you are going to tackle the work. This can be especially helpful if you aren't really sure how you're going to tackle work—which, let's face it, happens every now and again. Sitting down to craft a plan helps you figure out what your process should be.

Even if no one has directly asked you for a UX project plan, it's probably a good idea to put one together. There may come a time in the project when someone does ask you …and when they do, you'll be ready. Because UX processes and deliverables are sometimes unfamiliar and new, your non-UX colleagues may not know what to expect. A clear, jargon-free UX plan can help set their expectations. It's even better if you can include work samples. If you don't have examples from your own portfolio yet, borrowing examples from books or online works, too.

Average Time

2–3 hours, plus ongoing maintenance thereafter

- 1 hour to put together
- 1–2 hours to share and revise

Use When

- You start your first step in planning a UX project.
- Or, after doing some preliminary research, when talking to stakeholders, and once you're confident that you understand project goals.

Try It Out

1. **First, make sure that you understand the goals of the project.**

   Try to summarize them in a few short statements. The goals should speak to the business or behavioral change that you hope to create through your work. (If you've completed a "project brief," described later in this chapter, it will satisfy this step.)

2. **Brainstorm relevant methods.**

   Start free-listing activities that you think will help you achieve your goal. Sometimes, it helps to start by working backward. For example, if the project goal is to produce more inbound sales leads, you'll need to make it easier for customers to understand and be excited by your services and request more information. To do that, you'll need to redesign your landing pages. But before that, you'll need to understand users' perceptions of the landing pages now, why they're going there, and in what way the site *does* and *does not* currently meet their needs.

3. **Estimate duration.**

   Once you've got a solid list of activities that you think will help achieve the project goal, go ahead and estimate the time you think each activity will take. (For help with time estimates, refer to the average time estimates throughout this section of this book, and be sure to check out the tip on estimating complexity later in this chapter.)

4. **Place milestones.**

   Talk to your colleagues—especially those who are responsible for specific milestones relating to the product—and find out if there are key milestones or firm deadlines that you need to be aware of. Often, these will influence how much time you have for each step and, in turn, what type of activity you choose. For example, do you need to have a functioning prototype ready in four weeks? If so, maybe you don't have time for extensive in-the-field contextual research. Maybe aim for a day of "Guerrilla User Research" instead (see Chapter 5, "Research Methods").

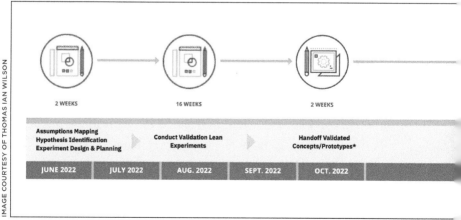

5. **Create a simple document.**

Put your plan together in a simple document that lays out activities, duration, inputs, outputs, and who needs to be involved. You can also show points of overlap or dependencies with the broader project plan. Avoid the tendency to spend too much time on this document overly finessing its design. Figure 4.2 shows a simple project plan outlining what work will happen when and who will be doing it. Figure 4.3 shows how you can lay out a project plan to communicate milestones and duration. Figure 4.4 shows that your plan doesn't even have to be digitized. A large whiteboard can be all you need.

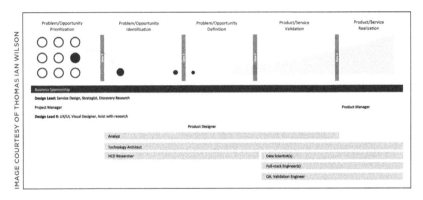

FIGURE 4.2
This project plan shows the core chunks of work to be done, along with when people in different roles come into the picture and where their work overlaps.

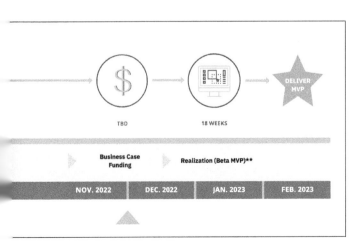

FIGURE 4.3
A visualization of the work over time, simplified to share with stakeholders who really only want the big picture—with an indication of where the project stands currently (see arrow).

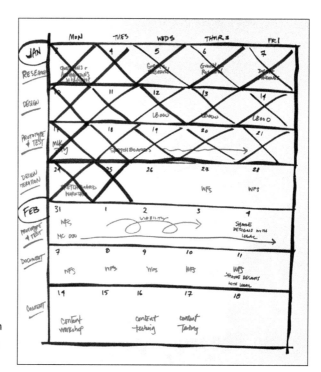

FIGURE 4.4

Of course, a whiteboard works just fine as well, especially if you have a dedicated workspace where the whole team can pop in and check on the plan as needed.

- **Scope and re-scope.** Often, your first pass at a UX project plan is luxuriously paced and, alas, unrealistic, given the time available. It's common to have to do another pass through the plan, to reduce it down to a manageable minimum.

- **Estimate complexity.** While reducing is often necessary, be careful not to shortchange yourself in the process. Use a complexity index like the one shown in Figure 4.5 to figure out which pieces are most likely to require extra time.

COMPLEXITY INDEX				
ACTIVITY	EST. DAYS	COMPLEXITY	WORST-CASE EST. DAYS	RISKS
User Research				
Recruit & Plan	5	3	10	Recruiting could take longer than expected; have had trouble finding target users in the past
Interview & Document	5	2	7.5	High volume of data to document and make sense of
TOTALS	10		17.5	
Product Assessment				
Heuristic Markup	2	1	2	
TOTALS	2		2	
Strategy Workshop				
Plan	2	1	2	
Conduct	1	1	2	
Document	1	2	3	Hard to estimate volume of data, content & documentation to make sense of
TOTALS	4		7	
UX Recommendations				
Prepare & Deliver	3	3	6	Contingent on approval; add'l discussion or data needed will add more time
TOTALS	3		6	
Initial Lo-Fi UI Concepts				
Team Sketch Sessions	3	2	5	Dependent on the number of direction changes uncovered by team & stakeholders during sessions
Refine Sketches	2	2	4	Dependent on the number of direction changes uncovered by team & stakeholders during sessions
TOTALS	5		9	
Iterative Hi-Fi UI Design				
Initial Figma Prototypes	10	2	15	May need re-adjusting and sprints and usability testing completes based on cust. feedback or tech feasibility; won't know until we test at end of each sprint
Iterations & Revisions	5		7.5	
TOTALS	15		22.5	
Usability Testing				
Task-based usability tests	concurrent w/ prototypes	2	15	Schedule will be impacted if UI prototyping and stakeholder review takes longer than expected (testing runs concurrent w/ design)
TOTALS			15	

FIGURE 4.5
The key to the complexity index is the rating given in the third column (how complex?).

continues

Here is how a complexity index works: give each task or step a number to indicate how hard or complex it seems. One equals not hard at all. Three equals pretty complex and unpredictable. Two would be somewhere in between. For the most complex items, pad the calendar with extra time. Alternately, you can ask yourself whether these need to be done as planned, or whether they can be simplified or reduced.

- **Use checklists.** Make sure that you are considering all the standard parts of the UX process and assessing *whether* and *if* each part applies. Use a simple checklist like the one shown in Figure 4.6 to mentally go over each part of a standard process and determine which should be included in your work.

- **Plan for triage periods.** In every project, there are rough patches and smooth patches. Usually, the rough patches correspond to important transition points. This is natural. Those are the moments when groups of people are working together to determine how to move forward. That inevitably requires some extra time for communication, thinking, and getting aligned. Being caught unaware inevitably makes it feel like the project is in trouble, but you can plan ahead for it by adding triage buffer zones into your project plan. There are a few places where triage padding is advisable:

  - **After research**, around the time that you are socializing the research findings and deciding what to do about them.

  - **Once the designs start to transition to higher fidelity** (for example, moving from sketches into wireframes). Seeing the designs become more *real* triggers all kinds of reactions and often a need to adjust based on those reactions.

- **If you work remotely**, find ways to make your plan easy for others to see and access. This doesn't necessarily have to mean heavy documentation: a Google Spreadsheet or an Excel document on a shared drive is probably all you need. It can also be helpful to set up a physical reminder of the plan (such as a printout or a whiteboard) to help keep yourself on track.

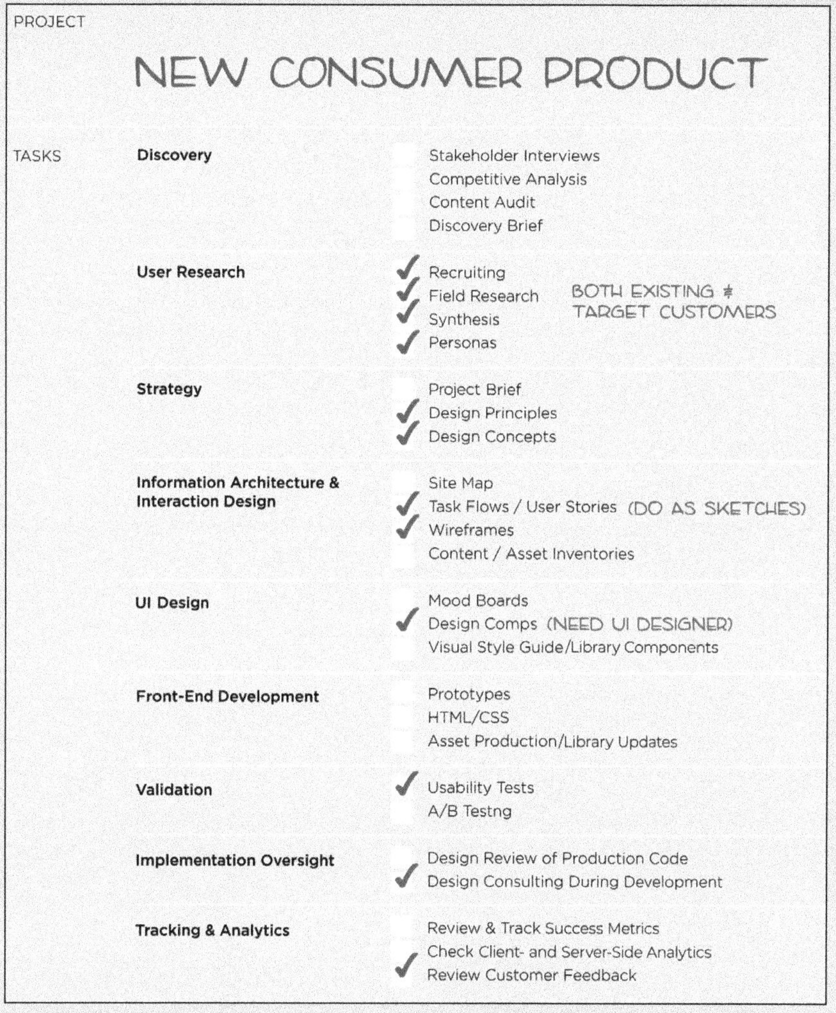

NEW CONSUMER PRODUCT

TASKS		
Discovery	Stakeholder Interviews	
	Competitive Analysis	
	Content Audit	
	Discovery Brief	
User Research	✓ Recruiting	
	✓ Field Research	BOTH EXISTING ≠
	✓ Synthesis	TARGET CUSTOMERS
	✓ Personas	
Strategy	Project Brief	
	✓ Design Principles	
	✓ Design Concepts	
Information Architecture & Interaction Design	Site Map	
	✓ Task Flows / User Stories (DO AS SKETCHES)	
	✓ Wireframes	
	Content / Asset Inventories	
UI Design	Mood Boards	
	✓ Design Comps (NEED UI DESIGNER)	
	Visual Style Guide/Library Components	
Front-End Development	Prototypes	
	HTML/CSS	
	Asset Production/Library Updates	
Validation	✓ Usability Tests	
	A/B Testng	
Implementation Oversight	Design Review of Production Code	
	✓ Design Consulting During Development	
Tracking & Analytics	Review & Track Success Metrics	
	Check Client- and Server-Side Analytics	
	✓ Review Customer Feedback	

FIGURE 4.6

Your checklist should be customized to the parts of the process that you typically include in your work.

Stakeholder Interviews

What are the team's priorities, and how much awareness and support for UX currently exists?

This is where you gather information and learn what matters to your colleagues. Knowing the priorities of others will help you identify where there are opportunities and problems to solve—and where user-centered design practices can help solve them. Stakeholder interviews usually take the format shown in Figure 4.7, just you and a colleague chatting informally in an office or conference room. No matter how you do this, the goal is to learn about your colleagues' priorities and goals, and to figure out and share how your UX efforts can help them accomplish those goals.

If you're lucky on your stakeholder interviews, you'll be pleasantly surprised by how much people already value human-centered products (as evidenced by code words like *user-friendly*, *intuitive*, and inevitably, *Apple*). If you're less lucky, you might find that people have a wary and seasoned caution about what can and cannot be done. But that's valuable information, too; in order to overcome those objections, you need to know what they are.

PHOTO COURTESY OF ALEX GREEN

FIGURE 4.7
Stakeholder interviews. A young woman taking notes while asking a
stakeholder some questions during an interview.

Average Time

5–8 hours total

- 1 hour to plan and schedule
- 3–5 hours to interview people
- 1–2 hours to synthesize your notes

Use When

- You're new to a company or team.
- You're trying to transition your responsibilities to include more UX and want to make a case.
- You're starting out a big project.

Try It Out

1. **Ask yourself what you want to learn.**

   This could be as broad as understanding the overall priorities of the company, or as specific as learning what each person on this project sees as your role. Having a few clearly stated learning objectives in mind will drive who you talk to and what questions you ask. To determine your key learning objectives, ask yourself, "If I learn nothing else, what are the two or three things I need to understand better after talking with people?"

2. **Next, put together your list of interviewees.**

   Ask colleagues or a supervisor whom they would recommend that you speak to. Leverage their knowledge of the organization. Or think in terms of roles and then attach names to those roles. For example, who has the *budget* for this project? Who will be *engineering* the product? Who's *marketing* it? Who's *selling* it? Who's *supporting* it? Who has ultimate *veto power* over the design? In any case, aim to speak to a cross-functional team so you can see the project or product from a variety of angles.

3. **Write down your questions.**

Basically, an interview guide is just a list of questions you want to ask. These questions should ultimately roll up to your learning objectives, but you may find that you need to ask them in different ways, depending on the role of the person you're talking with. Here are some good generic questions to start with:

- What's your role in the organization, and how does it relate to the product?

- What are your goals and objectives in your role? What are your top priorities? How do you know if you're successful? How do you measure success?

- How does your work impact customers? Who do you consider to be your primary customers? Can you describe them? What are their expectations, priorities, and goals? Why do they use your (or our) products? What prevents them from using your products if anything? What questions do you have about users/customers that you don't currently have answers to?

- Who are your competitors, and how well are you doing compared to them? What do you do well? What could be improved? What differentiates your company and your products in the market?

- [If there's a specific project underway that you're involved in…] What are your goals for this project? What is your vision for how this project will improve our product? Do you see any risks or red flags?

4. **Start listening.**

Schedule one-on-ones and ask your questions. Each conversation will probably be different but try to refer back to your learning objectives in each one, so you can compare answers and spot interesting differences in points of view. If you're the shy type, or you feel like it will be awkward to ask for people's time and start interviewing them in this way, here are a couple of things that may help:

- Offer to keep it short. Even 30 minutes of someone's time is better than nothing, and it's a lot harder for people to turn you down. You might even offer to take them out to coffee for this meeting, which tends to make conversation more natural and friendly.

- Explain (either beforehand, by email, or at the start of the interview) what you're trying to accomplish. Let them know that this is a big help to you. Even if you think they could care less about the potential improvements to the user experience, explain that this will help you improve the way you work. And, of course, be gracious and appreciative.

5. **Figure out what you heard.**

   After you have finished all your interviews, review your notes and tease out the big themes. Pay particular attention to:

   - **Expectations** that people have of you or of user experience.

   - **Assumptions and working knowledge** about users or customers. What do you absolutely know to be true, what things are merely hunches, and what gaping holes in your knowledge exist?

   - **Problems or concerns** with the existing product or the way people find it, pay for it, or use it.

   - **Failures**, such as things that have been tried in the past that haven't worked well, and why that happened.

   - **Questions** to follow up on at a later date.

   - **Involvement**, including who wants to be actively involved with UX and in what ways?

These interviews should help you see what parts of the product you should be focusing on, and what sacred cows are truly sacred (versus those that can be challenged). They may also help you see what technical and practical constraints you will need to work within. Without a doubt, they'll give you a sense of how success will be measured and judged. Finally, they will help you gauge how much support and enthusiasm there is for user-centered improvements. The art of the stakeholder interviews, and interviewing in general, is to *accept* and *believe* what your interviewee is telling you, but also to ask probing questions to try to understand what's *really* underneath their beliefs. When in doubt, keep asking *"why?"*

TIPS AND TRICKS FOR STAKEHOLDER INTERVIEWS

- **Share what you learn.** Offer to share your findings with your interviewees. Send a heartfelt thank-you and a summary of the themes that you heard from your interviews. This builds goodwill for the next time you need to interview these folks.

- **Take good notes.** If you are a competent typist, take along a laptop for note-taking and type your notes as you go. If you're more of a hunt-and-peck kind of typist, consider taking along a buddy to take notes, so you can focus on the conversation. While it's common to record interviews with users, it's probably best to put the recorder away when talking to stakeholders. Part of what you're trying to accomplish here is to build rapport, and being recorded can often make people a little cautious. If you're a truly terrible note-taker, leave a few minutes at the end of each conversation just for summarizing; ask your interviewee to sum up the most important things from their point of view. During this time, you can jot down just the high-level things as they rattle them off.

- **Plan ahead to share what you learned with impact.** Think in advance about how you need to report, share, or otherwise use your findings. Give away the ending of the story first—what improvements, actions, or decisions may be in the company's best interest, based on insights from these interviews. Frame these possible outcomes accordingly and succinctly. Let's say nearly all your stakeholders' chief concern is cutting user support costs. If you're presenting findings with a slide deck, suggest product changes based on the top three priorities for all interviewees on one slide. Frame it with a headline like this: "Top 3 ways UX improvement reduces support costs."

- **If you work remotely**, use a video conferencing tool like Zoom, Google Meet, or Microsoft Teams. Up to 80 percent of communication is nonverbal, so being able to take in the visual cues as well as the verbal ones is important.

Opportunity Workshop

What areas of the product are most in need of improvement from a UX perspective?

An opportunity workshop is a way to quickly assess what work needs to be done to improve user experience via product design, what's highest priority from a business perspective, and what will have the most impact from a user/customer perspective.

Average Time

3–4 hours total

- 1 hour to plan and invite people
- 2 hours to conduct the workshop
- 1 hour to document what you learned and plan the next steps

Use When

You find yourself having general discussions about the need for an improved user experience, but there is no clear momentum or sense of how to get there.

Try It Out

1. **Host a work session.**

   Block off at least two hours on the calendar and invite a cross-functional team together of people who all work on the product.

2. **State the goals of the work session.** For example:
   - Identify issues and pain points in the current product or process: What's occurring, how bad is it, and how often does it happen?
   - Prioritize those issues from a UX point of view. What can you actually do to solve these issues?
   - Decide on your next steps to address or improve any (or all) of them.

3. **Uncover problem areas.** Guide the team in a "pain storm" activity (see what we did there?) on sticky notes or index cards, as shown in Figure 4.8. Ask everyone to write down as many things they can think of that are:

   - A problem in the current product
   - A missed opportunity in the current product
   - Just plain important to get right in the product
   - One by one, ask people to share their sticky notes, and then put them on the wall where others can see them

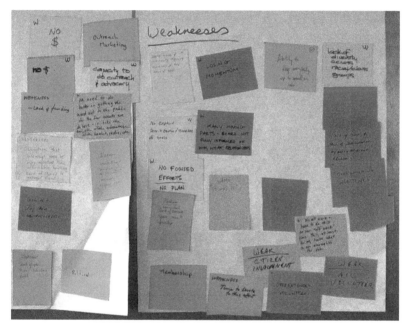

FIGURE 4.8
"Pain storm" opportunity areas.

4. **Discuss strengths.** Next, ask the team to write down the product's strengths—again, one strength per sticky note, as shown in Figure 4.9. It's useful to follow problem areas with strengths so that the team ends on a positive note, even if the overall discussion may have been constructively critical.

5. **Find themes.** Next, guide the team in an activity to organize the issues that were identified into related groupings. Once some clear groups begin to emerge, ask the team to label each group.

Put the label on another sticky note (preferably of a different size or color, to stand out from the other sticky notes) so that everyone can easily stand back and see the issues and opportunities as broad themes.

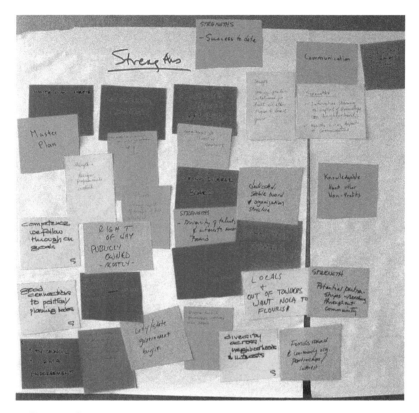

FIGURE 4.9
Brainstorm strengths.

6. **Prioritize.** Now, lead the team in a prioritization exercise. This could just be a discussion. Or, to make it more structured, give everyone a vote. Then ask them to put their vote next to the clusters that they think are most urgent to address, improve, or enhance.

7. **Discuss.** Once the priorities have been clearly identified, lead the group in a discussion about how urgently these should be addressed, and how you'd like to address them.

- **Use as a foundation for follow-up conversations.** Just because the team reaches some clear priorities doesn't necessarily mean that they will or should all be acted on; not everything is worth doing. You can, however, use those priorities as a starting point for tangible conversations with decision-makers about what changes the team is recommending and why. Remember that the *why* needs to be something those decision makers *care* about.

- **Don't skip user research.** An opportunity workshop is a great way to create a dialogue about how to improve UX, but it should not be considered a replacement for actually talking to users or customers. Issues raised here should be considered hypotheses to be validated or disproven through subsequent research and user testing.

- **If you work remotely**, it's definitely easier to do this kind of thing in person in a workshop setting. However, if that's not an option, you can probably gather much of the same information with a remote session via Zoom or Google Meet. If that's not an option, a survey, while not always completely accurate, is better than nothing. SurveyMonkey and Google Forms both create easy and free surveys.

  Set up your survey to ask people about the perceived strengths and weaknesses of the product. After you've gotten responses from everyone, do your own clustering and send a follow-up survey asking people to prioritize problem areas and provide thoughts on how urgently they believe these issues need to be addressed.

Project Brief

What are the expected outcomes for this user-centered design project?

Often, when a project is beginning, everyone involved has distinct ideas for what the right outcome looks like. In team discussions, it's possible for people to express their point of view and *think* they're all saying the same thing, but actually they might have very different ideas of what they expect to see. A project brief states directly what goals or expectations should prevail as the main mandate for the work. The brief, as its name suggests, is short, simple, and to the point, clearly summarizing the outcomes you expect from UX improvement, along with what you're doing, why you're doing it, and relevant constraints that will drive your work—*in that order.*

Another bonus of the brief is that because it's short—and gives away the ending of the story first (the expected outcomes)—it's more likely that people will actually read it. This creates an opportunity for everyone to agree on—or at least have a productive conversation about—the goals and focus of the project.

Average Time

2–3 hours total

- 1 hour to write the brief
- 1–2 hours to share with people (either in one-on-one conversations or a group meeting)

Use When

- You're starting a new project.
- You've inherited an in-progress project or have joined a team that's already been working together, but you need to get clarity and alignment on what you're ultimately expected to deliver (and how feasible it is you can do so).

Try It Out

1. **Determine the right building blocks for your project brief.**

   Based on your organization and what you're working on, here are some key questions to ask yourself (either on paper, or just in your head) when you're teeing up a project. Note that these questions reflect many of the same things you think about when doing a UX Questionnaire (described earlier in this chapter), so if you've already completed one of those, you can start by pulling your answers from there.

   - **Business needs.** What business needs are driving this project? If this is successful, what will be the impact on business? What is the revenue model for this product? What costs associated with it factor into this project? What measurable impact will improving this product have?
   - **User needs.** Who are your users or customers? What are their primary needs? What do you know about them? What don't you know about them? What assumptions are you making about them that you need to validate?

- **Goals.** What are your team's goals? What are your personal goals? How will you personally know if you are successful? When capturing goals, be careful not to confuse the what with the how. A how might be "redesigning the customer self-service support UI." The *what* in this case might be "to reduce the volume of phone calls to customer support."

- **Key expectations.** What are they expecting from you? Are there any discrepancies between *their* picture of your role and *yours*? What questions might they have? What things should you address prior to kicking off the work?

- **Consider also whether there are softer, but no less important, qualities of the work that are relevant to the overall project mandate.** For example, what is the product's value proposition, and what brand characteristics should the work reinforce or activate? If there are known design principles that should be reflected in the output, what are they? (If not, see the "Design Brief" method in Chapter 6, "Design Methods," for guidance.)

2. **Write up what you know, or your best guesses, into a short document.** Ideally, a project brief should fit on one page, so you can print it out and stick it on the wall for an ever-present reminder of top priorities. The example shown in Figure 4.10 has just a few key sections: what we're building, who it's for, and what the user experience should ultimately deliver from a user or customer's point of view.

3. **Circulate the document.** Share it with team members and key project sponsors; get their agreement or input if possible. If you have a hard time getting feedback by email, turn it into a meeting. Or visit people where they work.

4. **Regularly revisit and make sure that you're still on track.** After the team agrees on the brief, revisit it at major milestones of the project and use it as a framework for communicating how the work is progressing toward the overall high-level goals outlined in the brief itself.

Vision (Why)

We live in a fast-changing world. Modern technology encourages an always-on lifestyle that makes it hard to switch off and experience true rest and rejuventation. Partial attention and perpetual busyness have become the norm, and work/life balance seemingly a thing of the past.

But it doesn't have to be.

Equilibrium is a new offering that uses technology to your advantage to help you make better choices about how you use your time, and to maximize quality time in your life. For people who want to work less and play more, the Good Life Labs Consumer Product helps you become master of your own time.

Unlike to-do lists, complicated productivity systems, or ambitious bucket lists, Equilibrium takes the burden of maintenance off your plate and gives you options that lead to long-term happiness.

Requirements (What)

Socially networked. Integrates with other social networks. Easy for users to import data from other social networks, and easy for them to share what they've been doing in the consumer product with outside networks.

Device interoperable and mobile enabled. Designed for mobile first. Smartphone and SMS capabilities create a daily dialog with the user. PC and tablet experiences invite configuration and deeper integration with content.

Supports formal and informal goal setting. System suggests and detects possible goals, and also enables users to manually create their own goals.

Brings in data from a variety of places. This is the heart of the system. Integrates with tools like Outlook, iCal, Google Calendar, and other productivity software.

Rich information visualizations. Data is repackaged and displayed in suprising and engaging ways.

Design Principles (How)

It does the work for you
(minimal maintenance required)

It reflects your passions
(mirroring you and what you love)

It's the opposite of overwhelming
(calming and rejuvenating)

FIGURE 4.10
A sample project brief.

TIPS AND TRICKS FOR PROJECT BRIEFS

- **Make it ceremonial.** One way to turn the request for feedback on the brief into a more memorable and significant event is to turn it into a redlining workshop. Put together your best possible draft of the project brief based on everybody's feedback. Create multiple large-format posters of the brief, big enough to put on the wall and see from across the room: 2' × 3' is a good size. Then schedule a meeting for the redlining.

- **Invite the core team who will be working with you on the project, plus upper-level sponsors.** Working within teams or as one big group, facilitate a conversation about how the team would modify or change the project brief to better reflect the most critical project goals. Give everyone big red pens and ask them to work together to make changes directly on the project brief posters. (There may be multiple rounds of changes, so you want multiple posters.) You can also do this with a projector; project the brief on a whiteboard, giving everyone red dry-erase markers to write with. Afterward, update the brief to reflect the changes and send it around to the group.

continues

- **Keep the brief, well ...*brief*.** While assembling your brief, consider the rule of three. Try to avoid turning this into a laundry list of features that must be delivered. For each category, seek to summarize the top three *business needs*, top three *user needs*, top three *features and functions to be modified*, *added, implemented,* and so on. This will help you keep things short, simple, and direct.

- **If you work remotely**, a redlining workshop is trickier to pull off remotely, but it's absolutely possible. With collaborative feedback tools like Miro, FigJam, or even Zoom, you can share the brief and have participants mark it up as they would in person. If remote work limits you to only meeting one-on-one with key people, compile suggested changes from those sessions and share them with the broader group.

  It may also be helpful to pair up with a buddy on this, preferably someone who has responsibility for the overall project success—and who has a vested interest in the team having a shared vision. Work with that person to pull the first draft together, and then conduct your review sessions together. When you share the brief with others, it may have more weight coming from both of you.

METHOD 6

Strategy Workshop

What's our vision for the ideal user experience, and what do we need to focus on to bring that unique experience to life?

The ideal time for a strategy workshop is early in the process before design or development has begun. This is the time when optimism and interest in *what could be* are at their highest. This stage involves people when they're most likely to engage with an open mind, at the time when strategic thinking has the best chance of influencing and informing the ultimate work plan.

In a strategy workshop, you're leveraging the collective wisdom of a cross-functional team to establish a vision and a strategy for UX. When people talk about strategy, often they're using the same word to talk about very different concepts. To one person, strategy is about prioritization and having a timeline. To another, it might mean establishing a vision for the future. Neither is wrong, and a strategy workshop can help you get clarity on both.

Average Time

4–8 hours total

- 2–4 hours to plan
- 2–4 hours to conduct the workshop

Use When

- You have a product that feels like a loose collection of features that collectively don't deliver anything meaningful or valuable to users or the business.
- When the team is having trouble prioritizing what's worth doing.
- When you don't know what differentiates your product from its competitors.
- When you need to develop a shared vision with the team on the product's direction and future.

Try It Out

1. **State your goals.**

   Decide on your goals for the workshop. Are they to:

   - **Articulate** what makes the product unique?
   - **Create** an inspiring picture of the future of your product that can unify and motivate the team?
   - **Prioritize** features and areas to focus on?
   - **Determine** what your team should be focusing on now, next, and later?

2. **Make a plan.**

   After you've identified your goals, think about how you need to structure the workshop to achieve them. A strategy workshop can include an assortment of different activities, depending on your needs for that particular project, team, and time. Some of those activities you can try are described below.

Triads

Triads help you explore the identity of your product, starting with a simple word-listing exercise. For this activity, get the team to brainstorm a list of keywords that they think the product should embody, as shown in Figure 4.11.

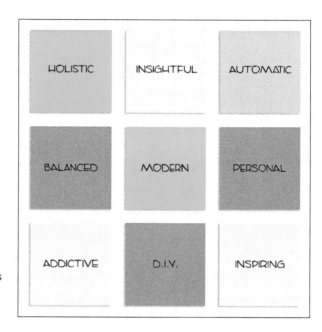

FIGURE 4.11

The first step in triads is to brainstorm words people think should describe the product.

The second step is shown in Figure 4.12. Pick three words that, when put together, describe the core of the product experience. Work with the group to identify combinations that are interesting to them. Then, for each particular three-word group, brainstorm related nouns, verbs, and adjectives that might go with a product built around this triad:

- **Nouns** help you think about objects that you might have in the system.
- **Verbs** help you think about actions that the system should support.
- **Adjectives** help you think about the more fuzzy and abstract parts of the experience, like how it should feel, how it should look, and what design principles should be evident throughout.

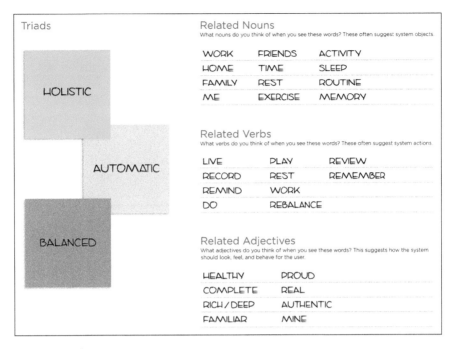

Triads

Related Nouns
What nouns do you think of when you see these words? These often suggest system objects.

WORK	FRIENDS	ACTIVITY
HOME	TIME	SLEEP
FAMILY	REST	ROUTINE
ME	EXERCISE	MEMORY

Related Verbs
What verbs do you think of when you see these words? These often suggest system actions.

LIVE	PLAY	REVIEW
RECORD	REST	REMEMBER
REMIND	WORK	
DO	REBALANCE	

Related Adjectives
What adjectives do you think of when you see these words? This suggests how the system should look, feel, and behave for the user.

HEALTHY	PROUD
COMPLETE	REAL
RICH / DEEP	AUTHENTIC
FAMILIAR	MINE

HOLISTIC

AUTOMATIC

BALANCED

FIGURE 4.12
Next, pick out three words that you think work well together to describe the core of the product experience.

It's okay to reuse keywords in multiple combinations. Figure 4.13 shows another triad that is built on a different three-word group. As you might expect, different word groups lead to different nouns, verbs, and adjectives. If you create a few different triads, you can use them to spark a conversation with the team about which direction feels more appropriate for your product.

For each triad, discuss what an experience characterized by those three words would look like. What would be the most important parts of the product? How would the product function or behave? What would users or customers use the product for? How would they feel about it? How would it fit into their lives? Allow at least 30 minutes for this discussion and capture the conversation on a whiteboard or poster pad.

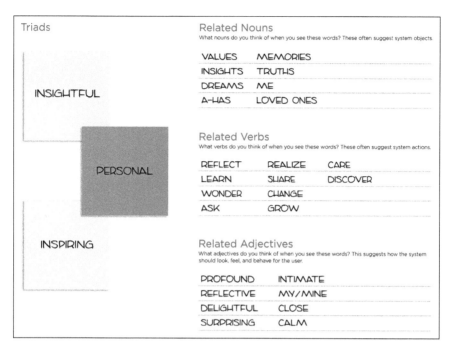

| Triads | Related Nouns |
| | What nouns do you think of when you see these words? These often suggest system objects. |

Related Nouns
What nouns do you think of when you see these words? These often suggest system objects.

VALUES	MEMORIES
INSIGHTS	TRUTHS
DREAMS	ME
A-HAS	LOVED ONES

Related Verbs
What verbs do you think of when you see these words? These often suggest system actions.

REFLECT	REALIZE	CARE
LEARN	SHARE	DISCOVER
WONDER	CHANGE	
ASK	GROW	

Related Adjectives
What adjectives do you think of when you see these words? This suggests how the system should look, feel, and behave for the user.

PROFOUND	INTIMATE
REFLECTIVE	MY/MINE
DELIGHTFUL	CLOSE
SURPRISING	CALM

INSIGHTFUL

PERSONAL

INSPIRING

FIGURE 4.13
Try creating a few different triads and exploring how those product experiences would be different.

Elevator Pitch

An elevator pitch helps you align around a shared description of your product and what's unique about it. For this activity, you can use a template to create a succinct statement explaining what distinguishes your product from its competitors.

To do an elevator pitch, provide copies of the template you see in Figure 4.14 and, working as a group (or broken into teams), have participants fill in the template. The elevator pitch can help everyone understand what differentiates the offering, along with possible features and characteristics that define the product's value. This also helps you prioritize, by shining a light on what matters most in delivering on the core value proposition of the product.

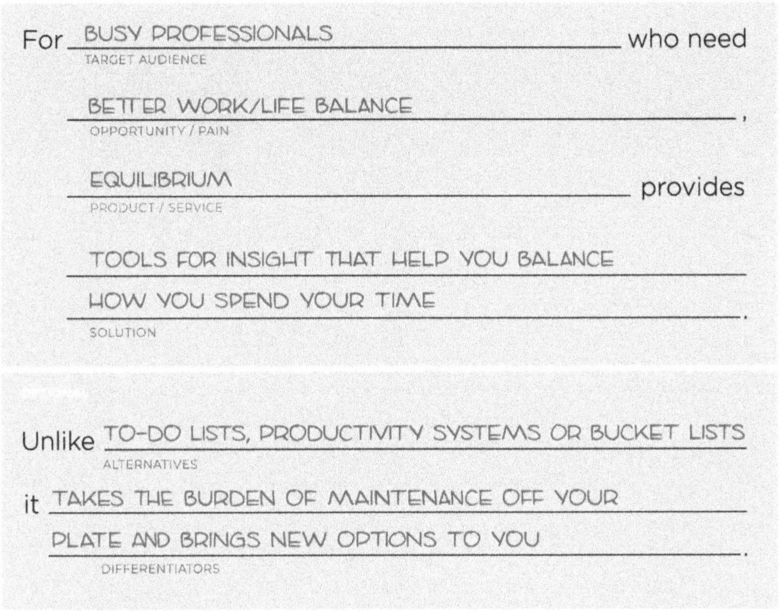

For **BUSY PROFESSIONALS** _____ who need
  TARGET AUDIENCE

  BETTER WORK/LIFE BALANCE _____ ,
  OPPORTUNITY / PAIN

  EQUILIBRIUM _____ provides
  PRODUCT / SERVICE

  TOOLS FOR INSIGHT THAT HELP YOU BALANCE

  HOW YOU SPEND YOUR TIME _____ .
  SOLUTION

Unlike **TO-DO LISTS, PRODUCTIVITY SYSTEMS OR BUCKET LISTS**
  ALTERNATIVES

it **TAKES THE BURDEN OF MAINTENANCE OFF YOUR**

  PLATE AND BRINGS NEW OPTIONS TO YOU .
  DIFFERENTIATORS

FIGURE 4.14
A variation on the elevator pitch template from Geoffrey Moore's book, *Crossing the Chasm*, this simplified template comes from Adaptive Path's User Experience Intensive Training.

Artifact from the Future

This is a technique for getting a team to think beyond specific features and functions and help them envision what impression the product will make once it's live in the world. An artifact from the future can take many different forms: a press release, a blog post, an online video review, or a customer testimonial (see Figure 4.15). The key here is to invite people on the team to create their own version of an artifact from the future.

Ask people to imagine that the future is *now*. The design of the product is complete, and it's out in the world. What does the press release say? What does a blog post say about it? What features and benefits would impress potential customers in an online video review? What would we hope customers say about it? Ask people to share their artifacts to understand their vision and then discuss what still needs to be built, what kind of personality the product will need to have, and how it will fit into their customers' lives for this vision to be realized.

FIGURE 4.15
An example of an artifact from the future. In this case, a Civility™ feature for the iPhone, which tracks instances of verbal abuse directed at Siri, locking users out once the threshold has been exceeded.

Storyboards

Storyboards are usually a tool for later in the process once you start developing product concepts and transitioning into detailed interaction and UI design. But in a strategy workshop, storyboards can get the whole team (even stakeholders who seem "too high up" to be participating in detailed design) to start thinking about the user experience. It's best to do a storyboard exercise after spending some time thinking about user or customer needs. The storyboard becomes a fun, visual way to explain how an offering can address those customer needs.

The storyboard in Figure 4.16 digs into the discovery and first-use experience. In a strategy workshop, you can break people up into teams and ask each team to make their own storyboard. You may find that people naturally dig into different aspects of the experience, which is great. That gives you more breadth in discussing options and priorities with the group. Reassure them that it doesn't matter how it looks; even the simplest, roughest stick-figure sketches will do.

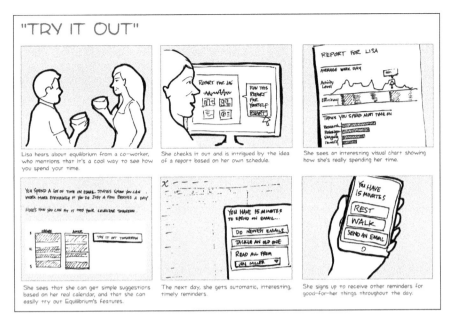

FIGURE 4.16

An example of a storyboard.

Mood Boards

Similar to a storyboard, the mood board is a tool traditionally reserved for later in the design process. But when turned into an up-front and collaborative exercise, the mood board can get the whole team to discuss their individual visions and begin to get excited about a shared vision.

Mood boards are essentially large collages where visual inspiration is carefully assembled to represent the feeling, appearance, and impression that the finished product should make (see Figure 4.17). The mood board typically brings together colors, photos, catch-phrases, and other visual stimuli to create visceral impressions that the team agrees will be the direction the product should aspire to.

Like an artifact from the future, a mood board can serve as a touch-stone throughout product design and development to allow the team to check back in and assess whether the product is coming together in a manner that is true to the team's vision. As you can see in Figure 4.17, you can bring in a range of pictures for participants to choose from or ask them to bring their own images and then work together to create a curated picture of how the experience should feel and function.

FIGURE 4.17
An example of a mood board.

2 × 2 or Kano Model

A strategy workshop has two goals: vision and focus. When you get a team together, all the good ideas often far outpace the team's capacity to develop them. For a team of one, it's important to manage expectations about how many of the items on the team's wish list can be done—and done well. This is important not just because teams of one are operating under resource constraints, but because those constraints impact UX. Users almost always prefer a simple product (fewer features executed extremely well) over a feature-bloated product (a lot of capabilities executed only marginally well). Establishing a focus helps you design to that preference (see Figure 4.18).

If you generated a lot of ideas in your discussions, do a team-based prioritization using a 2 × 2 structure. A 2 × 2 can be used to plot cost versus impact, as shown in Figure 4.19.

STEP 1 LIST FEATURES BEING CONSIDERED

SECURE SIGN IN

DATA IMPORT FROM OUTLOOK

DATA IMPORT FROM SOCIAL NETWORKS

DATA IMPORT FROM OS ACTIVITY

PERSONALIZED REPORTING / DASHBOARD

GOALS MANAGER

SUGGESTED ACTIVITIES & CONTENT

AUTOMATIC DATA SYNCING

"TRY IT OUT" CALENDAR

MOBILE REMINDERS

PROFILE

CONNECTIONS & INBUILT SOCIAL NETWORK

BEHAVIOR MODELS

FIGURE 4.18

For either a 2 × 2 or
a Kano model, step 1
is to list the features
that the team believes
should be included in
the product.

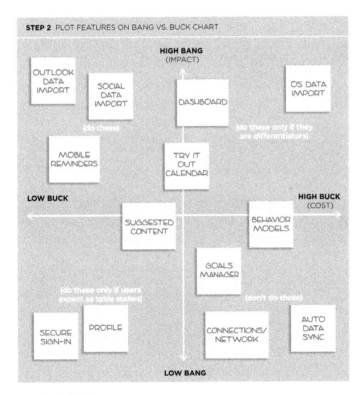

FIGURE 4.19

If you're doing a 2 × 2, step 2 is to plot each feature on the
cost versus impact axes. The plotting of features should be
a group activity, with everyone out of their seats and talking
about where they would place each feature.

Another alternative use of the 2 × 2 is the Kano model, as shown in Figure 4.20. Originally developed to support the product specification process in product manufacturing, the Kano model is a handy tool for plotting the value of features from a UX perspective. The Kano model helps you identify three categories of product features: *basic* attributes (bare minimum required to get users to try or buy), *performance* attributes (you've got to do at least some of them to remain competitive with the market), and *delight* attributes (people don't expect them, but they love you for having them).

Note that in the traditional use of the Kano model, you'd get this feedback directly from customers or users. In this adapted approach, we're using it as a tool for facilitating a discussion with a cross-functional team. Both structures can be used to facilitate a useful dialogue with the team on which features and capabilities should be the focus.

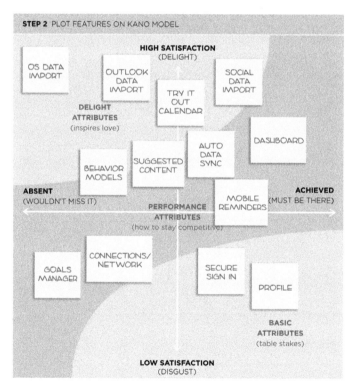

FIGURE 4.20

If you're doing a Kano model, step 2 is to plot each of the features on axes corresponding to satisfaction and achievement.

- **Pick and choose your methods.** Certain activities are optimal for answering certain questions:
  - How we are unique: triads, elevator pitch exercise, design principles
  - Our vision for the future: artifact from the future, storyboards, mood boards
  - Priorities: 2 × 2 or Kano Model
- **If you work remotely**, a strategy workshop should be done in person when possible; it's always worth making a special trip for it. If your whole team is remote, see if you can arrange a time to meet in the same city and to commit to this important vision-building exercise. And as always, if this simply isn't possible, Zoom or Google Meet is the next best thing.

If You Only Do One Thing...

...do the stakeholder interviews. Why? Because it does the best job of laying bare *other people's* ideas and hopes for the product. Even if you do nothing else, these conversations with stakeholders will give you valuable intel on organizational priorities, political considerations, and team dynamics—and will help you discover the assumptions and conditions you'll be working with as you set out to change and improve the user experience.

The methods in this chapter cover a range of activities you can use to get a clear understanding of project goals, opportunities for improvement, and how to get started. But at its heart, this chapter is about discovering the expectations your colleagues have for your product. It's also about giving yourself the time and space to think about your own expectations—what you believe needs to be done to create a satisfying user experience.

PHOTO COURTESY OF ARINA KRASNIKOVA

CHAPTER 5

Research
Methods

W hen you work on a product day in and day out, you can start to become *too* familiar with it, seeing and accepting all the pragmatic trade-offs that have been struck to make a complex thing possible. That perspective, however, can make you an unintentional apologist for that product's shortcomings. Users, on the other hand, have no incentive to apologize for your product. In fact, they have quite the opposite: a wealth of alternatives and the ever-constant option of voting with their feet.

Put simply, if your product doesn't support users in what they want or need to do, they'll go elsewhere. And even in situations where employees have no choice but to use in-house software, they'll often create workarounds to avoid the parts that make their lives harder, which results in redundancies, inaccuracies, rework, and in some cases, very serious mistakes.

The best way to provide experiences that satisfy users is to design with them in mind. The practices in this chapter can help you investigate what it's like for people when they use your product. These methods enable you to learn directly and indirectly what they need, want, and experience—and then build products that are optimized toward delivering on those needs. In this chapter, we'll continue our look at the following methods and the questions they answer:

- **Method 7: Learning Plan.** What do you know, what don't you know, and how are you going to learn it?

- **Method 8: Guerilla User Research.** What concerns are top of mind for users? How do they really behave? How are people using your product today?

- **Method 9: User Archetypes.** How can you think empathetically about your customers' needs, expectations, goals, and challenges when using your product?

- **Method 10: Heuristic Markup.** How does a user experience the product from beginning to end?

- **Method 11: Comparative Assessment.** What are the standards, best practices, features, and functionality that customers are likely to expect in a product like yours?

- **Method 12: Content Patterns.** What content and capabilities do users have access to in your product, how is it structured, and what is the overall quality?

Learning Plan

What do you know, what don't you know, and how are you going to learn it?

A learning plan sounds like a formal concept, but it really just means taking the time to learn where the gaps are in your understanding of what users need, want, and expect—along with how you can fill in those gaps in your knowledge. A surprisingly large number of organizations claim to practice user-centered design but fail to empower their employees to actually speak with or spend time with users. In other cases, designers and UXers are prevented from doing that research; sometimes executives are avoiding proof of what they already know is happening.

No matter the situation, it's critical that you learn as much as you can about the people you're designing for, one way or another. Committing to a user-centered philosophy means that you must respect and learn from your users' sometimes unpredictable lives. A learning plan is a simple tool that you can use by yourself or with a team to do this, by mapping out what you know and what you need to learn (see Figure 5.1).

Average Time

1–2 hours

- About an hour to assemble
- Ongoing discussions afterward

Use When

- You're first bringing a user-centered mindset to an organization (whether in an official or unofficial capacity).
- You first start out in a new job as a UX team of one.
- You've started a new project, and you need to know more about your product and your users.

BELIEF	CERTAINTY	NOTES	RESEARCH METHODS	EVIDENCE
Typical User Profile				
Busy Professionals - Our most likely users are busy professionals (e.g., work more than 50 hours a week. Probably skew more female, and many have children/families. Age range is 30s and 40s.	Medium	The high-level details are taken from our typical enterprise user. Need to confirm whether the consumer oriented product would appeal to the same type of user, or someone else.	[+] Doublecheck marketing reports and business case [+] Embed dry test in enterprise product and survey respondents	Marketing Segments
Needs				
Family-Oriented - Users are interested in family-oriented activities.	Low	Purely speculative. We need to do more to understand the variety of activities that users are interested in.	[+] Contextual interviews with 5-8 target users	Personas + Behavioral Dimensions
Stressed by technology - Our typical user feels some stress due to the "always on" nature of technology and devices. It's the desire to eliminate or reduce that stress that leads users on a search for products like ours -- therefore users may be having an experience of stress at the moment they first encounter our product.	Medium	True for enterprise customer; need to confirm with target consumer customer.	[+] Do market research review (especially Pew reports) [+] Contextual interviews with 4-6 target users	Marketing Segments Personas
Motivations				
Achieving and accomplishing - Users are high achievers and interested in accomplishing more outside of work, but not necessarily scaling back what they do at work.	Medium	True for enterprise customer; need to confirm with target consumer customer.	[+] Contextual interviews with 5-8 target users	Personas + Behavioral Dimensions
General goals - Goals tend to be generic: vacation, retirement, get in shape. Not a lot of adventure seekers and bucket listers.	Low	This is an assumption we've always made about enterprise customers, but never really confirmed.	[+] Contextual interviews with 5-8 target users [+] Intercept survey of current users	Personas
Behaviors				
Balance Achieved Through Activities - Ways they achieve a sense of balance now: church or spiritual practices, TV, exercise, commute time (listening to music, books on CD, etc.), shopping, reading print material (books and magazines). FaceBook for viewing photos and catching up with friends.	Medium	True for enterprise customer; need to confirm with target consumer customer.	[+] Contextual interviews with 5-8 target users (include journey lines)	Personas Experience Map Journey Line
Always On - Users are not early technology adopters, but they tend to be online a lot. Usually have computers at home and at work (personal computer at work, shared computer at home). Also likely to have a smart phone, and others in their household are also likely to have smart phones.	Medium	True for enterprise customer; need to confirm with target consumer customer.	[+] Diary study with 2-3 target users	Personas + Behavioral Dimensions

FIGURE 5.1

If possible, make this sample learning plan glanceable. A table is a great way to format all this information into an easy-to-scan, one-page plan that you can stick up on your wall or drop into a presentation deck as needed.

Try It Out

1. **Start with what you know.**

   Set aside 30 minutes or an hour to list everything you think you know about your users (see Figure 5.2). Just write, don't stop to edit; the goal here is quantity, not quality. What are your working assumptions? Think about things like the following:

   • What are your main segments/types of users?

   • What motivates them?

   • What frustrates them? What makes them happy?

   • What features and functions are most important to them?

   • What considerations are key in their purchase and reuse decisions?

   • Do they use your competitor's products? When and how?

   • What other products do they use?

- How much time do they spend with your product in a year? In a month? In a week? (You may discover that the number is surprisingly low.)
- What else competes for their attention?
- What frustrates them about your product?
- What do they like best about your product?
- What parts of your product do they use the most? The least? What parts of the product do you want them to use the most?
- What *is* the main goal your audience aims to achieve, and which parts or areas of your product help meet this goal?

ASSUMPTIONS ABOUT OUR USERS

TYPES OF USERS →	VIEWERS	ADMINS	BUYERS
GOALS/ STATE OF MIND	· Search + find correct answers · Want to be certain · Want to share what they find with others · Want to be good at their jobs/smart	· Dealing with piles/ lists/to dos · Provide good svc. · Solve problems. Repeat processes · "Add Value"	· Save $ · Ensure feature parity · Please their internal customers · Create automated processes.
PAIN POINTS	· Not sure if they've found the only/all the info. · Can't save + duplicate portfolios · Can't customize with their name/logo. · Not enough time	· Ability to compactly close a product in a timely fashion. · Listen for keywords · Creation of repeatable scripts for common issues	· Not aware of all the service options · Don't necessarily disseminate info... not everyone knows what they can do · Rigid systems
OTHER PRODUCTS THEY USE	Excel Word Dropbox Paper + Pen Sticky notes Binders + Photocopies Evernote	Sharepoint MS Access Email Archives Colleagues Intranet Evernote	Analyst Reports Procurement System Oracle email
COPING STRATEGIES	Email colleagues Create duplicates/clones Keep notes files Bookmarks	Support scripts Buy time Physical To Do Lists Relationship with other admins	Talk to colleagues at other places Look for good dashboards in other people needed

FIGURE 5.2

Give yourself 60 minutes in a conference room and invite a few team members to simply talk through your assumptions, capturing the discussion on the whiteboard.

2. **Separate certainties from assumptions.**

   For each assumption, indicate how confident you are in that assumption (and be honest about that). While you do this, look for any questions that can be simplified or grouped together.

3. **Brainstorm research methods.**

   Now, for each of your questions, think about how you might go about getting more data or info in this area. Also think about what resources you actually need to answer these questions (for example, face-to-face time with users, a survey, access to analytics or server log data, etc.). Keep in mind that not all research questions require direct and immediate access to users or customers. Some of those answers can come from tools or processes that users touch—call center transcripts, search analytics, and so on. Don't let limited access to users stop you here; be creative in thinking about where and how you can gather data to answer your questions.

TIPS AND TRICKS FOR LEARNING PLANS

- **Seek feedback**. It's one thing to write a plan. It's another thing entirely to get the necessary support to *execute* that plan. Share your plans with your team and your boss, and invite their feedback. They may encourage you to slim down your ambitions, and that's okay—this will serve to sharpen your focus. So, make sure you solicit, encourage, and incorporate this feedback.

- **Revisit from time to time**. Consider revisiting your learning plan at regular intervals (annually, for example) to keep it current and relevant. This periodic update is really important. It's more common than you think for companies to make future design decisions based on older research that was done years ago. The problem is that users, the products they use, and the technological landscapes in which they operate will have changed a lot since that research was done. So, get in the habit of revisiting and reassessing your working assumptions about user behavior throughout the year (every quarter)—and see if it's time to revalidate or update them.

- **If you work remotely,** you may want to brainstorm methods that are easier to conduct remotely, such as Zoom interviews, Slack chats, or remote usability tests. See Nate Bolt and Tony Tulathimutte's excellent book on remote usability testing for specific ideas: ⚲http://rosenfeldmedia.com/books/remote-research/.

4. **Plan outputs.**

   Finally, for each area that you'd like to research further, think about what form your evidence will take (for example, infographics or charts summarizing your data on use, presenting and distributing new personas, etc.).

Guerilla User Research

What concerns are top of mind for users? How do they really behave? How are people using this product today?

There is one key requirement of user research, and it's simple (but not always easy): **You have to actually talk to users.** It doesn't have to be a lot of them. Even just two or three is better than none at all. And as you've heard, once you get past five, you start hearing the same answers and feedback. At any rate, you make it a priority to talk to and learn from at least a few users, firsthand, by whatever means necessary. Guerrilla user research can take any number of forms, from social media DMs to Zoom calls to Slack conversations to approaching people in a coffee shop.

Average Time

About two days

- 3–4 hours to figure out where to go to find users and write your research goals
- 3–4 hours in the field, talking to users
- 4–6 hours to mine your data

Use When

- You're forming goals and priorities for design and feel that you need grounding in an understanding of user goals.
- The team is making decisions for the product without any primary or firsthand knowledge of user needs. You know this is happening when you find yourself in stalemate design arguments, or when you see people rationalizing product choices by speculating how a fictitious user (or even they themselves) would use the product.

Try It Out

1. **Think about your target users.**

   Start by asking yourself who you'd like to talk to and how. Think about what characterizes your users. How old are they, on average? What kinds of behaviors and interests do they have? Where do they live and work? How do they spend their free time? Once you have a basic idea of whom you're looking for, think about where this type of person might be likely to spend their time. If it's the type of situation or place you can easily get access to, go there and ask the random people you meet if they'd be willing to participate in a short study.

   For example, let's say your target customers are creative freelancers. True to stereotype, these folks are known to spend lots of time working in coffee shops. As such, you plan to spend an afternoon in a coffee shop, politely asking people you see working on their laptops if they'd be interested in doing a short user study.

2. **List your research questions.**

   Think about what you're trying to learn from your users and list your questions. Articulate why you're doing this work and what you hope to learn from it. Try creating a mind map, which gets your questions out of your head and onto paper or a whiteboard (see Figure 5.3). Start by writing the core topic you need to learn the most about in the middle. Now, when you think about what you need to know, what are the first things that come to mind? Write those around the central topic, connecting each of them to the center topic with a line. Repeat this process until you can't think of anything else that you want to learn from these folks.

3. **Go into the field.**

   Ideally, for a research session, you meet with the user in their own environment: work, home, or somewhere they spend a lot of time. Ask them to show you as much as they're comfortable with sharing about what's relevant and important in their own environment. With permission, take pictures or videos to document what you see as visceral artifacts to remind you of this person and the things you learned about them. And during your conversation, be sure you're covering all the research questions that you listed in step 2.

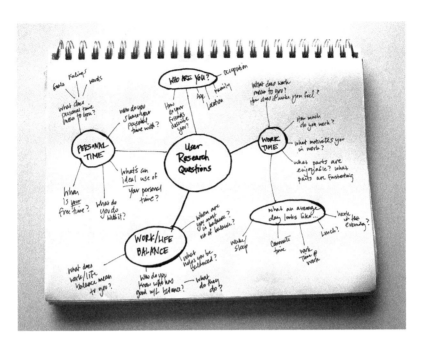

FIGURE 5.3

A sample mind map.

4. **Mine the data for insights.**

   After you're done with your research interviews, spend some time reviewing your notes from all the interviews, looking for the answers to those questions you listed at the beginning.

TIPS AND TRICKS FOR GUERILLA USER RESEARCH

- **Use your organization.** Are there existing people in departments within the organization that could provide direct access to your customers? Sales and support teams often have these direct connections, and they may be able to put you in touch with some of them. Another good place to connect with users is at industry-specific events or conferences. If there are existing marketing emails, newsletters, etc. that are regularly sent to customers, see if you can arrange to slip a sentence or two into one of those communications inviting customers to participate in a research study. If your organization uses LinkedIn, X, Instagram, TikTok, or other social platforms, send out a call for volunteers that way.

continues

- **Use your network.** If you're having trouble finding good research participants, send an email to your friends and colleagues saying you're looking for a person who fits this particular type of profile for some research that you're conducting. Often, the people in your community will have friends and acquaintances that fit the bill, and they can put you in touch with them.

- **Get their consent.** An important bit of housekeeping before any research interview is to inform the research participant of how you'll be using this research and get their official, written permission. This is called *informed consent*, and it is non-negotiable. Figure 5.4 shows a standard agreement template that you can use to cover both you and your research subject.

INFORMED CONSENT FOR RESEARCH STUDY PARTICIPANT

Purpose of this study
The purpose of this study is to learn more about how you manage work/life balance. Your participation in this study will help us to create new products and services for people like you.

Information we will collect
We will ask you about your experiences with planning, productivity, and personal fulfillment. We will observe you in your office, doing tasks you commonly engage in, and we will talk with you about these activities.

The information from this visit will be used, along with that from other similar visits, to inform the design of Equilibrium. Data gathered during testing is the intellectual property of Good Life Labs.

Permissions
We will take hand written notes, digital photographs, digital audio, and videotape the session. By signing this consent form, you are giving us permission to use your verbal statements, video segments, and still images for the purposes of illuminating, demonstrating, and evaluating research findings internally. This is in no way a product endorsement, and your interview will not be shared publicly in any way.

Non-disclosure
We may discuss ideas with you on not-yet-announced plans, concepts, products, and services. We are doing this so we can get your feedback only. By signing this form, you agree not to tell anyone about this or provide information about those ideas to anyone outside of this study.

Freedom to withdraw
You are free to refuse to participate, take a break, or withdraw from this study at any time. Please let us know when you need a break.

Questions
If you have questions, please ask them now or during the study.

Compensation
You will receive $100 as incentive for participating in the research session.

After reading this form, if you agree with these terms, please show your acceptance by signing below.

_____   _____
Date   Participant Signature

            _____
            Participant Name (Printed)

FIGURE 5.4
A standard consent agreement.

- **Ask open-ended questions.** There is an art to user research. The goal is getting people to open up and share relevant information about themselves without leading them into answers. One technique that helps is to ask open-ended questions—questions that require more than a single-word answer. Open-ended questions begin with words like "why" and "how." Avoid starting questions with words like "did" or "was." And when in doubt, employ the most powerful one-word sentence in existence: "Why?"

- **Don't ask about what's onscreen or about the product specifically.** Don't ask a participant to comment on what they see onscreen, or about what software or hardware they use; instead, ask them what they do, or how they would complete a task. Which means you don't ask a question like "What part of this app do you use to do Task X?" The reason is that this question focuses on the *tool* the person is using—instead of the *process* they go through. Usability and UX problems are very rarely the sole result of a technology issue. There are a handful of other seemingly unrelated factors that, in many cases, turn out to be the real problem: company policies, processes, politics, deadlines, stress, noise, interruptions, etc.

  So, if you only ask a user about the software they use, you won't hear about the other factors that may be directly responsible for the issues at hand. The software may very well suck—but if there's a process or policy in place that doesn't allow that person enough time or give them the right data to do their job, that's the real issue. And if you don't uncover it, the person and the organization will still have the same problem after the redesign launches.

- **Ask about past events.** Another technique for getting rich information without leading users to predetermined answers is to ask them to recall or remember events from their own lives. (For example, "Tell me about the last time you took a video with your phone." Or "Tell me about the last time you bought a car.") Ask people to recall the experiences chronologically, which can help them remember specifics that they might otherwise gloss over. The journey line is a simple pen-and-paper technique that you can do with users to facilitate this type of chronological conversation (as shown in Figure 5.5 on the next page).

continues

FIGURE 5.5
A research participant completing his journey line.

- **A picture speaks 1,000 words.** When sharing what you learned, include choice photos and audio clips to illustrate key concepts and bring the voice of the user to life.

- **Get into their environment.** The things that people do and keep in their environment, along with the hacks and workarounds they've created, are often your biggest source of realization and inspiration. For example, UX practitioners for a property website went into people's homes to watch them search for property online. They discovered that many people were copying and pasting URLs of property they liked into separate Word documents to find them again later, or to send a complete list by email. This led them to design an "add to list" feature with email capabilities.

- **Offer compensation.** People are often more willing to give you their time and insights when they are rewarded for doing so. Offering some form of compensation up front as a thank you for their time generally increases your odds of finding willing research participants. What you give them doesn't have to be a lot. Depending on how much time you need, a nominal gift card may be enough.

- **If research requests usually meet opposition, ask for less time.** If your organization's culture is one where the urgent always trumps the important and everything needs to be done yesterday, that request for a week of user research will probably be shot down in flames. Instead, ask for less. A lot less, in fact: be willing to settle for a single day split into 15-minute increments with each customer or user. Record the sessions, transcribe the audio, and look for commonalities across the sessions. For example, look for patterns where different people point out the same problems. That may be enough to point you in the direction of features or redesign opportunities that lead to increased use, revenue, or cost savings. And in the spirit of guerilla research, something is always better than nothing.

And here are some further **interview tips**:

- **Be confident.** If you seem like you know what you're doing, it will put your interviewee at ease.

- **Explain what's going to happen.** Tell them why you're doing your research. Explain what kinds of questions you'll be asking. Tell them what's required of them. Let them know how long it's going to take.

- **Allow silence.** Give them time to think about your questions before answering. Resist the urge to fill in silence by reframing questions or suggesting possible responses. Give them time to walk through the answers mentally and be careful not to finish their sentences.

- **Memorize a few sentences that will keep the conversation going.** For example, "That's interesting; tell me more." "Say more about that." "What's the reason for that?" "How come?" "Why?"

- **If you work remotely,** do this where you live and aim to take lots of videos and photos (with permission) to share with the rest of your team. Do it via Zoom and record the session (with permission) and share the recording. If traveling to a location where your colleagues are located is an option, take advantage of that and conduct some guerilla interviews with the members in tow. Research insights are always more profound for those who witness these sessions firsthand.

User Archetypes

How can you think empathetically about your customers' needs, goals, and challenges when using your product?

User archetypes are a technique to provoke empathetic, customer-oriented thinking, without requiring exhaustive customer research or loads of statistical data to underpin your thinking (see Figure 5.6). User archetypes are similar to and inspired by the UX technique known as *persona development*. Personas were invented by the brilliant Alan Cooper, and they are a time-tested tool of the user experience field. A persona is a composite picture of a collection of users, boiled down into one relatable, human profile. A persona is usually presented as an individual person with a name, a face, and a backstory. Personas usually explain that person's needs, values, goals, frustrations, and desires.

Personas are made as human as possible to further enhance the sense that this is a real person with a messy life and quirky ways of coping with very recognizable human situations. A persona is a fictitious composite based on extensive user research that you or someone else has observed firsthand. The trouble is, creating good personas takes time and resources.

User archetypes are a modified version of this. They simulate the same type of empathetic and user-oriented thinking but require a lot less time to create. They can be created with the help of a cross-functional team, which makes them a quick, inclusive tool for turning on the UX goggles. In essence, user archetypes are a persona hack that you create with the help of the team and using whatever data you have available—which can mean secondhand research, or even just the well-informed hunches of a team of people. If you have firsthand research to refer to, that's ideal, but absolutely not required.

While they're less scientific and rigorous than traditional personas, user archetypes can be equally effective for helping a team shift into a more empathetic mindset when designing and building for users. Above all else, they help clearly define your design target: who you're building for, and who you *aren't* building for. And in corporate environments where time available is never what you'd like it to be, that second part is much more important than the first.

Average Time

3–6 hours total

- 2–4 hours prep time
- 1–2 hours for the workshop

FIGURE 5.6
An example of a completed user archetype.

Use When

- You have an unclear picture of who your target user is and what they need or expect.
- You find that you and the team talk about users and their motivations in generic, nonspecific terms.
- You sense that the team as a whole needs a more empathetic and human-centered way of thinking about users.

Try It Out

1. **Plan a working session with the team.**

   Schedule an hour or so for a working session and invite a cross-functional team to help you create the user archetypes. Since this is a group activity, the number of people involved matters. Aim for no fewer than four people and no more than six—any more and the group becomes a bit unwieldy. Consider including people who have direct access to customers (for example, salespeople or call center representatives). They'll have great firsthand insights about customers.

2. **Set expectations.**

   Once you have everyone assembled, explain that thinking of users as individual people with unique needs helps you create products that are easy to use and lets you respect your users' time. Help your colleagues understand that UX is a frame of mind, and this activity will help get them in that frame of mind. Explain that what you are about to do is an *unscientific* technique that will nevertheless get everyone thinking differently about the people who use your products.

3. **Create teams.**

   Organize the group into small teams of about three people. Ask each team to discuss what they know or suspect to be true about your users and then focus on one particular type of user that they want to develop as a user archetype.

4. **Fill in basic information for each user archetype.**

   Give each team a poster-sized persona template and ask them to fill in the details of a fictitious but realistic person they might expect to use their product. Ask them to create a story for this person, including a name, where they live, what they do for a living, what frustrates them, what a day in their life looks like, and what they are doing before, during, and after the use of your product.

5. **Bring the user archetypes to life.**

   Ask each team to add photos, quotes, and other forms of real-life "color" to their posters. For this, you can use free stock photo sites like pexels.com, unsplash.com, or stocksnap.io, and have them pick images to represent their persona and what a day in their life might look like.

6. **Share and discuss as a group.**

   After the teams have assembled their posters, ask each one to share the story of their user archetype. As a group, discuss your reactions. What questions does each user archetype raise that you might want to explore or research further? Are there particular user archetypes that are especially relevant or effective in getting the team to think empathetically? How can you use these user archetypes in the future?

TIPS AND TRICKS FOR USER ARCHETYPES

- **Base them on whatever research you have.** Any pre-existing customer research can be a good starting point for your user archetypes. Gather any information available about the different types of customers who use your products. Look for any market segment information, demographics, or customer support insights. If you don't have any of that, just talk with the team about what types of people use your products. Salespeople or customer support people are often especially knowledgeable about customers and their goals and challenges.

- **Treat them as a hypothesis.** After the exercise, look for opportunities to validate (or invalidate) the details in the user archetypes against data from the field. In other words, don't let the process stop here.

- **Don't confuse these with real personas.** User research purists may have some concern about this method, because it's not necessarily grounded in directly observed user research. Be that as it may, user archetypes are actually very useful for generating empathy. And the fact that they can be done as a group activity makes them good for building interest and buy-in to provide a better experience to support users' needs. However, if and when the opportunity to do real personas arises, jump at it.

continues

- **If you work remotely,** it will be a bit more challenging to conduct a user archetype workshop remotely via Zoom, but it's still very much worth doing. And if for any reason that's not possible, doing this type of exercise yourself can still be useful in guiding you as you think about the design. If you're not necessarily planning to share the user archetype with others, you can take a lower-fidelity approach, like the one shown in Figure 5.7.

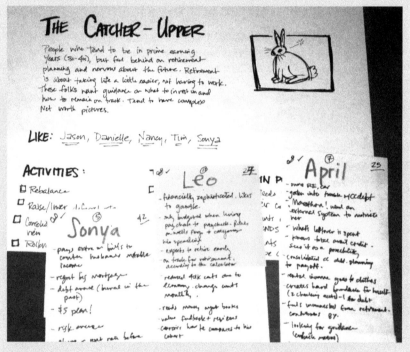

FIGURE 5.7

Here, notes from past research (in this case, individual interviews) are captured on sticky notes and then compiled into a single profile.

Heuristic Markup

How does a user experience the product from beginning to end?

Heuristic markups are inspired by heuristic evaluations; that's a fancy term for the review of a product to see how well it complies with recognized usability principles. In a typical heuristic evaluation, a UX professional audits a product and identifies any parts that don't conform to established standards and best practices. A heuristic markup is conceptually similar to a heuristic evaluation, but it places less emphasis on recognized standards and more emphasis on your own gut reactions and responses as you move through the product. A heuristic markup helps you tell the story of how a user might experience the product from start to finish (see Figure 5.8).

In a heuristic markup, you start at the beginning of the product and record your thought process as you move through the experience. A heuristic markup is easy to do and surprisingly fun. Plus, taking the time to really notice what you notice is a good way to lift the goggles of familiarity.

FIGURE 5.8

An example of a screen from a heuristic markup.

Average Time

4–6 hours to conduct and document the review

Use When

- You want to assess the basic quality of the product and spot potential opportunities for improvement.
- In the design process, if you want to check your work as new designs are underway.

Try It Out

1. **Block off a good amount of time.**

   Set aside some time to really use the product, from start to finish. Plan more time than you think you will need. This gives you enough time to take notes and capture your thoughts, reactions, and observations.

2. **Begin at the beginning.**

   Think about where a typical user starts with your product. A Google search? A visit to the app store? If your product includes a physical device, does their experience begin with the process of opening the product's box? Whatever it is, try to approach your offering from the same angle that first-timers would. Take screenshots or pictures; record your thoughts as you move from screen to screen or step to step. A Google doc is a great place to store these images and observations: at each step or screen in the process, paste a screenshot and add a note (or several) about what you're noticing and thinking about related to your user's mindset. Or use a screen recorder that also records sound (Loom, iShowU, Camtasia) and record your stream of consciousness as you move through the product, thinking out loud as you go.

3. **Pay attention to your reactions.**

   As you progress through the product, be alert to the subtle responses you have and the questions that show up. These thoughts often come so quickly that you're not always fully conscious you've had them, but they still influence your perceptions of the quality of the product. So, make an effort to go slowly—and pay attention to what your inner voice has to say along the way.

4. **Go from beginning to end.**

   Continue moving through the product, recording images and observations as you go.

5. **Share what you find.**

   When you're done, you'll have a candid, easy-to-share narrative that illustrates potential areas for improvement within the product. Keep in mind that you may be critiquing someone else's hard work here, so make it a point to soften any overly sharp or critical language before you share it with others. Capture the feeling but leave the expletives out. At the end, include a summary of the key takeaways—the small handful of things that you believe are most critical to research, address, or improve.

TIPS AND TRICKS FOR HEURISTIC MARKUPS

- **Adopt a persona.** If you have some sense of whom your users are, it can be helpful to create a backstory of their motivations and what they're trying to accomplish. This will help to guide your thinking as you move through the product. Use your user archetypes if you have them.

- **Record emotions.** This isn't just about what you think; it's about what you feel. There are seven universal emotions that drive behavior—anger, joy, sadness, disgust, fear, contempt, and surprise—and you should be watching out for all of them. So, make sure that you record your emotional responses to each step or screen (see Figure 5.9 on the next page) along with your thoughts. Did something make you feel happy? Surprised? Confused? Frustrated? Make an emotional graph of the entire experience to help you pinpoint the most critical areas to improve (or preserve).

- **Gather additional evidence.** Some people will likely question your process because it's not "expert" or quantifiable enough. Expect that and work to connect your observations to recognized standards or patterns, such as those described here:
  - **Jakob Nielsen's 10 usability heuristics:**
    www.useit.com/papers/heuristic/heuristic_list.html
  - **Bruce "Tog" Tognazzi's basic principles of interaction design:**
    asktog.com/atc/principles-of-interaction-design/
  - **IBM's Open-Source Carbon Design System:**
    carbondesignsystem.com
  - **Apple's Human Interface Guidelines:**
    developer.apple.com/design/
  - **Atlassian Design System:** atlassian.design

continues

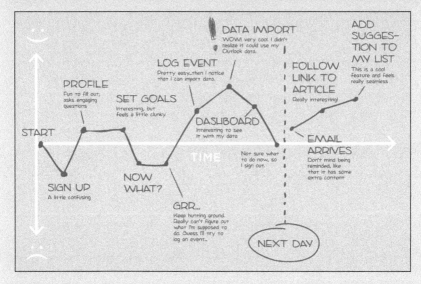

FIGURE 5.9

An example of a journey line that shows the highs and lows of the experience.

- **Share the experience.** Invite your colleagues to walk through the process of using the product as well. Ask them to bring their beginner's mind as they move through the process. Experiencing this type of walkthrough firsthand helps people see what you're talking about, and it provokes empathy and curiosity about how real users will experience the product. If you want people to truly understand where you're coming from, there's no substitute for actual use.

- **Think in terms of tasks.** You can structure your heuristic markup from start to finish, or according to common tasks. To do a task-based markup, identify a handful of core use cases or scenarios the product should support, and then follow the path for each one, reviewing each individually as you go.

- **If you work remotely,** the process itself is easy to conduct via Zoom or Teams, but sharing what you find may take a bit more coordination and, more importantly, tact. Try showing your walkthrough to a colleague whose perspective you trust first to get a second opinion on whether anything seems sensitive or incendiary. Once you've gotten confirmation that it seems good to share, set up a time for a share-out with a larger group. Use screen-sharing software and walk the team through your notes, inviting questions and commentary along the way.

Comparative Assessment

What are the standards and best practices that customers are likely to expect in a product like yours?

In a comparative assessment, you look at *indirect competition*: products and services that your customers are likely to encounter and use that aren't an apples-to-apples match for your product or service. This is often confused with a competitive assessment, where you evaluate your *direct competition*: products and services that provide the exact same features and functionality yours do.

The idea behind a comparative assessment is that people develop their expectations from the products and services that they use every day. And because of that, they're likely to compare things like ease of use, performance, or clarity of instruction with that of apps and sites that have nothing to do with your product or its business model— Amazon, Spotify, YouTube, and so on.

A comparative assessment uncovers those expectations and shines a light on how they influence people's perception of *your* product. It's a good way to start thinking about and discussing what an optimal experience looks like, before you start designing anything.

Average Time

4–8 hours total

- 4–6 hours to pick comparators and review them
- Plus an optional 1–2 hours to document in a guidelines document

Use When

- You're trying to establish vision and expectations for a new user experience.
- The team seems to be focusing on feature-by-feature comparisons against direct competitors and not aiming to create a simple, holistic user experience.
- You keep hearing comparisons like *"It should be the Apple of _____,"* but nothing more specific.

Try It Out

1. **Pick which products to evaluate.**

   Create a list of the products you want to include in your assessment. This should be a small, manageable number, three to five max.

2. **Create a list of areas to evaluate.**

   Next, determine the framework that you'll use to evaluate each product. A framework can be as simple as a spreadsheet with a column for each key question in your evaluation and a row for each product. The areas you focus on may be influenced by the domain you are evaluating and your goals for the project, but here are some common areas to make sure you focus on:

   • Content

   • Design

   • Features and functionality

   • Continuity or flow

   • Performance/responsiveness

   • Intuitiveness

   • Strengths, weaknesses, opportunities

3. **Walk through each product.**

   Now, with these focus areas in mind, begin to assess each product. Imagine that you've never encountered this product before; try to see it with fresh eyes. Take screenshots as you go and note your assessment of each product, as shown in Figure 5.10.

4. **Answer your questions.**

   Once you've assessed each product or offering, fill in your framework, so you can easily compare across offerings.

5. **Summarize findings or guidelines.**

   Finally, consider documenting key insights from your assessment in a guidelines document, as shown in Figure 5.11. This gives you a useful point of reference you can refer to as you design. It can also ensure that your work is truly user-centered design (and can be used in conjunction with the "Design Brief" from Chapter 6, "Design Methods"). Your guidelines can serve as a cheat sheet for fundamental design standards that you want to meet or exceed. This is simple, it's fast, and it goes a long way in helping teams establish shared best practices, along with a common language to talk about them.

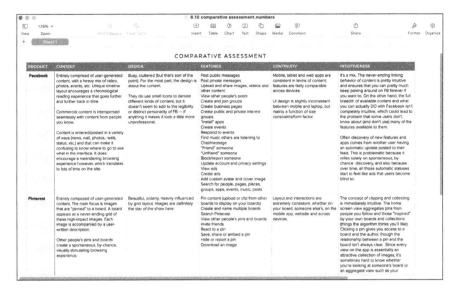

FIGURE 5.10

This spreadsheet is a simple way to capture what's special about the comparators that you're researching.

FIGURE 5.11

One way to make your most important findings a little more visual and
memorable is to take a few screenshots and assemble them into a series of
guidelines or best practices that you've observed through the competitive or
comparative review.

TIPS AND TRICKS FOR COMPARATIVE ASSESSMENTS

- **Go beyond mere features.** Your assessment should not be used to create feature comparison lists; this is dangerous. It encourages you to compete on feature parity, which all too often leads to bloated UX and a slew of features and functionality that no one wants, needs, or is willing to use. Instead, keep your assessment focused on the overall quality of the experience offered. Don't create an inventory of features; focus on the product's overall flow instead. How harmonious and consistent is the design? How readable, relatable, and human is the content? How intuitive are the categories in the navigation? What conventions will users expect to guide them through interactions and screens? How well does the experience flow from one type of device to another? Asking these kinds of questions can help you get a sense of the quality, appropriateness, and usefulness of the overall experience.

- **Plan it like a report.** Designing the kind of report you want to share at the end—before you do the assessment—can actually help you determine your question framework. For example, let's say you want to report on the voice and tone of content in the product, which means you need to examine these things specifically. First, decide on the key elements you want to compare and how you'd like to report them. Next, determine what questions you'll need to ask to get enough data to enable those comparisons. Finally, determine how you'll want to track them: in an open-ended way, on a numeric scale, through screenshots, in a yes/no fashion, and so on.

- **Share what you learn.** A comparative assessment can help you familiarize yourself with trends in the field, but using it to discuss those trends with a cross-functional team is infinitely more productive and valuable. A summary document like the one in Figure 5.11 can be the starting point for an informed, collaborative discussion about what matters most for your users, for your organization, and for your product.

- **Make it a group exercise.** Ask the participants to bring in sites that they think are relevant comparators, and then, as a group, review those sites and discuss significant trends.

- **If you work remotely,** although team collaboration is great, this is also an insightful, rewarding activity for a remote team of one. Have at it!

Content Patterns

What content and capabilities do users have access to in your products, how is it structured, and what is the overall quality?

In a content inventory, you sit down with the product or service and attempt to create a representative sampling of all the types of information, assets, and functionality that it includes—sort of an index of the world. And if that sounds like a massive, painstaking, time-consuming endeavor to you...it is.

Which is why we recommend focusing on *content patterns* instead; you can get many of the same benefits—an intimate understanding of structure and deeper familiarity with the content—with a *lot* less effort. While content patterns are less comprehensive than a traditional content inventory, they do expose the components most critical to good UX: recurring patterns of content and functionality that exist, along with how they're structured.

Average Time

4–8 hours, depending on how deeply you want to go

- 2–4 hours to review patterns
- 1–2 hours to create a content map or spreadsheet
- 1–2 hours to summarize key findings

Use When

You want to get deeply familiar with the structure, information, and capabilities of your app, site, or system (often this is at the beginning of a project).

Try It Out

1. **Pick key sections.**

   Start by picking a few representative sections to feature in your sampling. Within each of these sections, look for recurring patterns or structures across all the ways that content and data are configured and presented. For example, case studies, articles, help files, reports, and so on. This could also apply to features and functionality, which may have their own recurring patterns.

2. **Find the patterns.**

   List all the elements that come together to make up a unit of content. (For example, an article is comprised of a title, a byline, date, author, several long-form paragraphs, some images, and finally some tags and categories, which are used as metadata for searching and filtering.) Repeat this process for each new type of content that you find.

3. **Note potential mismatches in language, labeling, hierarchy, and priority.**

   Keep an eye out for obvious (and not-so-obvious) differences between what people expect and what they get—from what things are called to how they're organized, prioritized, related, and connected.

4. **Document what you find.**

   Put the patterns you've found into a spreadsheet or make a diagram or a map of the different types of content you find (see Figures 5.12–5.14). Diagrams and maps in particular often make it easier to visualize the structure, patterns, and relationships that exist in your content.

CONTENT INVENTORY

ID	TITLE	CONTENT TYPE	SAMPLE CONTENT	NOTES
1	Sign In	Navigation		Page is typically embedded within a corporate intranet, so it may have additional navigation around the perimeter.
1.1	Sign In Form	Form		Form contains the following fields: - Username - Password
1.2	Help	Support Content	For more information or if you're having trouble logging in, please call the benefits hotline.	Content would be more helpful if it included a direct link to a password reset and/or direct contact information.
1.3	FAQs	Navigation	Can I include my family in this program?	Accordion-style navigation. Clicking link opens additional content directly below the link within page. Clicking link again collapses content.
1.4	Tip	Navigation	10 Tips for Keeping It All in Balance	Links to article with tips for work/life balance.
2	Dashboard	Navigation		Page serves a navigational purpose, but is designed as a personal dashboard. Effectively the "signed in" state.
2.1	"How You Spend Your Time" Chart	Info Visualization	[Chart]	Info visualization showing users' data calendar overlayed on top of recommended calendar.
2.2	Suggestions	Editorial Content	You're in more than 40 hours of meetings a week. Lucky you! That puts you in category of busy professionals we call the "meeting masters." The challenge for meeting master is to find time to actually get work done outside of meetings. Here are a few tips for balancing it all.	Links to articles matched topically with recommendations that appear on calendar.
2.3	Network Feed	User Generated Content	Joseph just finished a playdate with his family.	Feed with updates from other users in network.
3	Goals	Navigation		
3.1	Overview	Instructional Content	Knowing your own goals is the key to a happy work/life balance. Use the goals manager to create an accurate picture of your values and aspirations, and we can make recommendations that are right for you.	Paragraph of text gets lost in the page design. May not really be necessary.
3.2	Goals List	Data Table	[User entered goals content]	Displayed as a simple table. Display could be made more visual and less dense, easier to

FIGURE 5.12

As you identify different types of content, you can track them in a spreadsheet.

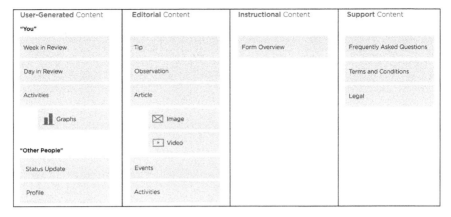

User-Generated Content	Editorial Content	Instructional Content	Support Content
"You"			
Week in Review	Tip	Form Overview	Frequently Asked Questions
Day in Review	Observation		Terms and Conditions
Activities	Article		Legal
Graphs	Image		
"Other People"	Video		
Status Update	Events		
Profile	Activities		

FIGURE 5.13

An example of a content map.

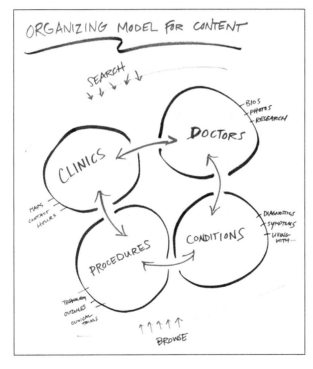

FIGURE 5.14

Even a hand-drawn model can be illuminating for clarifying the different types of content in the system and how they relate to each other.

- **Summarize what you discover.** Documenting content patterns can be a fairly technical exercise. This can make it hard to share and present to others. Present a spreadsheet, and you'll find people falling asleep in their chairs. So, to get people to pay attention and appreciate the significance of the findings, just talk through your high-level findings (which you identified in step 4 previously) and leave the spreadsheets at your desk (see Figure 5.15).

  And when you do this, give away the ending of the story first. Start with what you uncovered, what that information suggests should be done, and how doing so helps the organization achieve its goals. And show real, in-product examples to illustrate your points. If competing products already do what you suggest, and do it well, show those examples to give everyone a vivid picture of what those changes might look like in practice.

- **If you work remotely,** be sure to plan time to share your findings with your remote colleagues. A Zoom or Teams call with screen-sharing cuts to the chase for everyone. In this type of format, focus squarely on the outcomes of your proposed changes, a summary of those key improvements and why they'll likely produce that outcome, and examples from the actual content that supports your recommendations.

5. **Summarize key findings.**

   Finally, use this analysis to identify significant observations or findings. What are your top observations? Where are the discrepancies and mismatches in user expectation or understanding? What specific recommendations would you make to improve the product?

6. **Share and discuss.**

   Optionally, share your findings with the team and discuss what actions you'd like to take, based on what you've learned.

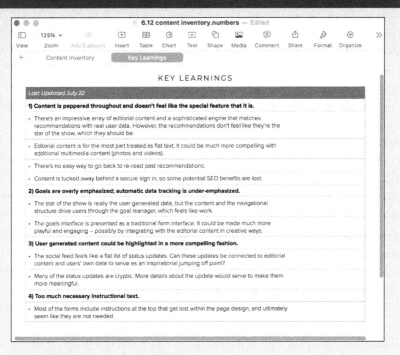

FIGURE 5.15

An example of a content inventory summary.

If You Only Do One Thing…

…**do user research**. It's the fastest path to helping you see the world through your users' eyes. Not only will it enable you to see areas for improvement in your product, but it will also give you a much more concrete sense of who your users are and what matters to them most.

The methods in this chapter cover a variety of investigative activities for learning more about your product, your users, your competitive landscape, and all the things you don't know now—but need to learn more about. At their core, however, *all* of these methods are about looking past what's familiar and known, in order to see the product with fresh eyes.

CHAPTER 6

Design Methods

D esigner Damien Newman created the design process illustration in Figure 6.1 to help illustrate a fundamental but little-known truth about the design process: the path to a clean, complete, well-considered product is messy, messy, *messy*. You generally have to throw away a lot of work before you get to something that you keep. And often you don't know what should be kept and what's headed for the trash until you get other people involved in the process. But showing your stakeholders or colleagues the messy design process can be a bit like making sausage: sometimes it can ruin their appetite for the meal. The trick is to follow an iterative design process that enables you to do your best work, but also brings people along for the ride.

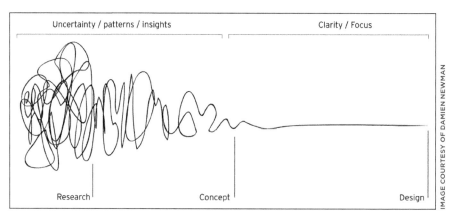

FIGURE 6.1
Damien Newman created "the squiggle" to convey the messiness of the design process.

The methods described in this chapter are tailor-made to get you through that process. They focus on iterative design coupled with structured, facilitative activities you can do with your non-UX colleagues to make them partners and co-owners of the UX design process. In this chapter, we'll cover:

- **Method 13: Design Brief.** At a high level, how would you describe your target design solution? What are the features and personality of the product? Who is it designed for, and what activities is it intended to encourage or enable? And the brief should include the overarching UX and design principles that will inform the work and answer the question: What should the experience of using the product *feel like* to a user?

- **Method 14: Task Flows.** How will the experience unfold over time? How do people expect those sequences to occur? How will you guide them through interactions?

- **Method 15: Sketching.** What are some different forms the product design could take? What might the overall system or product look like, and what range of ideas are possible at each point in the process?

- **Method 16: Wireframes.** How will the product look and function? What needs to be included and accounted for in terms of information structure, navigation, screen-to-screen interaction, content, and visual elements?

NOTE VISUAL/UI DESIGN RESOURCES

The methods in this chapter cover high-level design direction, flow, and interaction design. They do not cover visual/UI design, which would require its own book to do it justice. If you're interested in learning more about how to make smart, relevant, useful UI design choices, check out these resources:

- *Practical UI*, by Adham Dannaway, **www.adhamdannaway.com/ui-design-book**
- *Simple and Usable: Web, Mobile, and Interaction Design*, by Giles Colborne, **www.amazon.com/Simple-Usable-Mobile-Interaction-Design/dp/0321703545/**
- *About Face: The Essentials of Interaction Design*, by Alan Cooper, Robert Reimann, David Cronin, Christopher Noessel (4th Edition), **www.amazon.com/About-Face-Essentials-Interaction-Design/dp/1118766571**

METHOD 13

Design Brief

At a high level, how would you describe your target design solution? What are the features and personality of the product? Who is it designed for, and what activities is it intended to encourage or enable?

The design brief documents your working assumptions about the optimal design of the product and puts forth your hypotheses for how best to bring that design to life. Much like a project brief, a design brief is intended to be a clear summary of what direction you plan to move (see Figure 6.2). But the design brief is a little more focused on design specifics. It seeks to articulate the problems UX or UI improvement will solve (or the opportunities it will create) and connect the dots on how that will become reality.

The design brief is something you create for yourself first, and—if they have the time and interest—it can also be useful for your team and for any stakeholders who need to approve the design direction. A design brief helps you get shared vision on the intent and outcome of both the user experience and user interface design.

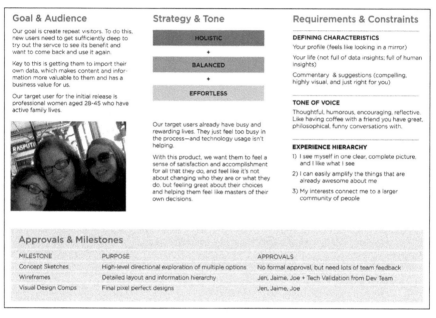

FIGURE 6.2
An example of a design brief.

Your brief should also include UX + design principles, which primarily answer the dual question: What should the experience of using the product look and feel like to a user—and how do you make sure your design creates it?

Sound design principles set clear standards that every person involved in UX, design, and development should strive to meet. They help you articulate the characteristics that should inform the user experience and the approach to product design. All of this is what creates products and services with a memorable *personality*, which may sound strange at first. But think about apps, sites, or systems you've used: while personality may not be intentional, it's there, nonetheless. Some feel confusing, complex, or technical; others feel fun, friendly, simple, smooth, or playful, social, productive, creative, and so on. Those feelings—and that user experience—is either intentional or unintentional. And when it's unintentional, it's usually bad.

Design principles, when shared with the team and with stakeholders as part of your brief, ensure that doesn't happen. They help you align the intent of everyone involved in the product's direction. And even if the only person who references these principles is you, they can serve as a barometer to continually gauge whether the designs (and builds) match the principles as the project progresses. These design principles form the foundation of a solid design system and also give invaluable guidance for how tough design decisions should be made (see Figures 6.3 and 6.4).

FIGURE 6.3
The UK government's thoughtful list of design principles.

---

6. This is for everyone

Accessible design is good design. Everything we build should be as inclusive, legible and readable as possible. If we have to sacrifice elegance - so be it. We're building for needs, not audiences. We're designing for the whole country, not just the ones who are used to using the web. The people who most need our services are often the people who find them hardest to use. Let's think about those people from the start.

- Using persona profiles to test accessibility by Anika Henke
- What we found when we tested tools on the world's least accessible webpage by Mehmet Duran

---

FIGURE 6.4

"This is for everyone" gives the team and stakeholders clear guidance on which side to err on when tough choices have to be made. And it clearly defines what distinguishes its products from others and what matters most to its user base.

Average Time

3–5 hours total

- 2–3 hours to create the brief and principles
- 1–2 hours to share with the team and incorporate feedback

Use When

- You want to clarify the team's expectations and intent where design is concerned and address any gaps or discrepancies in expectations early on.
- You need to set a standard for a way of working that creates great products, describes how they should feel and the emotions they should elicit, along with what distinguishes the product from the competition.
- You need a strong foundation for a design system that unifies the product experience in different circumstances, ensuring that it is both consistent and coherent.
- You're not sure what the vision or personality for your product is (or should be).

Try It Out

There are two ways to do a design brief. One way is to start from a good template and fill in the details (like the one shown in Figure 6.2). The second is to start with what you know, or have learned through your discovery and research work, and build on it. In either case, there are a few basic questions your design brief should answer (see Figures 6.5–6.7).

1. **Focus.**

   What is the focus of the design work? What will be created, improved, etc. as an outcome to this work? What are the reasons for that creation or improvement—to accomplish *what*?

2. **Audience.**

   Who will the design serve? Who are the primary audiences or personas that you will be designing for? Just as important, who are you *not* designing for? While a design brief is intended to be brief, this is an area where a little more description will enable you to double-check that your assumptions about users—their needs, mindsets, and priorities—match your teammates' assumptions.

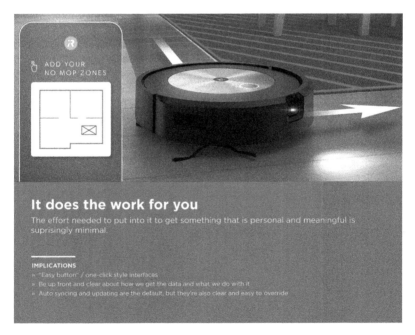

FIGURE 6.5

The design conveys that minimal effort will yield maximun results for its users.

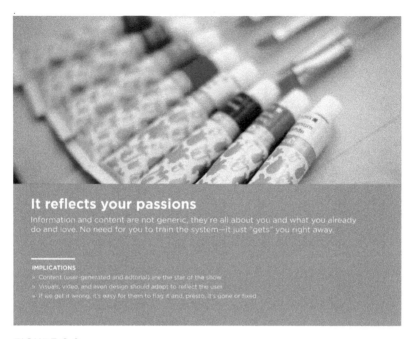

It reflects your passions

Information and content are not generic, they're all about you and what you already do and love. No need for you to train the system—it just "gets" you right away.

IMPLICATIONS
» Content (user-generated and editorial) are the star of the show.
» Visuals, video, and even design should adapt to reflect the user.
» If we get it wrong, it's easy for them to flag it and, presto, it's gone or fixed.

FIGURE 6.6

This company emphasizes "passions" to its users.

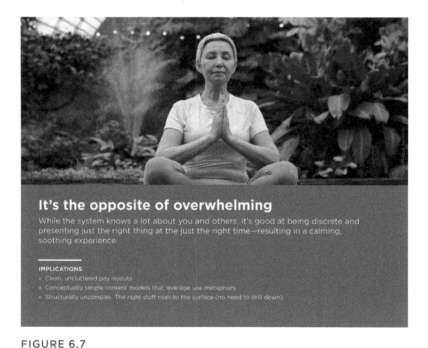

It's the opposite of overwhelming

While the system knows a lot about you and others, it's good at being discrete and presenting just the right thing at the just the right time—resulting in a calming, soothing experience.

IMPLICATIONS
» Clean, uncluttered pay layouts
» Conceptually simple content models that leverage use metaphors
» Structurally uncomplex. The right stuff rises to the surface (no need to drill down).

FIGURE 6.7

The image says it all here—your experience will be calm and soothing.

3. **Features and functionality.**

   What are the core screens, states, or scenarios? What workflows, use scenarios, and pieces of the experience will be central to the product and most useful and valuable to users?

4. **Feeling.**

   If you are successful, what will the feeling of the user experience be? This is emotion, which drives behavior. When people use the product, how will they feel about that use? As you're talking to stakeholders and team members, you'll find that people slip in words (usually adjectives) that effectively describe the desired feeling of the product. Notice that language, write it down, and put it in the design brief.

5. **Uniqueness.**

   Think about what you've learned through whatever research you've done. Have you discovered any differentiators and special characteristics that are key to your product? Are there any assets in your content patterns that are important to feature? Have you uncovered any interesting opportunities via user research that your product is uniquely positioned to address well?

6. **UX and design principles.**

   From this information, make a list of statements about what, ideally, the finished product should be like. Write short statements in a human voice. Capture how you'd like a person to describe your product after using it. Try to keep the list to no more than five. Prioritize the statements that directly give users what they need and create clear differentiation from your competitors.

7. **Restrictions and expectations.**

   What constraints must be obeyed, from technology or OS platforms to device form factor to accessibility? What is most critical to the success of the design? What parts must you absolutely get right, and what things can you absolutely not do?

8. **Share and discuss.**

   Once you're satisfied with your principles, share them (and the brief) with the whole team.

9. **Refer back to them regularly.**

   As you progress through design steps like sketching, wireframes, prototyping, and validation, continually refer back to your design principles and ask yourself, "Does what I'm designing feel like this principle?" If not, think about what should change to bring the design more in line with the principle.

- **Work within constraints.** One way to think about a design brief is that it clarifies the constraints that the design solution must obey. These constraints could include features and functionality, value, or brand propositions that the solution must reinforce or align with, and customers or users whom the solution should support.

- **Use it to validate assumptions.** One of the most important purposes of the design brief is to fully understand what ideas or expectations your non-UX colleagues have for the product. And it also uncovers things they want that you aren't aware of (but need to be). When you can provide a description of what the end result should look like, you're giving those non-UX folks something that they can respond and react to.

- **Add images.** Try to make a brief more than mere words. Embellish the brief with suitable imagery (icons or photos, for example) that give visual and emotional resonance to the ideas in the document. This helps the team connect emotionally to parts of the brief and remember it better later. It is also an opportunity for you to introduce visuals that foreshadow or allude to the quality of the experience the team is trying to deliver. For example, if the product should feel like a personal experience, include photos that seem candid, unstaged, and true to life. If the product should feel like a luxurious experience, include sophisticated, professional, polished imagery, and echo that in a clean, sophisticated layout for the brief document itself.

- **No generic principle statements.** Principles should help you make decisions in product design. This means they should be tangible and, to a certain extent, pointed. To test if a statement is specific and evocative enough, ask yourself if that statement could describe any competing product. If it could, the statement needs more work.

- **Go beyond easy.** Resist the urge to include a principle about being user-friendly, easy to use, or simple. Those things are all good, but they're table stakes for good UX and design. Given the rise of technology and the complex roles it plays in our lives, a simple experience isn't necessarily a differentiated experience anymore.

- **Make it a group activity.** If you'd like to include your non-UX team members in the creation of design principles, start by creating a big list of potential statements, as described earlier. Then hold a meeting or mini-workshop and invite the team to reduce the list and modify your draft principles to make them better. You can do this as a hands-on, lo-fi activity, creating design principles like the one shown in Figure 6.8. You can also invite the team to discuss what the implications might be for each principle as you apply it to product design.

FIGURE 6.8
Design principles don't have to be highly polished, as long as they capture a distinct feeling.

- **If you work remotely**, share your design brief with team members while it's in draft form and actively solicit their feedback—but don't hand them down like a decree; no one likes to be told what to do and how to do it. Instead, frame it as a conversation starter, and emphasize that you need and want everyone's input. Use it to get alignment before you start on the work. Getting people together in shared conversation to get their input makes this run smoother and faster.

Task Flows

How will the experience unfold over time?

People don't experience digital products page-by-page or screen-by-screen. They pop in the back door, jump erratically from one part to another, break your forms, and trick your logic. A task flow gets you thinking about how people *really* use your product. What are the most likely scenarios and sequences that users will follow? And what are some potential side doors that they may use to end up in the same place? The places where UX breaks down most often are the *moments in between*, when someone moves from one step or screen to another (no matter how carefully each step has been designed).

A task flow helps you design an experience that flows smoothly, even through the transition points. It also helps everyone get a handle on the back-end data, logic, and other systems that enable the journey. While you can make a task flow in any software program that's good for diagramming, we suggest you simply draw it out on a whiteboard, as shown in Figures 6.9 and 6.10. For our money, analog methods are a better choice since you'll rarely have the time you want to devote to this, and it is mission-critical that you *do not skip this step.*

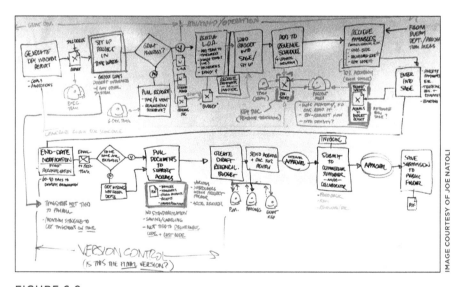

IMAGE COURTESY OF JOE NATOLI

FIGURE 6.9

A low-fidelity task flow on a whiteboard, focused solely on what interactions and system reactions need to occur during a user's journey.

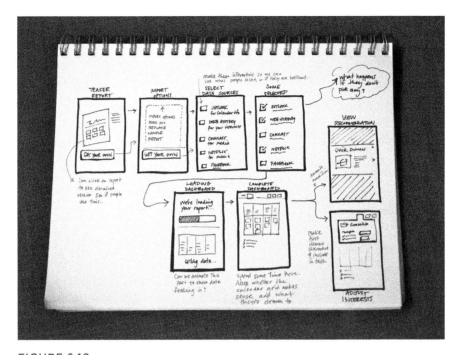

FIGURE 6.10

A low-fidelity task flow focused on the core UI states a user will see from screen to screen.

Working on a whiteboard allows you to work collaboratively with product managers and developers. The rough format keeps everyone focused on the task at hand, which is thinking through *how* people need to be able to use this thing—not what it looks like. It also prevents you from being precious about or protective of your work (overdesigning the look of the flow itself). And finally, it keeps everyone from making any assumptions about what something will *look like*.

The format Joe uses for this is simple: boxes and arrows, focusing on interaction and system behavior. Flows can also be made up of low-fidelity or sketched UI screens, illustrating what the user sees and can interact with at different points in the journey. Both are equally valid, useful approaches, so however you represent one step to the next is up to you. The only rule is that everyone in the room needs to be able to understand what your shapes and squiggles represent and mean.

Average Time

1–2 hours to think through and document a specific task flow. Unless you're doing a service blueprint, which can take a great deal more time (weeks) because it includes detail from front- and back-end processes.

Use When

You need a complete picture of how the broader user experience hangs together for yourself and for your team.

Try It Out

1. **Figure out your starting point.**

   You can do this in a top-down or bottom-up fashion.

   - **When you're thinking top-down, ask yourself what should a user encounter first?** What is the starting point? What are the major parts of the product? What comes first, and then what might happen as the user works his way deeper into the product?

   - **In the bottom-up approach, start with the most interesting steps in the process, or moments of truth, and ask yourself what comes before and after them?** Moments of truth are the points in your product that represent key destinations or transition points for your users. These moments are the reason they're here. For example, the purchase and confirmation screens on an e-commerce site might be a moment of truth. The activity feed or the reply function on a social network site could also be a moment of truth.

   - **Another alternative is to focus on scenario-based sketching, which is a bit of a blend of the top-down and bottom-up approaches.** Rather than just focusing on the top layer or the interesting moments, explore how users might start at the top and eventually work their way down to the interesting moments.

- **Pick your approach, and then draw or depict the initial screen or step as a small, thumbnail-sized representation.** (You don't need to show the entire screen, but giving just enough detail to convey the essence of the screen and the content and interaction available will make it easier to recognize it in your task flow.)

2. **Consider what comes next (or prior).**

   After you've picked your starting point, think about how your users would get to that point, and where they would go next. Repeat this process, either working your way from start to finish, or spreading out from the central moment where you began until you hit a reasonable start-and-end point.

3. **Think about alternate entries and exits.**

   For each step in the flow ask yourself, is there another way that someone could get here? Or is there somewhere else they're likely to go from here (not necessarily the next step in the flow)? Also, consider what should happen if people abandon at this point. If they come back later, what should they see? Similarly, if they come back on a different device or computer, what should they see?

4. **Think about decision points and branches.**

   Situations where a user has to choose between multiple options, or where the user's role changes (e.g., What an employee experiences in an internal app vs. a manager?) need to be explored. How do these choices or roles determine what the user can see and interact with? How does their path forward change as a result? How many possible paths are there (or should there be)?

5. **Add annotations.**

   Once you've captured all the key steps or screens for a particular task flow, go back through and add notes for how transitions should take place, or add other important points to capture that are not self-evident from simply looking at the task flow.

- **Keep it lightweight.** To go even more lightweight, use sticky notes on large paper or a whiteboard to plot out your task flow. Each sticky note represents one screen. Lay them out to figure out their relationship to each other and draw connector lines, annotations, etc. directly on the board or paper. If the flow changes, simply rearrange or redraw the sticky notes. (Thanks to UX designer James Goldsworthy for this tip.)

- **Don't boil the ocean.** Instead of trying to create a massive task flow that encompasses an entire system, create discrete flows that focus on core scenarios: the core tasks and activities that people use the app to do. It's less daunting, easier to think through, and can help you focus on getting distinct threads of the experience as fluid and accurate as possible. Afterward, you can go back through and think about how individual task flows connect to each other.

- **Use as a starting point for a clickable prototype.** This can also be a useful first step in determining what screens to include in a prototype and when interactivity should occur.

- **Think multichannel.** If you find yourself working on a task flow that switches channels or has nondigital components, consider creating an experience blueprint like the one shown in Figure 6.11 instead. Experience blueprints come from the field of service design, but they serve a function similar to a task flow—envisioning how an experience unfolds over time. To learn more about experience blueprints or service design more generally, check out the book *Service Design*, by Andy Polaine, Lavrans Løvlie, and Ben Reason (rosenfeldmedia.com/books/service-design/).

- **If you work remotely**, initial ideas for task flows are easy to put together wherever you are and can benefit from the focused thinking time that being remote sometimes provides. However, you do want this to be a group activity whenever possible. Your colleagues will be a useful resource for you in identifying edge cases and alternate paths that users sometimes take, which usually require separate discussion and exploration. Engineers are especially good at thinking through this sort of thing.

  So, we strongly recommend you set up working sessions via Zoom, Teams, or Google Meet to talk through what you have so far and get the team's thoughts, ideas, and feedback. Sketching or assembling a task flow on the fly, with collaborative tools like Miro, or by simply sharing your screen, will get you a lot further—a lot faster.

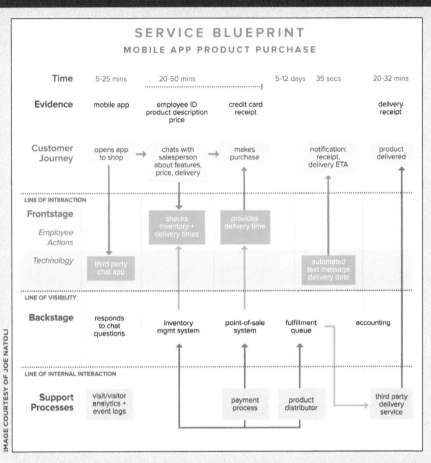

SERVICE BLUEPRINT

MOBILE APP PRODUCT PURCHASE

Time	5-25 mins	20-50 mins		5-12 days	35 secs	20-32 mins
Evidence	mobile app	employee ID product description price	credit card receipt			delivery receipt
Customer Journey	opens app to shop	chats with salesperson about features, price, delivery	makes purchase	notification: receipt, delivery ETA		product delivered

LINE OF INTERACTION

Frontstage *Employee Actions*		checks inventory + delivery times	provides delivery time			
Technology	third party chat app			automated text message delivery date		

LINE OF VISIBILITY

Backstage	responds to chat questions	inventory mgmt system	point-of-sale system	fulfillment queue		accounting

LINE OF INTERNAL INTERACTION

Support Processes	visit/visitor analytics + event logs		payment process	product distributor		third party delivery service

FIGURE 6.11

This simplified service blueprint example shows the various interaction touch points required to deliver a mobile purchase experience across frontstage, backstage, and support actions over specific intervals of time.

Sketching

What are some different visual forms the product design could take?

Sketching is an activity that should be familiar to pretty much all of humanity. It's when you sit down with pen and paper and allow yourself to start drawing out your ideas. However, in user experience design, sketching has added significance. It refers to the point in the process when you begin to explore different potential forms that the user interface design could take. This is an important step before beginning detailed designs.

Sketches are a vital design tool because:

- **They're cheap.** Sketching is a fast, inexpensive way to iterate and refine your ideas before transitioning to a higher-fidelity and more painstaking medium like wireframes or working code. If you discover that a certain idea won't work when sketching, you can quickly evolve or revise the idea. Erase, revise, move on.

- **They help you explore.** In user experience design, there are usually a variety of directions a design *could* take. Sketching is a thinking tool that you can use to explore your options, pinpoint an idea, and then adjust—and adjust again and again. This makes sketching an excellent tool for exploring constraints and trade-offs and thinking through the implications of one design over another.

- **They forestall perfectionism.** Because sketching helps you explore multiple directions, it's a natural deterrent to becoming too wedded to one particular idea too early. Sketching enables you to entertain a variety of ideas all at the same time, and often merge and evolve them into something greater than any one individual concept.

- **They invite conceptual feedback.** Sketches are messy, so no one can confuse them with finished designs (and get fixated on personal preferences or hang-ups). So, if you share a sketch with a team member or stakeholder, they're more likely to give feedback on the core concept—instead of on layouts, fonts, colors, and so on (none of which should be anywhere close to *real* at this point). And feedback on the concept is what you need most at the beginning stages of design. Conversely, if you show a more polished-looking design while you're still working on the basic idea, people will inevitably focus and fixate on surface aesthetics or assume it's too late to give feedback that might change or improve the concept.

- **They engage others.** Perhaps most valuable for a team of one (whose success often depends on getting support from non-UX peers), sketching gives you a way to translate abstract ideas into a tangible, visual language that you can share with others. Most people can't really envision something until they see it. Sketches bridge that gap, enabling you to confirm with the team what you're thinking and incorporate their feedback—before investing days or weeks of work into higher-fidelity design.

- **Anyone can do it.** This does not require precise artistic ability, and you don't have to be the only one sketching. In fact, inviting your cross-functional team to express their ideas with pen and paper gets them engaged, leads to great new ideas, and is fun!

For all these reasons, sketching is an essential tool in the UX team of one's toolkit that everyone should be able to use with a reasonable degree of confidence. Sketches also go beyond individual screens. They allow you to begin figuring out what the overall system or product looks like—along with the range of ideas possible at each point in the process.

Average Time

As much or as little time as you need. Quite often, 30 minutes of focused sketching time can make all the difference. For group sessions, you may spend anywhere from 1–3 hours to review with a team and determine the next steps.

Use When

- You're starting to explore design ideas.
- You want to engage the team in a constructive and tangible discussion of possible design directions.
- You're not really sure what direction the designs could or should go in, and you need a tool to spur your creative thought process and elicit feedback from team members and stakeholders.

Sketching is invaluable in helping to narrow down your ideas and get input from the team to move further into detailed design. This way of working settles design decisions. By doing the design thinking together and having critical conversations about the benefits and drawbacks of certain approaches, the strong ideas become self-evident. Rather than requiring you to preach or appeal to your colleagues' user-centered virtues, they can come to the same conclusions on their own by participating in the process.

Try It Out

1. **Use whatever tools allow you to think and draw quickly and effortlessly.**

   For some people, that means simple tools like an old pencil stub and a scrap of paper. For others, it means pens of varying weight and color, and a special notebook for sketching. And, of course, it may also mean using an iPad and stylus. Whatever imbues the sketching process with an air of thoughtful intention and makes your sketches clearer to other people is the right way to go. Sketches can also start with an existing screenshot of a current, coded build, where you draw over the top of it using tools like Miro, FigJam, Figma, or Adobe Illustrator. This can be a tremendous timesaver and gets everyone on the same page quickly. Do this in real time with a virtual audience, and minds will be blown.

2. **Consider using screen templates.**

   Every app, site, or system has to be designed for specific device types and multiple screen resolutions (breakpoints). Your sketches can be a lot more useful much earlier in the process if you start them on templates like those shown in Figure 6.12, which include a stencil or outline with an accurate sizing and aspect ratio for the target screen. And for digital sketching, it's even easier to find templates online for various mobile and desktop screen resolutions.

3. **Block off some time.**

   When you're ready to sit down and start sketching, consider giving yourself a time constraint—30 minutes, for example. The time constraint is useful because it forces you to move quickly and keeps your brain focused on creating instead of editing. The goal here is quantity, not quality—so no deliberating over an idea until it's perfect. "Perfect" doesn't matter when you're sketching; that comes later in the process. Here, it's about generating a lot of ideas for what's possible.

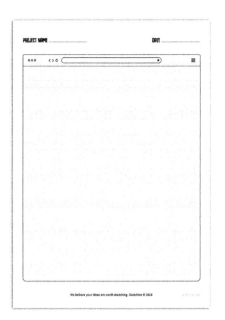
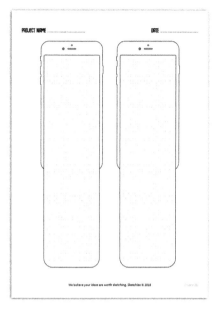
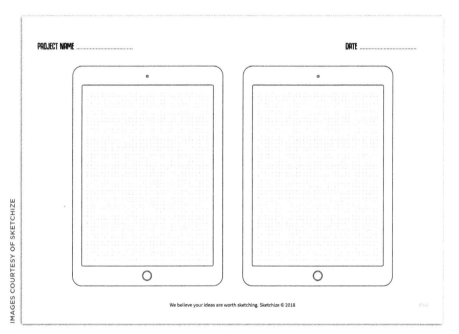

FIGURE 6.12

Sketching templates for smartphone, tablet, and web browser (available to download free from **sketchize.com**). Templates like this one aren't required but can help you remember to sketch multiple options before settling on just one.

4. **Sketch your first ideas for key parts of the experience.**

   Start by asking yourself, what are the most interesting moments in this product? If I'm the user, what point am I trying to get to? What screen, state, or configuration of data will be most compelling and most likely to impress me or give me the most value? What part of the experience is most likely to really impress me? Pick a key moment in the user's journey and start to sketch some potential screen layouts for them.

5. **Sketch alternatives.**

   After you've sketched one or two ideas for a particular state or screen, try to force yourself to sketch at least a few additional ways you could design that part of the product. For example, if the first sketch was a text-heavy design, how about a primarily visual way to present the same information? Continue this exploratory, experimental way of thinking as you drum up at least a few ideas for each screen that you're sketching. You can use a template like the one shown in Figure 6.13 to help yourself sketch quick, thumbnail-sized sketches for how you might design a specific page or moment of the experience.

   This may sound like extra work, but challenging yourself to continue and push past your first few good ideas inspires interesting new thinking. It's a way for UX teams of one to bring the same kind of rigorous, exploratory, generative thinking that a team of designers brings to a design problem.

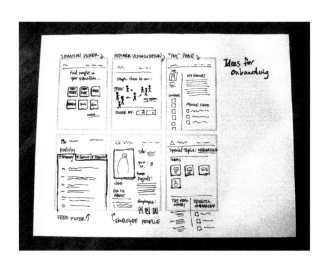

FIGURE 6.13

By forcing yourself to explore six different alternative approaches, you push past your first one or two good ideas.

6. **Review, critique, and revise.**

   Now comes the most important part. Assemble a group of fellow team members, co-workers, or even just friends. Each person presents and explains their ideas and solicits feedback. Start by explaining the inputs that informed your thinking, and then talk through your initial ideas for what the design solution might look like. While you're explaining your ideas, encourage people to ask questions and give their honest, off-the-cuff feedback. This is all valuable information about the impressions the design is likely to make in the wild, along with how people may interpret what they see.

   And while you're leading the charge as a UX professional, embrace and invite collaboration; be 100% willing to be wrong. Your work will be a thousand times stronger for it.

7. **Review the best ideas.**

   Your goal by the end of the sketching session is to come away with some sense of which ideas are promising enough to turn into higher-fidelity designs. Those higher-fidelity designs may just be more sketches, but they can also be wireframes, interactive prototypes, or even working code—whatever makes sense for the product development process that you're working with. You may find yourself mixing and matching some ideas from your initial sketches that are bigger than any one particular idea.

TIPS AND TRICKS FOR SKETCHING

- **Clarity before beauty.** You don't have to be a great artist to be a great sketcher. When sketching, aesthetics are low priority. You do, however, want to try to make sketches that someone else could look at and possibly make sense of—or that you yourself could make sense of if you pulled them out of a drawer two or three months later. To make your sketches clear, add annotations in a different color (e.g., red) to add visual clarity. Often, a short note and an arrow pointing to some part of the sketch are all it takes to clarify what makes a bunch of squiggles a solid gold idea.

- **Stick to drawing basic shapes.** The sketches in Figure 6.14 were created by designer Billy Carlson of Balsamiq. Billy's example, which mimics hand-drawn elements, shows that most user interface elements can easily be created with Balsamiq, using simple, low-fidelity elements.

continues

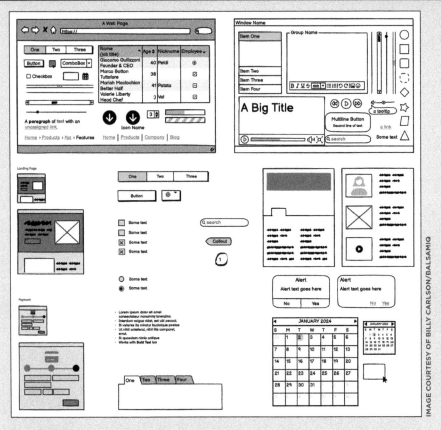

FIGURE 6.14
Focus on drawing simple shapes like these from the Balsamiq wireframing app.

- **Sketching tools.** If you're unhappy with the look of your sketches, there are tools that can help. Balsamiq is an online wireframing software with a sketchy appearance that you can use to put together sketch-like designs (balsamiq.com).

- **Sketch in words.** If you feel uninspired or stuck as you sketch, try to describe an idea in words before you attempt to draw it in pictures. Some of us are naturally word people; this sketching-in-text approach can be an equally valid way to explore the possibilities.

- **Be prepared to sketch anywhere, anytime.** Whatever your materials are, have them with you at all times so you can sketch on the fly, in meetings, or on a tablet in ad hoc conversations. When a conversation seems to drag on, with participants going back and forth about what they believe should happen to the product design, grabbing a pen and drawing what you or others have in mind can be very powerful. It can stop the circular arguments and debates and turn a purely speculative conversation into something a lot more tangible.

Also, the person who sketches directs the conversation—which is a very strong position to be in. Likewise, handing a pen to a colleague and asking her to sketch it out can give you a clearer picture of what she has in mind.

- **Frame the sketches for their audience.** To get people who are used to reviewing higher-fidelity designs to engage with sketches, it's helpful to spend a little extra time (but not too much) to scan your sketches and put them in a slide presentation. Use them as visual examples that support a written explanation of the design approach and the reasons for these visual choices. In cases of redesign, you can also project the current screens on a whiteboard and literally draw on top of it with whiteboard markers. This goes a long way in helping people understand what elements aren't working and how you plan to improve them.

- **Get people on their feet.** One reason group sketching sessions work so well is because they turn the traditional process of presenting and seeking approval for design on its head. Instead, they get people out of their seats and working together in an active, participatory, animated fashion. If you're all in person, have a "no butts in seats" rule during a session to make sure that you're truly keeping people active and engaged. Rough sketching turns passive recipients of the design process into active contributors to it. Group involvement also provides extra quality assurance for the UX team, minimizing or eliminating surprise reactions from those non-UX people later.

- **Know your altitude.** Sketches can be applied to design problems of varying specificity. You can use them at the start of a project to explore what major components or sections of the product you want to address, and to begin to develop preliminary ideas for what each could look like. Alternately, you can use sketches later in the process to figure out the details of a specific area or workflow. You might even have a collection of sketches that focuses on one single screen or moment—digging into all the permutations that one view might take, depending on the data the user has provided, what route they took to get there, if they're signed in or not, and so on.

continues

The important thing is to know the altitude of the problem you're trying to solve before you start sketching. The process can become hard to manage if you think you're doing a 30,000-foot, system-wide exploration but end up focusing all your ideas on a 5-foot view of a single state instead. Pick a scope for your sketching and stick with it.

- **Review with a focus.** Sketches can be an excellent tool for critiquing specific aspects of the product design. Consider having multiple review sessions with different types of people who will be focusing on different considerations, to ensure that you're thinking through all aspects of the product. For example, schedule a session with the engineering team to do a technical feasibility review and another session with the content folks to discuss whether the CMS can support these designs, along with how much of this content would need to be created or purchased.

- **If you work remotely**, group sketching sessions are very animated and physical. In general, that makes that makes them harder to do from afar. But even if you can't be there in person, you can still make sure that reviews happen as though you were together. You do that by setting up time and structures to enable the team to see your sketches, make their own, and have a highly detailed discussion around a collection of sketches. To do this remotely, schedule several larger blocks of time for an online working session with the cross-functional team. During this time:

  - Either block off a larger than average amount of time for the meeting (say, two hours), or explicitly give the working session a very narrow scope so you can be sure that you'll get through all the designs in the time available.

  - Ensure that the technology is set up for an optimal sharing experience. While this usually means Zoom, Teams, or Google Meet, tools like Miro, FigJam, Mural, and Scribblar are designed for visual collaboration online, and can be useful for sharing and annotating sketches, wireframes, and other visual artifacts.

  - In meetings like these, it's critical to have a clear agenda and a clear process for how content will be shared that everyone understands ahead of time. When technology issues derail a meeting, even if it's nobody's fault, it makes everyone annoyed (not the open, friendly, participatory vibe you're trying to create).

- If the meeting is focused on sharing (or co-creating sketches), you can make sketches ahead of time, scan them, and then send them around by email so people can refer to them during the meeting. Or, if you have a tablet, you can sketch real time during the meeting as you discuss ideas (see Figures 6.15 and 6.16). If colleagues aren't equipped to sketch and you're not using one of the tools mentioned previously, just ask them to sketch with pen and paper and hold their sketches up to their cameras—or snap a quick photo with their phone—and email it to the group.

FIGURE 6.15
In this collection of sketches, reference documents are posted on the left, and sketches are posted on the right.

FIGURE 6.16
You can tell by the annotations and copious notes in between sketches that they've been through a review session.

Wireframes

How will the product look and function in detail?

Wireframes are the meat and potatoes of user experience design. Many of the methods leading up to this point have all been geared toward enabling you to create smart, appropriate, relevant designs right here. A wireframe is a skeletal depiction of what a product should look like (see Figure 6.17).

If that sounds simple, let's not forget that a skeleton has an awful lot of bones. Like a skeleton, wireframes show you how the whole system hangs together to create a complete, interconnected structure that stands together as a whole.

Wireframes are typically black-and-white schematics or renderings of all the pieces and parts of the product or service. In a digital product,

IMAGE COURTESY OF BILLY CARLSON/BALSAMIQ

FIGURE 6.17

An example of a low-fidelity wireframe, based on the Spotify app.

they depict the parts of the product screen-by-screen. In a service, they may illustrate touch points that customers have with the service (be they digital, paper, or human).

Wireframes are (usually) black and white because they're focused on interaction, hierarchy, and content, not visual design attributes: What is the information that should appear on a screen? How should it be laid out? What details appear there? What navigation is available (if this is a digital product) to help someone move from one part of the product to another? Wireframes give some sense of how all the information and details relate to one another: How do you get from one step to the next, and what's the appropriate volume and hierarchy of information? What can people *see*, and what can they *do*?

In addition to black-and-white diagrams, wireframes usually include notes or annotations about how the product should behave. For example, what should happen when you press on a particular button? How should interactive elements change, in response to user

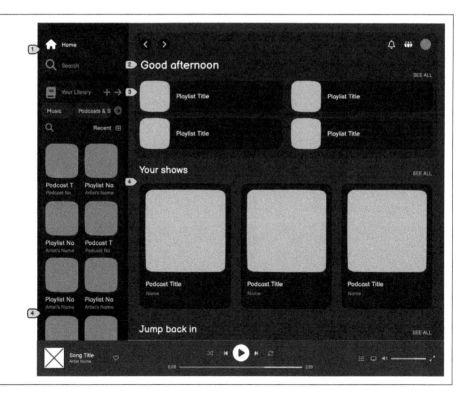

actions and given certain conditions? Those notes make wireframes an interesting bridge between a design document and technical specifications. Wireframes can also serve as a foundation for meaningful collaboration with engineers to make sure what's designed can actually be implemented.

Average Time

Hours, days, or weeks, depending on the scope of the system, the volume and complexity of data and content, as well as the volume and complexity of user interaction. When working on a digital product, each screen can take anywhere from 30 minutes to a couple hours on average.

Use When

You're ready to really nail down the details of the product design.

Try It Out

1. **Pick your tool.**

   With simple drag-and-drop components and seemingly endless template and component libraries at your disposal, wireframing and prototyping software makes short work of iterating on-screen design. Most apps, such as Axure RP, Figma, Sketch, Balsamiq, and many others, feature simple drawing tools that

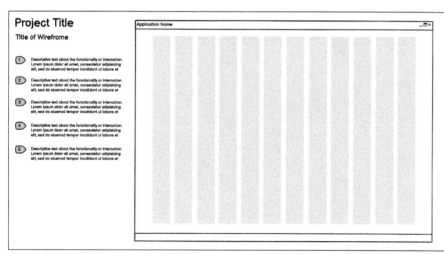

IMAGE COURTESY OF BILLY CARLSON/BALSAMIQ

allow you to easily approximate device form factors and screen resolutions, along with related OS-specific user interface and interaction conventions and elements in your diagrams.

2. **Create a template.**

Once you've chosen your tool, your impulse may be to jump right into designing screens. Consider taking a moment first to either create or select a template for your wireframes like the one in Figure 6.18—one that takes into account the device or form factor you are designing for. For example, are you designing for:

- A smartphone with a 6.1-inch (155 mm) display with Super Retina XDR OLED technology at a resolution of 2556 × 1179 pixels and a pixel density of about 460 PPI with a refresh rate of 60 Hz?

- A 1680 × 1050 HD Retina display on a ruggedized 13″ laptop for field use?

- An office full of antiquated desktop towers whose OS, browser, and monitors are more than five years old—and haven't been updated since then? (Yes, this scenario *does* exist.)

Specifics like these matter a great deal in determining just how much you can fit on the surface of the screen—and how people are most likely to interact with it. Start with a template like the one in Figure 6.18 that represents the aspect ratio and proportional measurements of the area you're designing for. You may need to scale down your measurements a bit to fit on the canvas of the software

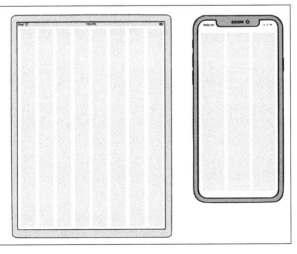

FIGURE 6.18
These are wireframe templates created in Balsamiq for laptop, tablet, and mobile screens. On the left side of the template are sample annotations. The colored boxes represent different grids.

you use; Figma, Sketch, Balsamiq, Axure, and others often have artboards available based on specific device layouts.

On your template, include a spot for a name to identify the page, screen, or design exploration. And make sure you add a spot for notes or annotations.

3. **Create a wireframe inventory.**

   One final step before you start creating your wireframes: make a list of the wireframes that you think you'll need to create and gather together any sketches that you're planning to turn into wireframes. If there are any screens in your list that you don't have ideas for yet, take the time to start sketching out the design *before* you start to create the digital wireframe. If you need to evolve any sketches further, do it on paper before you move into software. Once you go digital, it can be hard to separate the functional questions from the natural impulse to pretty up your wireframes—so try to have a basic plan before you get started.

   At the same time, your wireframes don't have to be a perfect copy of your sketches. In fact, it's likely that you'll go into more detail and think more about subtle nuances of the design, as you work through the wireframes. Some things that work on paper don't always work on screen, and that's okay; it's part of the process.

4. **Get wireframing.**

   At last, you're ready to start wireframing. Clear your calendar. Put on some good tunes. Pour yourself a nice cup of tea or coffee and prepare to settle into the time-eclipsing flow of wireframing. As you work, rendering designs for each screen or part of the product, think about things like the following:

   - **Sequence and state:** How will someone get here and where will they *go* from here? Does this step have multiple states, depending on which path the user takes to get there?

   - **Information density, priority, and relevance:** What's the main message or action from here? What should a user notice first? Is the most important thing on the screen also the most *obvious* thing? (Hint: It should be.) Does a user need to see all of this at the same time? How much do they need in order to take the very next step or do the very next thing?

   - **Grid:** How clean, balanced, and orderly does the design feel? How will those relationships change at various screen breakpoints? Where could this approach fall apart?

- **Design principles:** Is this screen or piece of the product delivering on the experience expressed in that handful of statements that were created?

- **Error messages and states:** What does the user see when things don't go exactly as planned?

Every once in a while, get up, take a walk, and then come back and try to see your wireframes with fresh eyes. When you do, ask yourself, "How can I make it even simpler?" Continue on this path until your wireframes are at a good stopping point to share with others.

5. **Seek and listen to feedback.**

Share your wireframes with the team (or anybody you can find). Get feedback on whether the designs make sense, if the flow matches how people would expect to move through or use the product, and if anything seems just plain funky. Ask people what they would expect to happen when interacting with certain parts of the design. Do their expectations match what you have planned? Accept this feedback for what it is—valuable and honest input that will help you make the design and intended UX even better.

TIPS AND TRICKS FOR WIREFRAMES

- **Show your work.** Wireframing can be the most labor-intensive part of the process. This makes it an important but tricky piece of work for UX teams of one. How do you ensure that you are doing great design work but not spending all day, every day, pushing pixels around the screen? Taking time up front to do sketching should help you balance the amount of time you spend working with others with the amount of time working on your own.

- **Whatever you do, make sure that you don't get too far along in the wireframing process before showing your work to other people.** Never go too far down the rabbit hole of ideas without having some basic conversations with your colleagues to see if what you're thinking is really viable. For a UX team of one, checking in and showing your work opens up the black box of design and helps your colleagues develop an understanding of the user-centered design process.

continues

- **Give it a grid.** A user interface grid is a foundational layout structure that organizes content into rows and columns, providing a systematic framework for arranging UI elements on a screen. Grid systems are mandatory for responsive design, ensuring that the interface design adapts seamlessly to various screen sizes and resolutions. Grid systems enable you to create fluid layouts that maintain consistency and visual hierarchy, providing an optimal user experience across multiple devices like desktops, tablets, and mobile phones. While there are many variations, essentially there are three common grid types:

  - A **column grid** divides the layout into multiple vertical columns, providing a flexible structure for organizing content. These are typically used for complex layouts, like web pages or app interfaces.

  - A **baseline grid** is a horizontal grid structure that ensures consistent vertical alignment of text and other elements across a layout. Baseline grids are good for typography-heavy designs to maintain readability and visual harmony.

  - A **square grid** is a modular grid consisting of evenly spaced, equal-sized square modules. It can be used to create a visually balanced layout, especially with square-shaped content like images or icons.

  - **For an excellent guide to all things grid, check out this article:** uxpin.com/studio/blog/ui-grids-how-to-guide/

- **Think about tool compatibility.** As you are selecting your wireframing tool, think a bit about whom you'll be sharing these documents with, how editable they'll need to be, and whether multiple people may need to be able to edit them. In addition, you may want interoperability with other applications and systems. Balsamiq, for example, is offered as a desktop version (Windows and Mac), cloud service, or as a plug-in for Google Drive, Confluence, and Jira. Figma integrates with just about every tool in existence in a corporate environment, including Jira, as well as developer tools like GitLab. Sketch, on the other hand, isn't a cloud-based app, and only works with macOS, making collaboration and integration extremely difficult.

- **If you work remotely**, design can be a tricky part of the process. Some design or UX problems require total heads-down focus (great for being remote). However, others require quick iterations, lots of subtle feedback, and an astute reading of body language to understand how people really feel about it (better in person). There's also a lot of talking and explaining that happens during this time, and doing it over Zoom is definitely harder than doing it in person.

There's often a point somewhere about halfway through the design work…when things finally seem to be taking shape and…SUR-PRISE! Suddenly it all seems to go off the rails, and your colleagues start to express big concerns about the design direction. This is when it's hardest to be far from the rest of the team. This moment often coincides with the point where designs have moved out of the ambiguous sketching phase and are starting to take a definite, digital form. Seeing something definitive and tangible can cause people to get worried about all the things that aren't right yet and become afraid they're being locked into a direction that's not all there yet.

In other words, people sometimes freak out. Leah calls this the *design triage period*. This is definitely a time to be with your team in a high-touch, face-to-face way, if you can. If possible, plan ahead and expect that there will be a design triage during the wireframe period—and expect to be onsite and in person with your team for a few days in the middle of it.

If You Only Do One Thing…

…**sketch!** And while FigJam, Mural, and Miro are common, in our experience the whiteboard variety accomplishes a lot more in less time. Going analog can be your secret weapon for getting people involved, excited, and engaged. This collaborative work will not only help other people see how the user experience design process works, but it will also help you improve upon your designs with the help of others. Across the three decades your authors have been doing this, we have yet to see anything that works as well, is as impactful, or saves as much time and effort across the board.

The methods in this chapter show the range of considerations that you have to think about when doing the heavy lifting of UX, UI, and product design, from the core positioning of the product, to what different forms the interface could take, to the tactical nuts and bolts of how the design will ultimately function.

The underlying spirit of it all is that design should be an exploratory, inclusive process that you invite people into—and help shepherd them through.

CHAPTER 7

Testing and Validation Methods

esting and validation methods help you figure out if your design will actually work. Will people be able to use the product or service as intended? Does it trigger positive emotional responses? How fluid and seamless does the user experience feel overall? Sometimes this kind of work is referred to as *usability* or *usability testing*—where the emphasis is clearly on whether you can use the product without error. Usability is part of it, but it's not the whole story. You'll also want to validate the emotional impact created by the experience, the fluidity of the product or service, and how well the overall product paradigm matches the mental models that people bring to it.

There's a popular misconception that this kind of research has to take a lot of time and effort to be done right. That's simply not true. Whatever enables you to validate designs quickly with real people and gain confidence that the design is moving in the right direction is fair game. The testing and validation methods in this chapter can be done on the quick and on the cheap. In this chapter, we'll cover:

- **Method 17: Interactive Prototypes.** Does it work and feel as intended?

- **Method 18: Black Hat Session.** What areas of the design could be improved?

- **Method 19: Rapid Usability Test.** Can people use this product as intended?

- **Method 20: Five-Second Test.** What impression is created by a specific screen, step, or moment within the product?

- **Method 21: UX Health Check.** Can you measure the baseline quality of a user experience and assess changes in quality over time?

METHOD 17

Interactive Prototypes

Does it work, feel, and behave as intended?

Prototypes are semi-functional models of a product that help you test how it will work and whether the interactions make sense to users. Prototypes can vary widely from the crudest paper-based explorations to highly realistic, functional models. This basic approach—idea first, then prototype, and then further improvement based on what you learn—is a powerful, time-endorsed method for any type of new product development.

And it's an excellent practice for you to get into as a team of one, because above all else, people expect UX practitioners to drastically improve product design. Some skilled UX practitioners just naturally know how to do that, but when you're just starting out, you won't always be sure of what needs to happen to make a killer design. Prototyping and iterating give you a method where you can comfortably trust your gut, but still give yourself space to learn and improve as you go.

Average Time

Varies based on format of prototype. Wireframing software makes it possible to create a clickable prototype in just a few hours or less. Building a more functional prototype with actual working code can take multiple days.

Use When

You want to validate the direction prior to investing the time and resources to make it fully real. Often, you'll discover that an idea doesn't work quite as well as you originally imagined. Discovering this information early on enables you to modify your design in a relatively cheap and efficient way, and to evolve the design with real-time feedback.

Try It Out

1. **Think about the purpose of the prototype.**

   Different points in the process argue for different types of prototypes. Ask yourself what type of validation you are trying to do and select the appropriate tool. Here are some different forms a prototype might take, depending on your goal:

   - To explore and validate early concepts, **paper** (sketches representing a few select screens or moments in the product) should be enough.

   - To get a sense of how a sequence of screens or moments flow together, a **low-fidelity clickable prototype** usually suffices to illustrate how a discrete experience will unfold. Low fidelity means your clickable prototype includes the bare minimum of interactivity: the visual attributes of the app, site, or system— are represented, but not styled in any way. A low-fidelity prototype lacks font style, color, and graphics, since the main focus is on organization, functionality, and priority of content and interaction.

Think of it as a "skeleton" for the digital product you've been tasked to design, using the term Jesse James Garrett first used to describe it (check out his book, *The Elements of User Experience*). A wireframe is essentially a rough sketch you can click through. The purpose is to allow you, your team, and your stakeholders to focus on how people will browse through and interact with the site, system, or app. You can use tools like Axure RP, Figma, Sketch, or Balsamiq to quickly create a low-fidelity clickable prototype.

- These same **tools** can simulate intended interactions more realistically, in higher fidelity. Axure RP, UXPin and Figma in particular enable you to integrate basic conditional logic— and, of course, there's always good old-fashioned HTML. If you have technical knowledge, you can also prototype directly in whatever the target technology is, which is sometimes the most efficient way because you may be able to repurpose the prototype into production code.

This type of prototype can be useful when you want to do rigorous usability testing before actually building the product, or when you want your colleagues or potential clients to get a realistic sense of what it will be like to use the product.

2. **Make your prototype.**

This is the fun part. Depending on your prototype fidelity and tool, this may be as simple as a low-fidelity approach like the Apple Music prototype in Figure 7.1, or it may require more time for writing code or setting up software to behave as you intend. A couple of things to think about as you work on your prototype:

- **You're trying to represent a sequential experience.** There is a beginning, middle, and end that correspond to how somebody might move through the product. Plan out that beginning, middle, and end on paper, and think about the states or screens that make up this sequence. Think about which transitions that take someone from one moment to the next should be included: Do you need to show how a user might move from field to field in an online form, along with validation messages that may appear, or is it enough to just show an empty form, followed by the screen people see after filling it out?

The answer depends on what you're trying to validate. If the purpose of the prototype is to show how form errors should be handled, then field-by-field is probably the best way to go. If it's to show how someone can create a profile and then get started using an app, maybe form-level interactivity is overkill. The main thing is to think carefully about *which states* you will need.

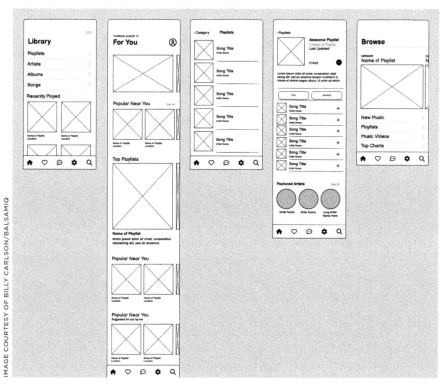

FIGURE 7.1

A low-fidelity wireframe for the Apple Music app.

- **A design is only as good as the content and information within it.** So, it's important to test the comprehensibility and usefulness of the information—the content, the data, and so on—along with flow and functionality. Without that content, you don't fully understand what needs to be communicated to the user via the prototype. And you cannot test or evaluate what you don't understand. That understanding has to drive every aspect of design, from the amount of content on a given screen, to the layers of navigation needed to access it, to determining the appropriate ways of interacting with it.

  The number one job of every single element on the screen is to allow access to content, expose and explain its relationship to other content, and present, communicate, support, and reinforce the meaning of that content so that it's clearly understood. And while people are remarkably flexible in looking at and responding to in-progress designs, your colleagues, stakeholders, and clients can make sense of what they're seeing more easily with reasonably realistic data. Remember that one of the goals of a prototype is to enable observers to see how information will unfold as they progress through the experience.

3. **Validate the prototype with yourself and others.**

   Use the prototype to observe how someone would really interact with the design if unaided and left to their own devices. To do this, put the prototype in front of a volunteer or a representative user and give them a task. Start at the beginning of the experience that you've prototyped and ask them to show you what they would do in order to complete the task. What would they interact with? What would they touch or click on to complete a task? Remind them that their only goal is to complete the task you've given them. Ask them to explain what they think they're seeing at each step along the way.

   Undoubtedly, you'll see things that surprise you when you watch people interact with the design. From this, one of two wonderful things happens. Either you learn that the design works as intended, which is great, or you learn what's not working well and you get some ideas for how to improve it—and *that's* great, too.

- **Know when to prototype and when not to.** Not everything you design has to be prototyped. Prototyping can save you time, but making a prototype takes time, too. You want to be sure that you're investing the time to validate something that *really* needs to be validated. In general, prototypes are ideal for evaluating new or nonstandard interactions or products, or for testing parts of the product that are simply too important to get wrong. To figure out what parts of the product are good candidates for prototypes, you can plot features and functions on a *Critical/Complex graph* like the one shown in Figure 7.2.

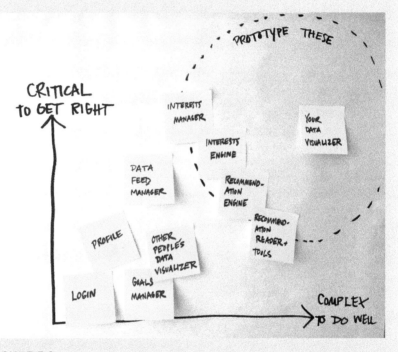

FIGURE 7.2

A Critical/Complex graph helps you identify which parts of the product are most important to prototype.

continues

- **Separate information from action.** Your task is to be ruthless in coming up with ways to segregate and separate the two, because this separation is the foundation of sound interaction design. As such, it's critical to keep two things distinct:

  1. Things the user needs to know.
  2. Things the user needs to *be able to do*.

  The latter should be up-front and center; the former has to be accessible but should be tucked out of the way and used only when needed—and in such a way that invoking it doesn't obscure or compete with the action the user is trying to take.

  What you're trying to do here is build a model in place for that separation: design patterns and interaction patterns that make sense. This, again, is why you should prototype in low-fidelity—to try, evaluate, and revise in quick, repeated cycles.

- **Don't fixate on the exact mechanisms used to display content or allow the user to interact with it.** It doesn't matter yet whether the final build will be a drop-down list, a menu of links, a button, or a hyperlink. It's far more important and valuable to figure out what's needed and how people will expect or want to interact with it. For example, you may use a traditional data table in the prototype, but that may not be the most efficient or appropriate way to expose this information. But you start with that table anyway, because it's a question that needs to be asked: "What's the best way to present this?" You start with your first best guess, and you change it as necessary across your iterations.

- **If you work remotely**, always walk people through your prototypes and review them together. Prototypes are almost, by definition, incomplete—if they were fully complete, they'd be the finished product. So, with any prototype, there's always a certain degree of imagination required to envision how the rest of the product functions beyond what has been prototyped in detail. If the viewer isn't familiar with how the prototype is meant to work, confusion can ensue. For that reason, unless they're very functional and self-explanatory, don't just release prototypes into the wild and ask people to send feedback. Instead, schedule time to review it with the team and do some basic usability testing—remotely via Zoom or Teams, if not in person.

Black Hat Session

What areas of the design could be improved?

Black Hat sessions are inspired by Edward de Bono's "Six Thinking Hats." This is a facilitative framework where teams adopt deliberate mental attitudes to make group work more dynamic and directed. Each participant in a group discussion figuratively puts on a hat of a certain color, and each hat signifies a particular point of view. For example, there's a hat for optimism (the yellow hat), one for emotion (the red hat), one for creativity (the green hat), etc. The black hat, according to the de Bono Group, is the judge's hat:

> It offers logical reasons for concern and invites us to explore with caution. One of the most powerful hats, it encourages us to identify, consider, and weigh risks. A person wearing the black hat is obliged to point out weaknesses or risks, and to be frank about what's confusing or seems like it could be further improved.

All of the hats are interesting, but for the purposes of design critique, the black hat is especially powerful. It's the essential part of a framework that can put your teammates in a state of mind that enables candid and productive feedback on designs. This is valuable for several reasons:

- **People don't necessarily know how to give critical design feedback.** This can be even truer for your non-UX partners. When presented with a set of wireframes, it can often be hard to know where to start in evaluating them. For someone new to the experience design process, it may be difficult to know if what you're looking at has issues or not. A Black Hat session gives a group of people permission to call things as they see them, which releases them from worrying about whether their feedback is relevant or even correct. Black Hat sessions provoke honest, constructive conversations.

- **Because a Black Hat session is all about pointing out the hard stuff, it accomplishes a few very important things.** First, it gives anyone who is unhappy with certain aspects of the design a constructive forum for sharing their concerns and instills confidence that they're being heard. Second, it creates a safe place where people who are less comfortable giving negative feedback can express their concerns as well. Third, it puts all of these data points into a format that you can see, track, manage, and take charge of.

- **By running a Black Hat session, you show you're not protective and defensive about the designs that you are creating**, and that you are serious about doing what needs to be done to make a great product. It also shows that you are the driver of a process where designs get better and better through continuous input and iterative improvement. Figure 7.3 shows what a typical Black Hat session looks like.

FIGURE 7.3
A cross-functional team conducting a Black Hat session.

Average Time

30–60 minutes

Use When

- You're too close to the designs, and you need honest feedback on what's working and what isn't.
- You sense that the team is holding back or not fully engaging in design reviews.
- You want to do targeted reviews with subject matter experts (for example, technical feasibility reviews with the engineering team).

Try It Out

1. **Make time for a group work session.**

   Once you have designs in a shareable form, schedule a Black Hat session. Block off an hour on the calendar, find a room or area with large, usable wall space, and assemble a group of people to help you critique the designs. It's ideal if this group is actually the cross-functional team that works on the product together, but barring that, even a group of friends or uninvolved colleagues should be able to provide feedback on potential stumbling blocks from an end-user perspective.

2. **Explain the rules.**

   With the group assembled, tape to (or project on) the wall any designs you want to critique. Explain the rules of the Black Hat session. Everyone has one job and one job only: to assume *the most critical, judgmental perspective they can muster*, and look at the designs from that point of view. Ask participants to write down every problem or issue they see on a sticky note (one issue per sticky note) and place the note on the designs near where they spotted the problem.

   One easy way to "put on" the black hat is to pretend that you're a grumpy, skeptical user who is short on time and trying to do four different things simultaneously. Or pretend that you're a tough, very senior leader who will be approving these designs before they are considered final.

3. **Start the clock.**

   Give the group 15 to 20 minutes to walk through all of the designs, reflect on what they notice, and write their sticky notes. You can have participants do this as a silent exercise, or you can invite them to discuss what they're seeing as a group. You can participate as well, writing your own sticky notes. Either way, make sure that everyone writes lots of notes. If they seem hesitant, you can give them some guidance as they go. Ask them things like:

   - When you look at each screen or step, do you understand its fundamental purpose?
   - What jumps out at you? Is it what should jump out at you?
   - Do you know what to do in order to advance to the next step?
   - What questions do you have about the information and functionality that you're seeing?

- Do you feel like this is a reasonable number of steps?
- Does anything feel too complicated or cumbersome?
- Is there any language that doesn't make sense? Instructions? Button labels? Anything else?

4. **Review and look for common themes.**

   After all the sticky notes have been written, invite the team to step back and look at other people's sticky notes, looking for themes and issues they might have missed. Are there issues or complaints that come up repeatedly across the majority of participants?

5. **Discuss and synthesize.**

   Now, engage the group in a discussion about the big themes that emerged. You may find that the issues identified run the gamut

TIPS AND TRICKS FOR BLACK HAT SESSIONS

- **Use them whenever, wherever.** Black Hat sessions don't require a lot of prep and material—just some people, some designs, some sticky notes, and a little bit of time. That makes a Black Hat session a durable, self-contained pop-up exercise you can use whenever and wherever it's helpful. For example, if you're having a difficult design review meeting where the team seems to be rehashing the same issues again and again, call a timeout and run a Black Hat session. You can even do these by yourself, as a form of quality control.

- **Focus feedback.** Black Hat sessions can be general, as described previously, but they can also be focused on specific topics. A Black Hat session that focuses on, say, technical feasibility can be a great way to quickly involve engineering and identify designs that may prove problematic from an implementation perspective. Similarly, you can run Black Hat sessions that are focused on content, usability, conversion, pretty much anything.

- **If you work remotely**, giving critical feedback can be uncomfortable. So can receiving it, even if you're the one requesting it.

from language, flow, and ease-of-use, all the way to core assumptions about the design concept. That's great; you've just gotten a lot of help to make the design even better. During the group discussion, record the points on a flipchart or whiteboard. That list effectively becomes the synthesis of all the individual sticky notes. Close with a discussion about what's most successful in the designs, in order to end the session on a positive note. Or close by discussing the top areas that need to be improved and what the next steps for making those improvements are.

6. **Update the designs.**

   After the meeting, revisit the designs to address the issues that the group identified. Some may be simple, quick fixes. Some may require more thought and rework to the designs.

For that reason, it's ideal to do this sort of activity in person. The in-person dynamic makes it easier for you to read nonverbal cues, diffuse any awkwardness, and encourage your colleagues to be open and honest. It also makes it easier for you to use things like humor to defang the process. If you can't do this in person, here are some tips for conducting this kind of review remotely:

- Set expectations as you would at an in-person session. Explain that you need the team to provide critical feedback; set time limits; and provide a mechanism for them to capture and share their thoughts screen by screen and one by one.

- Make the feedback visible by adding annotations directly within screen-sharing software. Or use tools like FigJam, Miro, or Mural to get your team to go through the product and give feedback asynchronously.

- Regularly remind them that this kind of feedback can be uncomfortable to give, but that you really need their honesty and candor to do your work well. Give them permission to say hard things.

Rapid Usability Test

Can people use this product as intended?

A rapid usability test is a natural output to many of the design methods described in Chapter 6, "Design Methods." The essence of the rapid usability test is that you do it quickly—like the name says. With this method, you'll forego rigor and perfectionism to make it possible to get rapid feedback on designs. You'll let go of recruiting and scheduling time with real users and just test the designs with anyone available. Think of it as putting the design in front of the first person you find (who is unfamiliar with the product) and seeing if they can make sense of it.

Ideally, you should test designs with people who truly represent the intended end-user, and if you have the time and team support, you should go that route. But if you're just trying to get a gut check on whether a design direction works or doesn't, any fresh pair of eyes can help you see things from a new perspective and settle wavering questions.

Average Time

As little as 10 or 15 minutes per person, whenever you need it.

Use When

- At any point during the design process when you want to do a quality check on the designs.
- As often as possible to check your work along the way.

Try It Out

1. **Find someone, anyone.**

   As you're working on a design, when you want to see if it makes sense to others, print out the design or grab your laptop and wander over to anyone who hasn't seen it yet. This could be someone who sits in the desk next to yours, someone you encounter walking down the hall or in the cafeteria, or if you truly work alone, a friend or family member.

2. **Ask them what they're seeing and how they think it works.**

   Think about the purpose of the page, screen, or section of the design that you're working on. What are the main things people should be able to use it for? With this list of primary tasks in mind, show your design to your volunteer. Ask them how they think they could interact with this design to accomplish a particular task. If there are multiple screens or steps that you're designing, proceed through each screen, asking them to explain what they're seeing and what they would do to advance to the next step. That may only take 5 minutes, or it might take 20.

3. **Find a few more volunteers.**

   Once you've shown your design to one person, try to find a few more people to run through the same process. Your colleagues may enjoy getting involved, since it's a break from their normal routine and shows that you value their perspective.

4. **Iterate the designs.** If you identify anything that's especially confusing to people or that they interpreted differently than you had intended, go back and revise the design.

TIPS AND TRICKS FOR RAPID USABILITY TESTS

- **Not for expert users.** Rapid usability tests are preferable for products that don't have a highly technical purpose or very specific audience. They're for situations where the average person is a reasonable stand-in for your actual users. If you *do* have a very technical product and you're trying to run a rapid usability test, you should try to find someone who is a good stand-in for a typical user. At a minimum, you may need to spend a few minutes up-front explaining some concepts and terminology.

- **Be willing to stop and fix things.** If you discover after your first few conversations that something in the new design is just not working for people, stop and fix the design before continuing. Ultimately, it's more productive to test three different designs of progressively improving quality with two people each than to test one bad design with six people.

- **If you work remotely**, enlist the help of family, friends, acquaintances, or people you meet on the street. You can also use online tools like Chalkmark (optimalworkshop.com/chalkmark), UserTesting (usertesting.com), Lookback (lookback.com), or Maze (maze.co) to create test scenarios and record users going through these scenarios remotely.

Five-Second Test

What impression is created by a specific screen, step, or moment within the product?

First popularized by Christine Perfetti at User Interface Engineering, a five-second test is a lightning-fast but surprisingly insightful method to quickly assess the information hierarchy in a product. (Read more at articles.centercentre.com/five_second_test.) A five-second test helps you see how clear and memorable a given moment in the product or service is to users (see Figure 7.4).

FIGURE 7.4
In a five-second test, show a design to a user for five seconds, and then remove it from sight and ask her what she remembers about the design.

PHOTO COURTESY OF CASTORLY STOCK

Like a rapid usability test, a five-second test can and should be done regularly to check your work as you progress through the design process. You can even combine a rapid usability test with a five-second test for a rapid but rich round of validation. In a five-second test, you expose the user to a screen or moment in a product, ask them to look at it for five seconds, and then remove the screen from view. Once the screen has been removed, ask them what they remember seeing, and what they thought the overall purpose of the page or screen was.

Considering that people often use products in a distracted, multitasking state, the five-second test is a pretty good indicator of how people really experience your products.

Average Time

5–10 minutes per screen

Use When

- You want to test the information hierarchy of a page, screen, or state.
- As often as possible to check your work along the way.

Try It Out

1. **Find a volunteer to test your designs on.**

   This can be anyone handy (as in the rapid usability test) or actual, representative users. Explain that you're going to show them a screen in a product, but only for five seconds, after which you'll take it away and ask some questions about it.

2. **Commence the five-second countdown.**

   Show your participant the design that you are testing and silently count off five seconds. You can do this in person by showing a printout or a design on the screen of your computer, mobile device, or tablet. If you're doing this remotely, you can do it through screen-sharing software, such as Zoom or Teams.

3. **Ask the volunteer what she remembers.**

   After five seconds have passed, remove the picture from view. Now ask your research participant what they remember seeing on the page or screen. Also ask what they think the purpose of the page was, and, if they're unfamiliar with your product, what they think the product was.

4. **Did they get it right?**

   Did they notice the most important messages or information you're trying to convey in that moment? If not, your information hierarchy may be off. Did they correctly interpret the purpose of the product and the screen? If not, the balance of messaging and basic affordances (what it *looks like* you can do with that screen) may need more work. Could they correctly identify the type of product this is? If not, you may need to think about navigation, branding, or messaging.

5. **Repeat regularly.** Repeat as many times as needed to vet key screens or moments in the product.

- **Test a variety of screens.** This is a great way to validate important parts of a product, like the start or home screen. But people sometimes enter products through the back door, too. They poke around online; they save bookmarks; they follow links in emails. To test that the product design is robust at all levels, consider running five-second tests on random lower-level pages as well.

- **If you work remotely**, consider using online tools. Check out Five Second Test (fivesecondtest.com), as well as UserTesting and Maze, as mentioned earlier.

METHOD 21

UX Health Check

What's the baseline quality of the UX, and how does it change in quality over time?

In a UX health check, you regularly assemble a cross-functional team to do an audit on the quality of the product's user experience. This technique was developed by Livia Labate and Austin Govella at Comcast. It's a way to figure out how well the product is currently measuring up against user experience expectations (Figure 7.5). It's an unscientific method, but has the benefit of inclusivity; you are measuring this baseline with the help of your colleagues. If you conduct this process regularly, you demonstrate and agree collectively on changes in quality over time (see Figure 7.6).

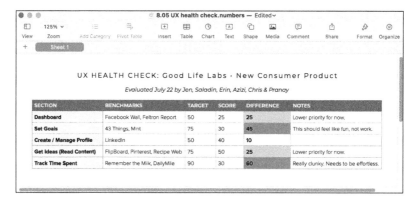

FIGURE 7.5
An example of a UX health check spreadsheet.

Average Time

1 hour on a recurring basis (could be weekly, monthly, quarterly, etc.)

Use When

You want to start tracking the quality of UX over time and don't have other formal measures in place.

Try It Out

1. **Designate a team.**

   Identify a cross-functional group of people to be the health check team and set up a recurring meeting: monthly, quarterly, weekly, or whatever duration makes sense for your product. Ideally, this is the team who is responsible for the product on a day-to-day basis.

2. **Break the product into sections.**

   Looking at your overall offering, break it down into sections or areas of focus. This could correspond to the sections of the product from a navigational perspective (for example, registration, account, homepage, etc.). Or, alternatively, this could be layers of the experience (content, brand, interactivity, cross-channel consistency, etc.).

3. **Set competitive benchmarks.**

   For each section or area of focus, pick a relevant competitive benchmark to serve as an inspiration. For example, you want your product suggestions to be as good as Amazon's. Or you want your cross-channel consistency to be as good as Apple's, and so on.

4. **Set a target.**

   Next, for each of those sections, decide how good your product actually needs to be, compared to its competitive benchmark. You may not be able to make your cross-channel consistency 100% as good as Apple's, but maybe 50% as good would be a significant improvement. As a team, assign a target percentage for each section and its benchmark. As you discuss why you've chosen the target percentage that you have, note and document your rationale. This is so that you and the team can remember your thought process in the future and explain it if anyone asks.

5. **Measure yourself against the benchmarks.**

   Now, for each of these sections, give the product a rating. You might want to be 50% as good as Apple, but after discussion, you decide that you are presently only 25% as good. Discuss how well each section measures up against its competitive benchmark and give each section a percentage number that reflects where you think you are today. The team may need to have a bit of discussion to arrive at a number that everyone can agree on. That's good! The discussion is the most valuable part.

6. **Spot the biggest opportunities for improvement.**

   Once you've agreed on your rankings, identify the biggest gaps between your target and where you stand today. Then discuss what you're going to keep, what you're going to improve, and how you're going to improve it.

7. **Repeat regularly.**

   As you continue to evolve the product, keep checking back and measuring yourself against your benchmark. Where your product is improving, congratulate yourselves. Where your product is underperforming relative to your baseline, focus on your next round of improvements.

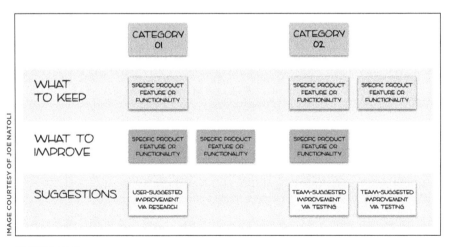

FIGURE 7.6

Example of a model for synthesized results of a UX health check, using sticky notes or a Miro board to categorize what's changing (and what isn't).

- **Don't pretend it's hard science.** This is definitely an unscientific approach. Basically, it takes a subjective measure—who you like and want to be like—and layers on further subjectivity by asking how good everyone thinks you are compared to them. Don't pretend that this is anything but a thumb-in-the-wind measurement. However, what is effective about this technique is that it gives a cross-functional team a shared, familiar language to talk about product quality. It's a low-overhead activity that you can do regularly. This helps you develop a long view of your own product—and to look backward and forward in time—in discussing what you're improving now, next, and later.

- **Use it to prioritize.** One of the subtle benefits of this method is that it helps you easily see where to prioritize your resources and effort. Often, there's a need to improve the user experience throughout the product, but wholesale redesign from the ground up isn't realistic. A far more pragmatic approach would have you focus on improving one small set of things at a time. The group-led process of the UX health check makes it clear to everyone (including you) what that handful of priorities should be.

- **If you work remotely,** you can do this process via a conference call with screen sharing to ensure that you're all looking at the same part of the product as you provide your assessment. Keep in mind that the discussion is the most important part of this process, so resist the urge to turn it into an asynchronous activity where everyone just sends in their individual scores.

If You Only Do One Thing…

…run a Black Hat session. Of all the methods in this chapter, the Black Hat session is the fastest and most blunt instrument for satisfying your curiosity about what isn't working. Black Hat sessions clear away all the niceties and expose bad or unworkable designs with striking efficiency.

Falling in love with your own ideas is an ever-present risk in UX and product design. Being proud of your work is great, but you never want it to prevent you from seeing that designs can evolve, simplify, and improve. This chapter offers a variety of methods for assessing how well a design is working—quickly, and with minimal overhead. The spirit of this chapter is simple: always be more curious about what isn't working than what is.

CHAPTER 8

Evangelism Methods

In addition to actually designing great user experiences, it's important that a UX team of one spends time building awareness of how UX benefits the business side of the house. Often, we think of this as spreading the word of UX, and so the methods in this section are described a tad facetiously as *evangelism* methods, which implies that it's about preaching to the unconverted. Well ...it is, and it isn't. While growing support for UX certainly requires introducing it to new people, we also don't want to appear insensitive to the other side of the conversation. In fact, it's the other side of the conversation—welcoming it and being willing to listen and understand it—that's key.

The methods in this section are about creating awareness, to be sure, but more importantly, they're about provoking conversations that will help you identify opportunities for UX, build support for your work, and learn more about how you can help other people using your UX and product design skills.

The happiest and most successful teams all talk about the same thing: having the support of peers and leaders. Now, it isn't required that your manager and colleagues are also UX aficionados. But it *is* important that colleagues have an open mind and are supportive of what you're trying to accomplish. If you don't have these kinds of supportive relationships, these methods will help you start *making* them. This may not even be that difficult. At this point, UX is commonplace in most organizations, so it's likely that people you work with are already familiar and interested. These methods will help you identify and mobilize your base of supporters. In this chapter, we'll cover:

- **Method 22: Captive UX.** Builds awareness of user-centered design and keeps people interested in your work.

- **Method 23: Mini Case Studies.** Summarizes your work and turns it into compelling, bite-sized stories that you can share with others.

- **Method 24: Peer-to-Peer Learning Community.** Mobilizes support and knowledge within a community of interested colleagues.

- **Method 25: Org Chart Evangelism.** Builds relationships and potential opportunities for UX in an organization.

Captive UX

Captive UX is a technique for building awareness of user-centered design and keeping people interested in your work.

Captive UX gets its name from the environment in which it is practiced—one where you have their captive attention (for example, on the inside of an elevator or restroom stall door) and post bite-sized notices to create awareness for UX and promote what's been going on (see Figure 8.1). Captive UX can be used in public meeting rooms, cafeterias, stairwells, and heavily trafficked hallways as well. The basic idea in all cases is to do a little informal promotion and awareness building.

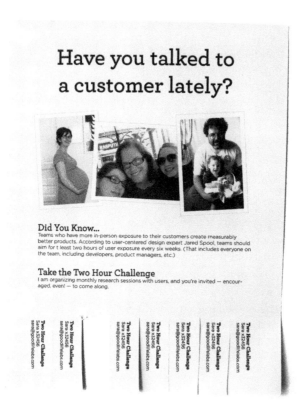

FIGURE 8.1
This flyer reminds readers of a core principle of UX and challenges them to get involved.

Average Time

An hour or two to design flyers and post them around the office.

Use When

- You want to build awareness for UX quickly, creatively, and with minimal effort.
- You have recently completed some UX-related work that you'd like to showcase.

Try It Out

1. **Think about your message.**

   One approach is to create a UX newsletter. Include some news from recent projects and their outcomes, and how that benefitted a department or the organization as a whole. This is effective if you're trying to build interest and trust in UX services. Another approach is to build awareness of the UX resources available to other departments (which could be you).

   Maybe most importantly, you can use captive UX to help people on the business side of the house see how the UX work you do helps them hit the KPIs and business results they're on the hook for, which will change the way they see you and your work. In all cases, include some information about how to get in touch with you if someone is interested in learning more.

2. **Make it fun to read.**

   Design a one-page flyer (or a few different types of flyers that work together to form a little campaign). Show your flyers to a friend to make sure that they make sense and cast you and UX in a flattering light and focus on what UX can accomplish for the company. At the same time, keep it understandable—no UX-specific jargon; speak the language of the folks you're talking to.

3. **Distribute.**

   Print a bunch of copies of your flyers and post them around the workplace. (Remember to clean up after yourself a week or two later by going around and removing any flyers that are still hanging.)

4. **Repeat.**

   Plan to do this again once every few months. *The UX avenger strikes again!* A surprising location, plus a novel message, will definitely get people's attention.

- **Permission vs. forgiveness.** Should you notify someone or get advance permission to do this? You will be the best judge of what's acceptable where you work, but generally in this type of situation, our motto is it's better to ask forgiveness than get permission. Going the permission route can turn a simple idea into a big deal and slow the process. And in some cases, you're asking to be told "no." The whole point is that this should be light and easy to do. So, if you *just do it* and see how people react (assuming your flyers are tasteful, appropriate, and informative), usually it's not a big deal.

- **Don't be shy.** Capers like this elevate what you do from undercover UX to something that's public and you're proud of. That kind of exposure can be a little intimidating, especially if you're the shy type. Here again, you will be the best judge of what you're comfortable with. However, when someone shows passion and leadership, people usually appreciate it and are attracted to it. Here, you're demonstrating that not only do you care about creating great products for real people, but you also have vision and a clear process for how to make it happen.

- **Be patient.** In contrast to the previous point, there's also the possibility that your first foray into captive UX won't suddenly have your phone ringing off the hook. The intent is to begin creating awareness and familiarity with UX. As people become more familiar with something over time, they often grow to like it more. This first batch of captive UX flyers may not necessarily have people banging down your door to lead the next user-centered redesign of the company's flagship product, but the flyers *will* start to create awareness and receptivity, which over time helps build opportunities and relationships.

- **If you work remotely**, turn it into an email newsletter that you send to your colleagues from time to time.

METHOD 23

Mini Case Studies

A mini case study summarizes your work and turns it into compelling, bite-sized stories that you can share with others.

Mini case studies are good hygiene at the end of every project or sizable piece of UX work you've conducted. *Mini* is a strategic choice here: by focusing on bite-sized stories, you create easy-to-remember, quick-to-tell, simple-to-share anecdotes. This also makes them easier for others to hear, understand, and make sense of. By keeping them mini, you also make less work for yourself, which means that you're more likely to actually *do* them. If possible, see if you can tell the whole story in one page, like the mini case study in Figure 8.2. Then it's easy to send this one page around and share it. Or you can put all your mini case studies together in a presentation or a document, and it becomes a self-contained portfolio of your UX work.

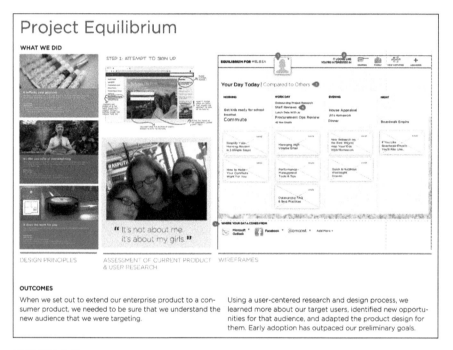

FIGURE 8.2

A sample mini case study.

Average Time

About two hours per case study.

Use When

- You need examples of past UX projects to share with colleagues.
- You want to get better at explaining your work clearly and succinctly.

Try It Out

1. **Ask yourself some questions.**

   For a given project, consider the following questions:

   - **What was the impact of your work?** If you have access to any quantitative measures of impact, that's ideal here. If not, even anecdotal evidence of impact, such as customer or stakeholder quotes, is good. Lead the case study with this information; give away the ending first. Why? Because it's the only thing that will compel the majority of your non-UX colleagues to keep reading.

   - **How can you describe the project goals in just one or two sentences?** Try to think about the *why*, not the *what*. Instead of *redesign the website*, a more compelling and interesting goal (for your non-UX colleagues) would be *help more customers sign up (and increase conversion rates)*.

   - **What did you do, and whom did you work with?** Don't think too hard about this. Keep it high level; just a few bullets will do.

   - **What's one interesting thing you learned in the course of the project?** People love these kinds of details. They're often described as the big "ah-ha's." If you can identify one or two, it makes your mini case study more interesting and makes people curious about what kind of ah-ha's there might be to unearth in their project or product.

2. **Gather visuals.**

   Pull together three to five interesting, attractive images—either of the final design, or of some particularly visual working documents that were developed in the course of the project. Having a few pictures in your mini case study pulls people in and makes them more memorable.

3. **Create a one-pager.**

   Put your images and mini write-up into a nicely formatted document. Ideally, it should all fit within one page.

4. **Memorize it.**

   Try to commit your mini case study to memory, so you can easily share your story when the right opportunity arises. And, of course, be prepared to send along your document when someone expresses interest.

- **Tell a simple story.** When you do your mini write-up, try to think about it from the layperson's perspective—or even better, the businessperson's perspective. UX experts tend to be interested in craft and process, so it's tempting to fill in a lot of details about the work that you did. But someone who is unfamiliar with UX is likely to have a more basic set of questions: What kind of problems did this solve? What kind of impact did it produce? How much did it cost in terms of time and resources? Was it worth it for the benefit that it gives us? Try to craft your mini case study to tell that story.

- **If you work remotely**, this technique is tailor made for you. It's great for remote practitioners because it produces an overview of your work that is self-explanatory and easy to share with people who are far away.

METHOD 24

Peer-to-Peer Learning Community

A peer-to-peer learning community mobilizes support and knowledge within a community of interested colleagues.

While you may be the only one practicing UX where you work, you may find that engineers, product managers, marketers, and others are all at least nominally familiar with the concept and eager to learn more. Host a peer-to-peer learning community to create a voluntary forum for sharing information that also uplevels the knowledge of user experience within your organization (see Figure 8.3 for an example).

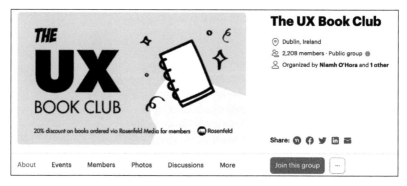

FIGURE 8.3

One example of a peer-to-peer learning community: The UX Book Club, found on **meetup.com**.

One important aspect of a peer-to-peer learning community is that everyone is interested in learning, and no one claims to be an expert. This engenders a participatory, open attitude that invites people in.

Average Time

Depends on your format, the frequency with which you meet, and what role you take. If you're the one organizing it, assume at least two to four hours of coordination effort per meeting.

Use When

A peer-to-peer learning community is appropriate at any time but is a particularly good idea once you've built some initial awareness.

Try It Out

1. **Invite everyone.**

   Send out a broad invitation announcing the community and inviting people to participate—and be sure to invite people from your organization in non-UX and product design roles! Include a date and time for a kick-off meeting, which ideally takes place in person (although remote and via video conference will work too, if that's your only option).

2. **Agree on format and goals.**

   In the first meeting, discuss goals of the community. What is everyone hoping to learn or do? How much working knowledge of UX is there, and how much do people want to learn? Record this conversation on a whiteboard or flipchart. Also, discuss what format people are interested in following to foster learning. This could take a number of different forms. Any of these models can work well—or even a combination of them—to give a group just enough structure and a reason to stay engaged.

   - A book club (where everyone agrees to read and discuss a UX book)
   - A discussion list (where people can share interesting examples and links)
   - A brown bag or lunch-and-learn series (where outside presenters can be brought in, or community members can volunteer to research and share on specific UX topics)

- A whitespace learning project (where the community decides to work together to design a solution to an interesting problem)

Finish the meeting by agreeing on a topic, format, frequency, and date for the next community meeting.

3. **Pick a leader and plan ahead.**

   Communities generally need organizers. That's probably you unless someone else has volunteered to organize it. You can also share responsibility, putting a new member of the group in charge week by week or month by month. If you agree to follow a format that requires some work in between meetings (for example, to find a presenter or organize an activity), be sure to plan for and block off enough time for adequate preparation. Even if your format is as simple as a book club, sending out one or two reminder emails in between meetings is a good idea, to keep the community in people's minds.

4. **Meet. Learn. Have fun.**

   Pay attention to what's working well, and what could benefit from a revised approach. Check in regularly with individual participants to see that they're getting value from the community. Continue to fine-tune and tinker with the format as needed.

TIPS AND TRICKS FOR PEER-TO-PEER LEARNING COMMUNITIES

- **Estimate and block off prep time.** A common mistake with community efforts like this is underestimating the amount of time needed for organizing and administration. Try to make a realistic estimate up front of how many hours per week or month this will probably take and be sure you're in a position to make that commitment. If not, consider asking someone to be a co-organizer.

- **Give it a time limit.** If you're not sure if your organization has the appetite for an ongoing peer-to-peer learning community, consider pitching it as a fixed-length experiment (say, three to six months). That way, you're not committing to do this forever, and there's also some urgency for people to get involved, or else they'll miss the opportunity.

- **If you work remotely,** keeping up momentum can be difficult when you lack the in-person element. A format such as an internal discussion list may work better in this case.

Org Chart Evangelism

Org chart evangelism builds relationships and potential opportunities for UX in an organization.

The basic idea of org chart evangelism is that you make it a priority to connect to people at every level of the organization—at the base, in the middle, and even at the top. For example, instead of trying to win an executive over in one single presentation, you build an army of supporters *throughout the organization*, at every level. The approach is simple: connect to people, introduce yourself if you haven't met before, ask them about their own work, listen sincerely and carefully, and discuss any ways that you think UX could help them do what they do better (or faster, or more efficiently, or more profitably, etc.).

In addition to doing your regular job, have a parallel track of influence and information sharing that's always in the back of your mind; seek out opportunities for one-on-one conversations to spread the word. In org chart evangelism, the lunch date is your most powerful weapon.

Still, there are many ways to connect to people at various points in the org chart, and the format that you use may depend in part on whom you're connecting to. The goal when connecting to people at any level is to share how a user-centered design approach can help get them the results they're already after. And it also serves to help you find more opportunities to apply UX practices to improve the products and services delivered by your organization. John Griffin, Director of Customer Experience Design for Blue Cross NC, puts it this way: "Doing great work, at whatever level you have permission to play at, is the non-negotiable thing that gets you in the door to have bigger conversations."

Average Time

Ongoing

Use When

You've done the undercover UX thing and would like to start building a recognized UX role or practice.

Try It Out

1. **For people you feel comfortable approaching directly, the best format is usually a casual, social conversation.**

   Ask people out to lunch, or to have a drink after work, or even share a coffee break. Tell them that you've been working on some things that you'd like their advice and input on. This works well with people whom you already feel friendly and social with, but it can also be surprisingly helpful with those people that you feel *least* inclined to spend time with: perhaps that coworker who always seems grumpy, that person you've had some workplace tension with, and so on. Treat this as an opportunity to learn about their priorities and what they're trying to accomplish. This is less about pushing your perspective on them, and more about listening and offering to help where there's good alignment between their needs and yours.

2. **For people who operate more at the "managing lots-of-stuff and always-busy" level, position it as a sharing of capabilities and services.**

   Ask them if they'd be interested in hearing about some projects that you've been working on that use new kinds of techniques for product design and have the potential to help that person and their department achieve its goals. If they say yes, schedule a half hour or an hour for a casual walk-through of your work and approach. *Don't* make this formal; no one likes to feel as if they're being "educated." Leave time to discuss in case they have questions about any of it, or if they see anything in your work that seems relevant to what they're working on.

3. **Getting access to people at the most senior levels in the organization and finding a way to connect your passion with their priorities may be more daunting.**

   Two good paths for connecting with these kinds of people are first, to use the guise of sharing and briefing them on the status and outcomes of current project work, and second, to connect with them through the people who work directly for them. In either case, you may need to work with other people in the org chart—to get yourself invited to a project update meeting, for example, or to get to know people at lower levels and ask them to help you represent your message higher up in the organization.

- **Give it time.** Be patient with yourself and other people, and don't expect that one conversation will be enough to win support and a home for UX (it won't). One of the most important lessons for UX teams of one is that a UX practice isn't built by delivering great projects (although it certainly doesn't hurt). It's built through relationships, trust, and goodwill *over time*. If you arm yourself with that expectation from the beginning, you'll have the endurance, patience, and flexibility to build a good idea into a flourishing practice.

- **If you work remotely**, the truth is that it's definitely easier to build relationships face-to-face. If you'll be meeting with other members of your team in person any time soon, think ahead about whom you'd like to meet with, and drop them a note in advance to set up a little extra time with them while you're there. At the same time, if a Zoom call is all you've got to work with, then go for it. An honest, personal invitation by email can often work as well, particularly since remote meetings have become commonplace these days.

If You Only Do One Thing...

...focus on building relationships with Org Chart Evangelism. And if you don't have time for the whole org chart, start by identifying a few key supporters and asking them to lunch. It will lay the foundation for more discussions—or more work together—in the future. Even more importantly, it will help you feel that even though you may be a UX team of one, you are certainly not alone.

The methods in this chapter are all focused on building visibility and support for UX, whether that's project-by-project, with mini case studies, or moment-by-moment, with Captive UX. The ultimate goal of all these methods is to build rapport, goodwill, and relationships with others who could be potential supporters of UX. It's about demonstrating that you care about the goals and results *they* care about, and the UX work you do can help them accomplish and achieve those things.

CHAPTER 9

Growing
Yourself and
Your Career

For teams of one, it's important to establish a few growth strategies that are just for you, regardless of what your colleagues think or say about UX or product design. These strategies will keep you passionate, motivated, and may even give you skills that you can bring back into your practice to help advance the commitment to UX shared by all. In this chapter, we'll look at a range of resources for continual growth. This includes not only finding opportunities in your own organization, but also taking advantage of the extensive range of external options that are available for UX and product design professionals of all kinds.

Online Professional Communities

Be it formal or informal, having a community of like-minded professionals can be one of the most important things you do for your career. It will give you people you can learn from (or mentor), people you can share experiences and best practices with, people to commiserate with, and in some cases, active participation in these communities can lead to future job opportunities. In short, engaging with peers and mentors will keep you *sane*. Professional communities come in lots of different flavors, and some have free online groups, as well as paid memberships that provide access to special events and other benefits.

While there are far too many to list here, the following groups and organizations are the largest or most active (meaning there's a lot of interaction and engagement among members) at the time of this writing. When you join an online group, you want it to be one where people are talking *with* and *to* each other, not *at* each other. If you don't see comments and discussion following a post, it's a sure sign that the original posts are self-promotional and self-serving, and those people are posting about things no one else cares about.

Finally, if you don't currently use social media on a regular basis for all the benefits we mentioned above, we strongly suggest you do so—your career will thank you.

LinkedIn Groups

From a professional perspective, LinkedIn is by far the best place to grow your career, from networking to job hunting to learning and mentorship. What's more, LinkedIn does a great job monitoring engagement, and it labels engaged communities with the "Active Group" tag (see Figure 9.1). The following groups are among the most active, supportive, and engaged.

User Experience Design (UX)
iii Public group
Active Group ❓

FIGURE 9.1
LinkedIn's Active Group tag tells you members are actively engaged in discussion.

User Experience Design (UX)

784,000+ members | linkedin.com/groups/3209228/

From the group's page: A place for Visual, Product, UX & UI Designers, UX Researchers, UX Writers. No links to Behance, Dribbble, Fiverr, daily UI challenges, UI shots, or portfolio showcase.

UX This Week

329,000+ members | linkedin.com/groups/1875717/

From the group's page: This group is to learn, reflect, and share about user experience. New trends in experience design for AI, machine learning, voice, and conversations to Internet of Things (IOT). You are welcome to discuss the design process. You are requested to learn, reflect, and share in order to help, coach, or become a mentor to the members who need it.

We are learners and practitioners of UX design, UX strategy, design thinking, product management, and everything around it. We create emerging experiences for products and services, for the users or those trying to learn how to create one. We share our own experience with the group, meet new aspiring UX designers, junior product managers, and people from other fields who want to move to UX and learn it. We try to help them by answering their questions, help them clear their fear, encourage them to take on the opportunity, and help them by guiding, coaching, and supporting them in any way possible.

Interaction Design Association (IxDA)

151,000+ members | linkedin.com/groups/3754/

From the group's page: Welcome to the Interaction Design Association (IxDA) LinkedIn group. IxDA is the first global professional organization devoted exclusively to the needs of interaction design practitioners and the growing discipline of interaction design. We invite you to join this vibrant community that exists to improve the human condition by advancing the discipline of Interaction Design.

This group is a space for conversations with colleagues around the world to ask questions and share your thoughts. There are more than 100,000 IxDA members and 200 local groups around the globe. Get involved in the discussions and let's make this a venue where new things happen in our profession.

There is no fee to become an IxDA member. Members of the community are invited to contribute to various volunteer capacities—you can get involved in a local group, work on local or global initiatives, and become part of the IxDA leadership.

Agile UX

51,000+ members | linkedin.com/groups/3803162/

From the group's page: The Agile UX group was created to highlight trends, best practices, and insights for LinkedIn users interested in Agile development, user experience, usability, user testing, and user experience research.

Our research indicates that the optimum manner to apply user research, user testing, and usability testing to software development is through an Agile iterative process, combining the best of both Agile SW development practices and user experience research/testing. This group is dedicated to this mission: Making iterative, Agile UX discovery and optimization a reality for all organizations, large and small.

User Experience Professionals Association (UXPA) International

39,000+ members | linkedin.com/groups/717/

From the group's page: User Experience Professionals Association (UXPA) International supports people who research, design, and evaluate the user experience (UX) of products and services. Founded in 1991, the original 50-member group has grown to serve a community that includes nearly 2,400 members worldwide by promoting UX concepts and techniques through our annual international conference, publishing new UX findings through both the *Journal of Usability Studies* (JUS) and *User Experience Magazine,* and our 59 local chapters in 30 countries around the world. In 2004, UXPA International established World Usability Day, which in 2011 was celebrated in 44 countries.

Interaction Design Foundation (IDF)

32,000+ members | linkedin.com/groups/2529386/

From the group's page: Founded in 2002, the Interaction Design Foundation (IDF) specializes in education and career advancement for designers: we offer self-paced online courses on design, as well as networking events in 84 countries in all major cities across the globe. Course certificates issued by the Interaction Design Foundation are recognized by industry-leading corporations. Course materials are developed by leading practitioners as well as by academics from top-tier universities like Stanford University and MIT.

HCI/UX Mentoring Circle

26,000+ members | linkedin.com/groups/6623413/

From the group's page: There are a number of LinkedIn groups that sometimes touch on career-related issues in HCI and UX, but none that focus on them and provide a forum for long-term advice and feedback. Issues of interest include skill development, educational programs, how to work with other team members, jobs, dealing with management, and any other career-related issues that people would like to discuss.

UX Writers & Content Designers

25,000+ members | linkedin.com/groups/8251547/

From the group's page: So many groups for designers and content marketers, so few for UX writers! Welcome to UX Writers, where we share questions, advice, tips, best practices, and open roles with fellow writers, designers, and content strategists.

Slack Groups

An untold number of organizations and generous individuals have started Slack groups for UX and product designers and researchers of all kinds. Slack can be a much more direct—yet comfortable and casual—means of communication where you can message members directly or take part in topic-specific channel discussions.

Mind the Product

60,000+ members |
mindtheproduct.com/product-management-slack-community/

From the group's page: Join 60,000+ product people in the world's most dynamic Slack community for anyone who cares about building products people love (see Figure 9.2). Sometimes you just need to ask a question or debate a solution. Sometimes you want a second opinion on something you're building. Sometimes you just want to vent and get commiserations from fellow product managers. The Mind the Product Slack channel is an amazing tool for all of this and more—and we have 60,000+ product managers actively engaged every day. Join us!

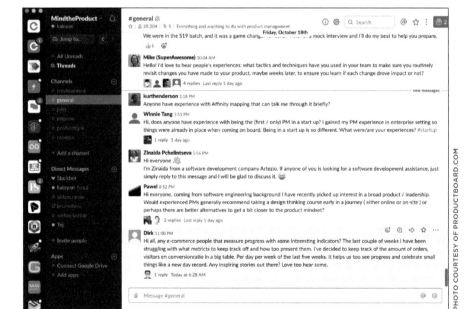

PHOTO COURTESY OF PRODUCTBOARD.COM

FIGURE 9.2
Founded by product managers, the site is filled with insight valuable to the UX and product design professionals who work with them every day.

Designer Hangout

18,000+ members | designerhangout.co

From the group's page: Designer Hangout is a dedicated, invite-only network of UX designers and researchers who discuss trends, give advice, share stories, uncover insights, surface opportunities, and connect in person. As a UX practitioner, Designer Hangout is your "secret weapon" to progressing your career and accomplishing your life goals. Together, we're creating the world's most reliable brain trust for UX designers in a fast-paced age.

Mixed Methods

16,000+ members | mixed-methods.org

From the group's page: Mixed Methods is a community interested in the hows and whys of user experience research. Through interviews with industry experts and hands-on trial and error, we indulge and celebrate curiosity. Expect to test assumptions, examine methods, and engage in some old-fashioned experiments.

Hexagon UX

7,000+ members | hexagonux.com/join-us

From the group's page: Hexagon is a non-profit aimed to empower and support womxn and non-binary folx in UX through community, events, and mentorship. We believe in fostering relationships both online and offline. There is no formal membership required to join Hexagon. Connect with your local Hexagon chapter, apply for the mentorship program, or join us in our global Slack group. Participate in conversations about all things UX—from portfolio reviews to sharing research discussions to learning about leadership and various career paths and more.

Service Design Network (SDN)

7,000+ members | service-design-network.org/slack

From the group's page: Our Slack workspace offers a community platform for service designers around the globe, with direct community interaction, discussion, and knowledge sharing. It will also benefit from the unmatched depth of the SDN's existing resources—from our publications and awareness initiatives to our growing network of 30 chapters worldwide and to an exciting new series of online events.

Rosenfeld Media Communities

12,000+ members | ♏rosenfeldmedia.com/communities/

Books and conferences are polished versions of important conversations that are already taking place within UX communities. Rosenfeld Media amplifies those conversations by supporting a variety of communities—and you're welcome to join them:

- *DesignOps Community*, for people interested in Design Operations and Research Operations.
- *Enterprise Experience Community*, for people with a stake in developing successful enterprise experiences.
- *Advancing Research Community*, for people interested in innovations in user and customer research.
- *Civic Design Community*, for people interested in the intersection of design and the public sector.

When you join a Rosenfeld Media community, you'll get access to monthly community videoconferences and past recordings, a semimonthly newsletter with industry news, articles, and other relevant content, and first dibs on discounted tickets for Rosenfeld Media Conferences. Best of all, participating in our communities is free!

Creative Tribes

1,700+ members | creativetribes.co/slack/

From the group's page: Find, connect with, and grow your tribe—no matter your particular niche, profession, or creative endeavor. Join 1,700+ folk—startup entrepreneurs, strategists, marketers, writers, developers, designers, remote workers, and other creatives—to share and discuss tribe-building strategies, experiences, and resources.

Discord Groups

Fairly new on the scene in terms of tech platforms, Discord is an instant messaging and VoIP (Voice over Internet Protocol) social platform (see Figure 9.3). Users have the ability to communicate with voice calls, video calls, text messaging, media, and files in private chats or as part of communities called *servers*. These online hangouts allow UX and design professionals of all kinds to get together to share interests, design techniques, inspiration, and resources. It also fosters opportunities to meet new colleagues and collaborate.

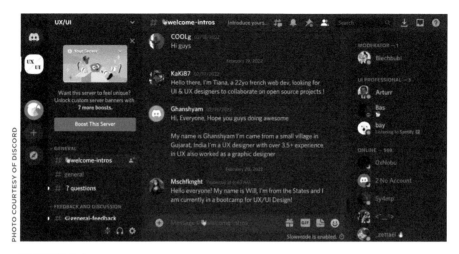

FIGURE 9.3
Discord servers enable communication and learning through voice, video, text messaging, and media.

Design Buddies

59,000+ members | discord.com/invite/designbuddies

From the group's page: Design Buddies is a global design community to help designers level up. Founded in April 2020, we offer events (online and in person), job boards, design challenges, content, give-aways, resources, and more.

Web Dev and Web Design

31,000+ members | discord.com/invite/web

From the group's page: Web Dev and Web Design is a Discord server for developers and designers. It has almost 30,000 members and plenty of channels to discuss programming, accessibility, and ask your specific questions. As a member, you will find channels with job opportunities, and spaces to request feedback and improve your work. But also, the community meets in online events to discuss the challenges of the industry and explore how to balance life and work.

Get Started in UX Design (GSIUXD)

15,000+ members | discord.com/invite/yEtXavWKS5

From the group's page: GSIUXD aka Get Started in UX Design—A community driven to spread awareness and help new UX designers transition into the field and make a place for themselves. Discord is your new platform where you can exchange ideas, tips, and many more from product designers, UX designers, user researchers, visual designers, freelancers, product managers, just to name a few. Our primary goal is to help each other to learn by sharing our experiences and knowledge gained in the past. Are you excited?

Design Squad: UX Community

15,000+ members | discord.com/invite/gjeETK58kN

From the group's page: Welcome to the Design Squad: UX Community! This is the go-to spot for UX professionals to connect with each other, collaborate on projects, and get the latest industry insights. With thousands of members, we provide a safe and friendly environment to share and exchange knowledge and experiences. Get access to the tools and resources needed to thrive as a UX practitioner, including live discussions, project feedback, exclusive tutorials, and more. Join us as we support each other in this rapidly growing field!

Floxies Community

1,400+ members | discord.com/invite/SspKVnQX4k

From the group's page: Floxies Community is an international community for women around the world who share a passion for UX/UI design and Webflow Development and support one another in their tech journeys. Join the Floxies Discord Server and connect with a Community of Women from all over the world who want to grow together and support each other on their journey.

Subreddits Groups

A subreddit is a specific online community, and the posts associated with it, on the social media website Reddit (see Figure 9.4). Subreddits are dedicated to a particular topic that people write about. While there are many on the topics of UX, product design, UX research, and design in general, these are the most popular subreddits we're aware of.

FIGURE 9.4

Designers frequenting the web design subreddit often ask questions and get advice on a number of tough issues related to UX and web design, like getting paid on time!

r/web_design

832,000+ members | reddit.com/r/web_design/

From the group's page: Anyone who designs websites will find this subreddit useful. It's a community for discussing all aspects of web design, from coding to aesthetics and everything in between. Subscribers can submit links to their work for critique from the rest of the group or ask for help with any aspect of online design. You'll also find posts for web design jobs here.

r/userexperience

111,000+ members | reddit.com/r/userexperience/

From the group's page: A community where professionals, enthusiasts, and individuals interested in the field of user experience can share knowledge, ask questions, and engage in discussions about various UX-related topics.

r/UI_Design

143,000+ members | reddit.com/r/UI_Design/

From the group's page: User Interface Design (UI Design) is the design of user interfaces for the web and devices using design and typography principles with a focus on maximizing usability and the user experience. Discuss the principles of design and typography with a focus on usability and maximizing the user experience.

r/UXresearch

36,000+ members | reddit.com/r/UXResearch/

From the group's page: A community for sharing and discussing UX research. The goal is to think about UX research broadly and consider studies from related/overlapping disciplines (e.g., market research, medical anthropology, public health, design research). Open to both academic and applied research.

Online and Local Meetups

Many cities have local groups with their own active programs of events and meetups. Some events are topical and deliberately focused on learning (book clubs or bringing in outside speakers, for example). Some are purely social and geared toward giving people opportunities to meet and mingle. In either case, these are fantastic occasions to gain professional connections, talk shop, and trade war stories.

The easiest way to find events and groups near you is the Meetup app, or **meetup.com**. Just search for "UX" in your area, and you're sure to find a group. And if you don't find a local group in your area, consider starting one. Post to social media and see whose game to help you. Or, if you know of companies in your area that do UX work, consider reaching out and introducing yourself to see if people there might be interested in co-hosting a meetup. If there are schools or universities in your area with formal programs in UX or even related disciplines like HCI, graphic design, or information science, get in touch with them.

In the meantime, here's just a small slice of what's available to you via Meetup.

The UX Book Club

1,900+ members | meetup.com/theuxbookclub/

From the group's page: The UX Book Club will help you reach your reading goals with must-read UX, Product, Tech, and Innovation books in a global community of design thinkers and doers. Whether you want to read more, learn together, network, or talk with more confidence in professional discussions, anyone is welcome to attend our FREE, online book club meets. Our focus is UX, product, tech, and innovation, but book choices range in focus and perspective. All levels and backgrounds are welcome: We run bi-monthly global online book clubs focusing on our featured book via Zoom. We also run one-off virtual events and masterclasses featuring authors and contributors. We are always on the lookout for contributors, so get in touch with suggestions!

UX Support Group

5,800+ members | meetup.com/ux-support-group/

From the group's page: We're here to empower UX professionals of all levels to get to the next level in their professional journey. In short: Become more --> produce more value. Between events, we continue conversations, sharing resources and opportunities via Slack. Join us!

UX + Data

6,660+ members | meetup.com/ux-data/

From the group's page: The UX + Data Meetup explores the experience around data itself—how to make data easier to work with, how to get more value out of data, and how data enriches our work and lives.

User Experience HQ

3,900+ members | meetup.com/userexperiencehq/

From the group's page: This group is for people working or interested in user experience, design thinking, product management, experience design, UX research, and prototyping. This meetup features different event formats, including product & UX hackathons, panel discussions, workshops, learning sessions, presentations, and more!

Ladies That UX NYC (multiple local communities worldwide)

3,098 members | meetup.com/ladies-that-ux-nyc/

From the group's page: LADIES THAT UX doesn't run for profit but seeks to make the world of work better for women around the world! 2015 Winner of Net Awards Grassroots Event of the Year and growing to OVER 50 cities worldwide, we are a friendly, welcoming, and collaborative community for women in UX.

LTUX NYC aims to foster an inspirational and supportive space where women in UX can feel secure sharing their ideas & industry experiences, growing together in all levels of their career, and asking questions they might not feel as comfortable asking in other environments. We organize events throughout vibrant NYC that encourage women to be public speakers, engage in lively discussions, informally meet and greet, and learn from each other.

> **NOTE** **CONSIDER HOSTING A LOCAL MEETUP**
>
> Brian is a team of one who started a local IxDA chapter. He has found that in addition to putting him in touch with other UX professionals, it has actually sparked more interest in UX in his organization. His current manager and his previous manager both now attend IxDA meetings with him, and he's talking with his company about the possibility of sponsoring a future IxDA event. This is a great approach because it not only makes you feel less isolated as a UX team of one, but it also helps your coworkers see that UX is part of a larger trend that goes well beyond the walls of your organization.

Mentors and Buddies

Some professional associations offer mentorship programs, where you can pair up with someone who is more experienced and establish an ongoing relationship to seek guidance, wisdom, and periodic sanity checks. Or, if you'd like to share your own experiences to help another practitioner, you can volunteer as a mentor. Either way, you are guaranteed to learn more about how to balance perspective, people skills, and practical expertise. Again, check your professional association's website to see if this service is offered.

If it isn't, consider looking to the people you already know. Is there someone you met in the professional community who might make a good mentor? Why not ask them? Or maybe someone you work with might be helpful. This person doesn't necessarily have to be a UX-savvy individual. Even someone who can help you examine and evolve the way you position your work for maximum effectiveness can be a tremendous support.

At the same time, we want you to understand that mentorship does not have to be formal. You don't have to have a specific one-to-one relationship with someone you label as a *mentor*—reality is that you can gain advice and guidance from anyone, anywhere, over time. Social media channels like LinkedIn, X, or any of the communities we just mentioned are perfect places to ask for and absorb wisdom from people who have been there and done that. So instead of seeking that one perfect, be-all-end-all mentor, commit to asking questions anywhere and everywhere, participating in discussions and learning along the way.

NOTE THE RULE OF THREES AND SOCIAL MEDIA

Here's a fun fact. Social network theory has a concept called the *rule of three*, which states that you're likely to feel a network effect at up to three degrees of separation. Here's what that means in terms of social media. Your *first-degree* connections are the people you are directly connected with on social media platforms, such as friends, colleagues, and acquaintances. Your second-degree connections are the friends of your direct connections. When you share content or engage with posts, they can be seen by these people. Your third-degree connections are the friends of your second-degree connections. Your content can potentially reach them as well.

To make the most of the rule of three, start by building a strong, diverse first-degree network. Connect with people who work in UX and product design who post often about topics you care about as well. You build that second-degree network by creating and sharing high-quality, UX, or product design-focused content. When your direct connections engage with those posts, you reach a broader audience through their networks. And finally, when you actively join in discussions, groups, and communities related to UX, you start engaging and connecting with people in your third-degree network.

It stands to reason, then, that if you want to increase your opportunities—for mentoring, for job opportunities, or to increase your visibility to potential clients—you need to grow your second and third-ring networks (see Figure 9.5). Becoming a part of the large, diverse UX and product design social media community, along with actively posting and participating in discussion, is how you do it.

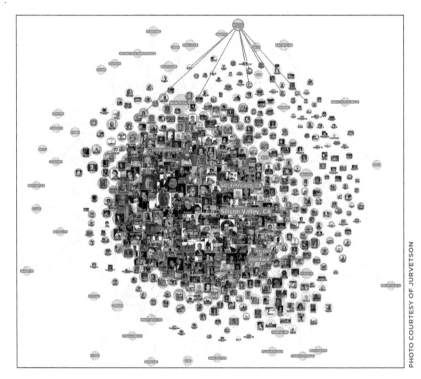

PHOTO COURTESY OF JURVETSON

FIGURE 9.5
The bigger your professional online community, the more opportunities you're likely to encounter, for mentoring, job opportunities, client work, or simply for friendship.

Continuing Education

One reason why continual growth is a good idea for teams of one (or indeed, any UX practitioner) is that the field is changing fast. Maybe you started out focusing on the web, and then gradually discovered that now you need to conduct research and design for everything from mobile apps and devices to automobile command centers to appliance interfaces. Tomorrow, it might be AR- or VR-driven, device-independent, connected service strategies. The simple truth is that technology is a fast-changing field, and since you are responsible for designing people's experiences with technology, you need to be able to move fast, too. To keep up with the pace of change, UX teams of one can benefit from a variety of continuing education options, ranging from classroom learning in degree-granting programs to online education in the comfort of your own home.

Online Resources

You can find an abundance of informative, well-written online articles, magazines, and newsletters that focus on UX, which you can sign up to receive by email. These sites are filled with curated, authentic, and useful content from fellow user experience professionals. Here are some of the most popular ones:

- **A List Apart:** alistapart.com/
- **Smashing Magazine:** smashingmagazine.com/
- **UX Magazine:** uxmag.com
- **UX Planet:** uxplanet.org
- **UXmatters:** uxmatters.com/

Online Courses and Workshops

For more guided learning in the comfort of your home or office, online workshops or learning modules can pack a lot of information in an hour or two of dedicated learning (and provide tangible how-tos and examples). Online learning generally gives good value for your buck. Many resources are free. The ones that charge tend to be relatively inexpensive (far less than the cost of attending a conference or taking an in-person class).

In person, group-based training can cost a bit more than an online course or workshop, but can also serve as a boot camp or intensive to take you quickly from a newbie level of knowledge to expert. These options tend to be more limited, but the organizations that do them often schedule tours, taking their curriculum to different parts of the world.

Before we get to the list, a word of cautionary advice for those new to the UX and product design professions: no online course or bootcamp program is enough, in and of itself, to get you a job.

While all learning is valuable—you should absolutely learn as much as you can as often as you can—what any recruiter or hiring manager will want to see on your resume and in your portfolio is experience. Real work done for real businesses. Even entry-level positions in the UX (and related) fields now require two to three years of work experience. While we don't believe that's right or fair, it's reality. So, any organization, individual, or bootcamp that "guarantees" you a job—especially with a promise of "or your money back"—is one you should absolutely be skeptical about.

The internet is littered with stories about bootcamps that promised things they did not deliver, and students deep in debt and still jobless. And as of this writing, one of the largest, most high-profile bootcamps has been banned for predatory lending practices and false job placement "guarantees." So please, *please* do your homework before committing by finding and talking to people who have been through those programs. Especially those for whom things didn't work out.

What's more, bootcamps are largely focused on what you can do with your hands: skill development, software proficiency, and the ability to follow a prescribed process. What isn't taught are the skills you need most—the ones

Now, none of this is meant to discourage you from learning. Put simply, the more you learn, the better you'll be at just about everything you ever attempt. So, taking courses or attending workshops is *always* a worthwhile pursuit; just be wary of anyone who positions doing so as a shortcut to landing a job.

OK, without further ado, here are some of the most widely frequented places for online learning:

- **Udemy:** udemy.com
- **Coursera:** coursera.org
- **LinkedIn Learning:** linkedin.com/learning
- **Nielsen Norman Group:** nngroup.com/
- **Interaction Design Foundation:** interaction-design.org/courses
- **Rosenfeld Media Workshops:** rosenfeldmedia.com/events/
- **Treehouse:** teamtreehouse.com
- **UX 365 Academy:** ux365academy.com

we discuss in this book, the ones between your ears. Specifically, the ability to think critically and strategically, to research and analyze well, and to ask the right questions and investigate the right issues that lead to designing something that delivers value to both businesses and users.

Next, you need to understand that there is no such thing as "certification" in the United States and in many other countries as well. Not in the way that architects, lawyers, or doctors are certified. There is no independent body that administers a standardized test in order to determine your ability to practice UX or design. There are only organizations that give you a certificate of *completion*—a file or piece of paper proving you took the courses and did the work—and disingenuously refer to it as a "certification." As such, more often than not, it doesn't carry the weight with potential employers that students hope for.

The only thing close to actual certification we know of is the International Usability and User Experience Qualification Board (UXQB), but the weight it carries with employers is still up for debate.

Finally, if you're reading posts, videos, and articles all praising UX and design bootcamps, we advise you to look a little more closely and do some digging. All too often, you'll find that the majority of them are often created by people employed by those programs. Are there people who have gone through bootcamp programs, gotten jobs, and succeeded? Of course. But the war stories are many—and growing. So, keep your eyes open. Be realistic.

Local colleges, universities, and community colleges may also offer relevant courses that you can sign up for without being required to enroll in a degree program. Check your local school's catalogs under design or computer science to see what courses are available.

Finally, many conferences offer optional workshops before or after the conference where, for a little extra money, you can get comparable training tacked on to your conference.

Degree Programs

While the UX field tends to welcome self-taught folks with open arms, eventually you may decide you want to go back to school. Degree programs can go a long way in sharpening your skills, simply because of the long-term, narrow subject matter focus that a four- or five-year degree program offers. At the same time, a significant portion of undergraduate degree programs in UX we're aware of are still very uninformed and immature. Many still have a very high concentration of fine arts or graphic design–based curriculum, and very little UX other than learning tactical methods and basic software skills. Others rely heavily on human-computer interaction (HCI) principles from several decades ago, which won't help you much in today's iterative software, app, and web development environments.

With all that said, formal education is still very much worth investigating. Three programs in particular—Purdue University Polytechnic Institute, Savannah College of Art and Design (SCAD), and UC San Diego's Cognitive Science program in the U.S.—seem to have strong, thorough, real-world-informed programs that appear to cover the skills students need to work in this industry. That isn't to say there aren't others, so you should check out the following list of schools that offer undergraduate and graduate degrees in UX as of this writing: **uxmastery.com/resources/ux-degrees**.

And when you do, consider the following criteria when evaluating whether a school's program will give you what you need to succeed:

- **Look for required courses covering essential UX topics** like user research, usability testing, UI design, interaction design, and information architecture. Opportunities to explore related areas like cognitive psychology, communication, and writing are a big plus.

- **Research faculty expertise.** Investigate the qualifications and experience of the program's faculty members. Working professionals with real-world UX expertise will do a much better job of preparing you for landing and working in your first job. Check out faculty research interests as well; that work can reflect the strength and focus of the program.

- **Look for partnerships and internships.** See if the university has partnerships with UX- or design-related companies, as well as coordinated internship opportunities, co-op programs, or networking events.

- **Avoid programs whose entire four-year curriculum is loaded with fine arts or illustration classes.** While a foundation in the fine arts is helpful, beyond your freshman year, it won't do much for you. Programs filled with these classes are a sign that the university doesn't really know much about this industry.

- **Avoid programs whose curriculum primarily consists of classes teaching you purely tactical skills, like how to code or use software.** While those skills are valuable, they can be learned easily online, often for free. And they are not the skills that will make you a successful UX or product designer.

Conferences

For what you pay, conferences provide a straight shot of inspiration, information, and networking in one very effective, compressed chunk of time. Going to conferences is a little like going to a professional spa, where you refresh and revitalize your energies for the work to come. If possible, we recommend going to at least one conference a year, and even trying to identify your "home" conference—the one that you attend consistently and where you can catch up with your UX buddies every year. Having a home conference also enables you to see how the content and issues in the field evolve over time. You can find multiple, comprehensive lists of conferences via Google; just search for "UX conferences list."

So, how do you cover the cost of traveling to and attending a conference?

- **Start by asking if your employer will pay for it.** Many companies recognize conferences as a beneficial form of continuing professional development and are willing to cover your attendance as a reasonable part of continuing education costs.

- **If your employer balks at the cost, don't give up.** Many conferences actually have scripts and other resources you can use to convince your boss! Here's a particularly brilliant letter provided by the ever-generous Vitaly Friedman's *Smashing Conference*: smashingconf.com/live/convince-your-boss.

- **Another way to attend a conference and get some or potentially all of your costs covered is to be a presenter.** This may sound intimidating if you have never spoken in public before, but many conferences openly solicit submissions for talks, workshops, and poster sessions, and they're often seeking to balance known speakers with new voices. Check the conference website for information about submissions.

NOTE FINDING YOUR CONFERENCE PRESENTATION

Don't think you have a talk in you? Spend some time brainstorming topics that you know the most about. Or think about projects you've worked on that are interesting or notable (either because they went really well, went really poorly, had some new angle or technique, or some combination of all of the above). Pick your two or three best ideas, give each one a title and a few sentences of description, and submit them to the conference organizers.

You might be surprised by what happens. In our experience, once you've got your title, your abstract, and a looming deadline, the rest of the content pretty much takes care of itself. But if you'd like some inspiration for how to structure your talk, check out past conference presentations on YouTube to see examples of what works well in other people's presentations.

The most beneficial thing you can do at a conference is to meet other people (see Figure 9.6). It's often said that the best part of the conference happens in the hallways, but only if you make the effort. How? Just by showing up. Attend the happy hours, dinners, and informal mixers that the organizers inevitably offer as opportunities for socializing. Introduce yourself when you sit down next to someone at a session. Be friendly and forward, even if just for a few days.

Trust us, you'll be glad you did.

PHOTO COURTESY OF COTTONBRO STUDIO

FIGURE 9.6
Networking and meeting people is the best part of any conference.

In Your Organization

For some, your own organization may not be the first option that comes to mind. In many instances, you'll be trying to help *them* grow a UX practice. How can you expect them to help *you*? Even though they may not be experts in user experience, well-intentioned employers often have programs and structures in place designed to help their employees continue to grow and ensure that their work contributes meaningfully to the organization's goals. Training in areas related to or even outside the UX or design discipline can be infinitely valuable as well, such as product management, general management, time management, or presentation and communication skills. Any training that gives you a chance to meet other people from across the organization can be worthwhile, too. Sometimes you learn valuable new things when you have an opportunity to work with people outside the context of a project.

Whatever your path to improvement looks like, the first place to start is to come up with goals for yourself—and write them down. In some respects, goals are the agreement you make with your employer about what you'll focus on in the next year, and where you can expect support from the organization. Consider making specific aspects of UX work and training explicit goals. This will make others (e.g., your boss and your boss's boss) aware that these are priorities for you and will invite a useful conversation about the lengths to which your organization will go to support your goals.

A less formal way to leverage your organization is to create a voluntary peer-to-peer learning community where you and other people who are interested in user experience commit to learning more with each other's help. (See "Peer-to-Peer Learning Community" in Chapter 8, "Evangelism Methods," for more details.)

Finally, your organization may be able to provide support for your growth in the form of resources—such as time to learn, money to take a class or group conference, or, the biggest coup, people to help you. If you can get help in the form of other people, you've taken the first step toward transitioning from a team of one to a full-fledged team. When your workload becomes heavy enough that it's more than one person can handle, resist the urge to take on more work and prove how industrious you are. Instead, be smart and ask for help: Can they open up headcount for a fellow UX practitioner, or even a temporary allocation for a freelancer or contractor to help until things ease up? Any feint in this direction (even an unsuccessful one) starts to position UX as a legitimate hiring concern—and not just your personal pet project.

Making a Case for Career Growth

Leah personally knows a team of one who actually has to sustain her own position and budget by writing grant proposals to fund her work. Granted, having your own budget sounds like an incredible luxury to most teams of one. But for *this* team of one, the internal grants process is smart (if painstaking); it communicates very clearly that UX initiatives take time and money, just like any other organizational initiatives. In writing that grant, she must make the case for *why* to do the work, *what* the work will entail, and what *outcomes* can be expected. And she can put a *dollar amount* next to that.

In business-speak, this is called being *numerate* (literally, the ability to understand and work with numbers), and it's usually what is required before anyone will entrust you with the budget to build a team. To be numerate, you need to understand how your work contributes to the company's profit, and how you're going to sustain that over time:

- **Align with business goals.** Sometimes when you start digging into your organization's business goals, you learn that it doesn't really *have* any. Or, it has a lot of them, but they're all set at the individual business unit level, and in fact, some compete with others, and good luck dealing with all that. If the UX work you're proposing doesn't align with business goals, or you can't explain how what you're cooking up will support what the business is trying to accomplish, no one outside your discipline will see the value of that work.

  Talking with business stakeholders and managers across multiple departments, from sales to marketing to finance to product, can help you assess how your organization sees UX goals aligning with business goals (or doesn't, as the case may be).

- **Measure your progress.** If you can get everyone to agree to a minimum but standard UX measurement process and then diligently and regularly measure it, your colleagues and managers will have a better understanding of the impact of your UX improvement work. For a simple way to start measuring your progress in user experience, try a "UX Health Check" (see Chapter 7, "Testing and Validation Methods").

- **Strategic planning.** When it comes to product development, businesses often plan and budget around projects. They deliberately attempt to manage risk and minimize complexity by scoping things as narrowly as possible, even in Agile or iterative environments. They put a lot of effort into defining what's in and what's out, especially when operating in time-boxed sprints. With your broad, how-people-really-work purview, you may be seen as the harbinger of unnecessary overhead, scope creep, or the dreaded "big design upfront." Here is where having some long-term strategic priorities—ones that connect directly to bottom-line business goals—can help greatly. Combine a "Strategy Workshop" with a "UX Project Plan" (see Chapter 4, "Planning and Discovery Methods") to create a big picture vision, and then plot out what needs to happen now, next, and later to get the business results everyone is after.

Moving Out and On

Hey, it happens. You may at some point decide that you've exhausted the learning opportunities and resources that your current situation can provide. If that happens, the most important thing a UX team of one can do is to take their career into their own hands and decide the next step. At this point, there are a few important questions to ask yourself:

- **Team of one, or team of many?** Do you prefer to continue being a solo UX practitioner, or do you want to work with other user experience and product design folks and learn from them? There are pros and cons to both situations, so there's no one right answer, only the right answer for *you*, right now. Some people even like to go back and forth between big teams and teams of one to keep their skills sharp.

- **Innie or outie?** Do you want to work inside an organization, or do you prefer to consult with a variety of organizations? Being on the inside can give you lots of practice in owning and evolving your own product, not to mention the interesting interpersonal and political muscles you flex in an organization (which will serve you well as a freelancer or consultant). Being an outie can give you an opportunity to work on a variety of new and challenging problems, although sometimes you don't get to see them all the way to market.

- **Employed or independent?** Do you prefer to work for a company, where the work is steady (if not always of your choosing), or do you prefer to be your own boss, making your own hours and running your own show (but also responsible for drumming up your own business)? Note that certain parts of the world may be easier to freelance in. Urban centers with a sizable UX community tend to provide more opportunities to work with UX-friendly companies and to subcontract for firms that specialize in user experience services.

- **What topic or touch point?** Are you passionate about AI? AR? VR? Voice? Mobile? Enterprise? Social? Search? Consider whether there are certain areas of user experience that you are particularly inspired by and where you would like to focus your work. Or you may like working on a variety of touch points and problems, and that's okay, too.

- **Specialist or generalist?** Finally, what do you want the balance of your work to be? When you're a UX team of one, usually you don't have a choice. You're doing your own research, creating your own designs, running your own validation testing, and even managing your own project. By default, that makes you a generalist. However, you may find that there are parts of the work you enjoy most or that you do best, and in that case, it's fair to ask yourself if you'd be more fulfilled (and have more impact) by going deeper into one specialty rather than staying broad.

  A caveat here: If you're choosing the path of self-employment, you're almost always better off starting as a generalist and specializing later; doing it the other way around can be pretty tough in terms of finding work and gaining wide experience.

All of these questions are basically filters to help you clarify and focus on the right next step for you personally. While many of us, at first, are thrilled just to have the opportunity to start doing UX work anywhere, make no mistake: your skills are needed and in ever-growing demand in an ever-increasingly digital world. So be deliberate and choosy as you grow your career and plan your next steps, both for yourself and for the people who will use the products you create in the future.

Going Independent

The UX field has a lot of independent practitioners. Many organizations can't justify hiring a full-time UX person, or simply don't want to, so an expert-on-call is just right for them. In today's volatile economic climate, often driven by shareholder speculation, a company's bottom line simply looks better with fewer employees. So, for organizations that see UX as a nice-to-have, outside contractors are always the way to go.

As a result, those going the route of UX independence can command relatively high fees, particularly if they've been doing this for a while and have a strong list of positive project outcomes, clients, and testimonials to show for it. And because the UX and product design community is highly networked, with an always-on social media backchannel, opportunities to demonstrate expertise and self-promote are in abundance (see Figure 9.7). So going independent can be a very viable option—but if you do, just be aware that you may find yourself dealing with the following challenges.

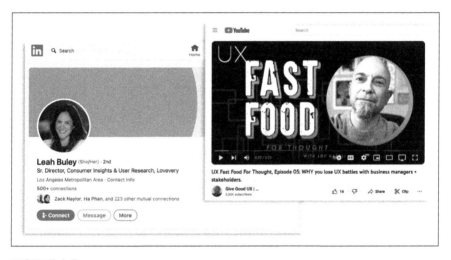

FIGURE 9.7
Social media channels like LinkedIn and YouTube are effective tools for independent practitioners or employees to demonstrate expertise and notify the business community that they're available for work.

Getting Paid

Your fees will be affected by several factors: your experience level, norms in your local market, and how aggressive you are about what you charge. The following techniques can help you make sure that you're earning enough to keep yourself in business.

- **Calculate your fees.** UX professionals who go independent and stay independent have figured out their fees, along with stipulated payment schedules that put enough in the bank, even if they encounter a slow period. Be thoughtful when you set your fees (see Figure 9.8). Spend some time thinking about how much you actually plan to work, and how much of that time you can reasonably expect to be billable hours. And be sure to check the salary surveys regularly published by professional associations like the UXPA to get a sense of standards in your area.

And while hourly rates are sometimes required by companies that contract freelancers, we strongly suggest you advertise and present your fees as full-or half-day fees instead. For far too many clients, an hourly rate is an invitation to debate how long your work should take (even though they have no idea what that should be).

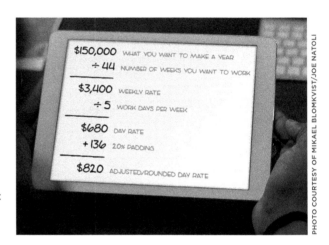

- **Negotiate.** If a client immediately says yes to your fees and you don't have to negotiate, you're probably pricing yourself too low. See the previous guidelines for pricing yourself. Establish your lowest number for every project you estimate—one where, even if the agreed-upon fee is lower than you proposed, you still make a healthy profit on your effort. Be prepared to stand firm on that number and refuse to go below it. All project work isn't created equal; if it isn't truly profitable, it will hurt you and your business in numerous ways.

- **Establish a fee schedule that protects you.** You always ask for a portion of the project fee up front, and then the rest upon completion (or to coincide with the delivery of major deliverables). This non-refundable deposit is typically 25 to 50 percent of the total project fee. If your client isn't paying you, the strongest leverage you have is to withhold or stop work. Asking for some payment up front or along the way means there's in-progress work left for you to stop. Otherwise, you can find yourself in the uncomfortable—and powerless—position of begging for payment for services already rendered.

- **NEVER work without a contract.** Some people may argue that this kind of formality isn't really necessary if you have good relationships with your clients. Those people are wrong. You must commit to protecting yourself first, before serving your client relationships. Contracts with a clearly delineated scope of work remove the possibility of heated, emotional debates about what you did and did not agree to do, or how much you agreed to do it for or when and how you should be paid—which ensures that you can stay in business to serve those relationships longer.

Position Your Engagements for Success

Let's face it. Some organizations have serious problems. Some take forever to make decisions. Some are so politically fraught that nothing ever gets done. Some are just not nice environments to be in. Any of those things can certainly impact how successful and enjoyable the engagement will be for you. Here are a few tips to make sure that you really know what you're getting yourself into.

- **Do a project brief.** Ask good questions about the project and the organization up front. Take a moment to ask yourself and your client contacts hard questions about timelines, goals, your role, their team, total team skills, ultimate decision-makers, and how success will be defined and measured. Ask them what obstacles currently stand in the way of that success. Ask who their competitors are and what level of parity they need with those organizations. Ask about the consequences of not succeeding. Then ask yourself if you still want to do it. When your gut tells you *no*, respect it. Taking the time to complete a project brief can help with this (see "Project Brief," Chapter 4).

- **Be choosy about what you call yourself.** If you can position yourself as a consultant rather than a freelancer, your time and work may be perceived as more valuable. It's a semantic sleight of hand to call yourself a consultant instead of a freelancer, but we believe it makes a difference. As a freelancer, you run the risk of being perceived as staff augmentation. And because the company has no long-term commitment to you, it's okay to give you the dirty jobs. As a consultant, however, you're enhancing what they can do by bringing a particular, specialized expertise into their office—one that they perhaps could not afford to hire full-time. Think of yourself and talk about yourself as a consultant. The key difference is that consultants bring a unique expertise, so ask yourself: *what's yours*?

Manage Your Time

In UX and design work, there are usually two things that contribute to how long something takes: first, how much time it takes you to do the thing, and second, how much time it takes to research, communicate about, revise, and get buy-in on the thing. You want to be able to bill for *both*. One of the biggest threats to scope creep (and your profitability) is when you have accurate estimates and agreements for the first part, but not for the second. To manage the first part well, know thyself and know thy process. To manage the second, know thy client.

- **Estimate conservatively.** There's a popular misperception that going independent makes life less busy. You're doing 60 hours a week in your current job, working for the man? Scale back! Become your own boss! In an ideal situation, independents can make as much as a full-time employee in a fraction of the time. But that outcome requires formidable time management skills, a keen sense of focus, and a very healthy client list. It's very common, at least initially, to find yourself working more hours than you would in a 9–5 job. The key is to make brutally realistic estimates about how long something will take and track your time well. That will allow you to recalibrate your estimates, learning as you go.

  To develop realistic estimates, don't just guesstimate how many hours it will take. A far better predictor is how complex the problem is. A complexity index (as described under the "UX Project Plan" in Chapter 4) can help you gauge where in the work there's the greatest chance for a slowdown in the schedule. Then you can plan extra buffer time accordingly.

- **Create timeboxes.** Your own perfectionism can be another risk to timely completion. It's dangerously easy to lose yourself in your work and suddenly realize that something has taken far longer than it should have. That creates problems whether you work for a company or for yourself, but it exacts a particularly personal toll when you're working for yourself. Ultimately, it sacrifices time that you would otherwise have for yourself and the people you love. It's also sometimes questionable whether you'll get paid for that time. Timeboxing can help. In other words, give yourself small chunks of time to complete discrete, well-defined portions of your work.

Leah freely admits that she is a terrible procrastinator and will take every opportunity to put off finishing her work, so it helps to have immovable boundaries boxing her time. (Such as a train that absolutely can't be missed, lest she be stranded. Sometimes, setting an alarm can also help.)

- **Manage feedback loops.** Managing that second category of time—the time it takes for others to digest, give input, and approve—can be its own full-time job. At a minimum, you should assume that there will be some communication time at major decision points. Often, it's not just communication time but full-fledged freak-out time. That's OK—natural, even. However, because it's charged with the extra energy of humans discussing and in some cases disagreeing, you don't want to exacerbate it by pinching or curtailing the discussion to protect the schedule. Instead, plan ahead for it to ensure that there's time for necessary conversations (and that you get paid for them). Plan for triage periods, as described in "UX Project Plan" in Chapter 4, and include reasonable estimates for discussions, weekly check-ins, presentations, and client review time in your project plans.

If You Only Do One Thing…

…focus on finding your community and getting plugged into it. Use whatever format makes sense, whether that be social media, virtual hangouts, or live and in-person.

This chapter hopefully reinforces that UX teams of one are not alone. Far from it—you are part of a dynamic, ever-growing community. How you choose to engage that community is a matter of personal preference, but *whether* to engage should not be. Keeping yourself connected to other UX and product design professionals outside your organization is especially important. It will put you on the path to continual learning and growth, along with greater professional satisfaction as your knowledge and skills expand.

CHAPTER 10

What's Next?

The idea for this book was born in 2008. That's when Leah first saw that there were people who, like her, felt that they were staking out a user experience practice in a place where it had not previously existed. It is now sixteen years later. And it's a gross understatement to say that an awful lot has changed in the user experience field.

The Evolution of UX

Almost two decades ago, web and software design were the standard. Today, mobile and app design have taken the lead. Back then, it was more common to talk about user experiences as existing within the context of a single channel or touch point. Today, we understand that a digital product is almost always a full, multichannel experience, and that our job is to give people a seamless product experience, even as they jump from desktop to laptop to mobile to tablet and back again. And to take this even further, digital experiences are now embedded in our homes, in our cars, and in what we wear on our bodies—making the idea of a stand-alone user experience of any kind seem terribly old-fashioned.

Open APIs mean that pretty much all the digital products we use now exist in an interconnected ecosystem of interoperable services. Chatbots and AI enable us to create and communicate and learn in ways that were previously unthinkable. AI in particular can help UXers and product designers streamline their workflow in ways previously unimaginable; some of the tactical work covered in this book can be sped up, enhanced, or cleaned up by ChatGPT. Storyboard images can be created almost instantly with the help of text-to-image generators like Midjourney, DALL·E, or Adobe Firefly. Augmented reality (AR) and virtual reality (VR) give us complete immersion in the kinds of worlds and interactions previously only available in our imaginations. The user experiences enabled by this new ecosystem are sometimes awesome and, more often than not, still pretty fragmented. And AI in particular poses significant ethical issues around privacy and intellectual property—challenges that UXers and product designers will have to wrestle with, navigate, and hopefully help to define.

Despite the seemingly endless warnings that new tech is going to take our jobs and replace us, the truth is that all of this change just means more opportunities for UX teams of one. At this point in history, the fact is that there are now more UX education options, more UX practitioners, and more open UX jobs than ever before. Undoubtedly, many of these jobs will require teams of one who are prepared to lead multifunctional teams to better designs. And how will they do this? By focusing on the durable value and purpose of design.

The Endurance of Design

Design is the act of creating new solutions under constrained circumstances, whether those constraints are aesthetic, technological, or resource-driven. That may sound like a restriction, but it's actually a gift. Constraints, in the end, are a designer's best friend. They give you boundaries, sure—but those boundaries become landmarks of inspiration that are just as instrumental for expanding your thinking as they are for limiting it.

For UX teams of one, constraints largely come in the form of other people. The product managers, engineers, marketers, and decision-makers you work with to put products into the world challenge you to be creative within constraints.

Successful teams of one know that this is the role that their teams and colleagues play, and like a master designer working with the best materials, they work within these constraints in a purposeful way. Just as much as your non-UX counterparts constrain what's possible, they also shine a light on opportunities for improving user experience. Your colleagues, and the constraints that naturally accompany them, focus your thinking on the issues and opportunities that matter most. They provide supplemental thinking to your own singular point of view. They help you be a better designer.

When handled confidently and patiently, your colleagues can become your own landmarks for inspiration, and they can help you make far more impact than you could on your own.

The Secret Agenda of the UX Team of One

As much as a book and its authors can have a secret agenda, here's ours:

To give you the confidence and ready tools to take on the non-UX world as unwitting allies, essential and welcome co-conspirators in creating the human-inspired, technology-enabled world of tomorrow.

Hopefully, this book has given you some comfort and confidence in knowing that you are by no means alone—neither in your passion for user experience nor in the constraints that shape your work. You may even have seen that you're already doing a lot of the best practices and techniques that work well for UX teams of one. Maybe you've added some new tools to your toolkit as well. But our goals in writing this book reach far beyond methods and tools: our true aim is to inspire you to think about what it is that you're trying to accomplish in your work. To encourage you to consider what changes you're trying to effect—and what kind of future you're trying to make possible.

If You Only Do One Thing...

...get clear about what parts of this work matter most to you.
While we've focused heavily on methods here, winning the hearts and minds of the non-UX world requires much more than method-by-method or project-by-project thinking. It requires you to get clear with yourself on your own master plan (see Figures 10.1 and 10.2). Sure, a master plan might sound daunting—but it doesn't have to be. So, we'll close out this book with one final method, one that's just for you:

1. Clear ten minutes on your calendar.

2. Grab a piece of paper and something to write with.

3. Quickly, without thinking too much about it, write down 3–5 things that you want—or that you want to be true about your work.

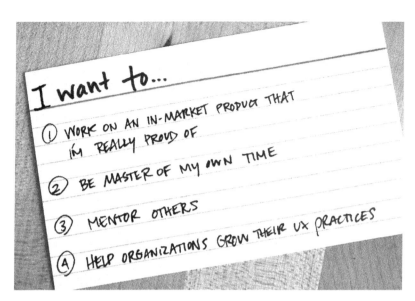

FIGURE 10.1

You don't have to name the job title that you want or the company that you want to work for—although that's certainly fine if that's what comes to mind—but think in terms of what qualities you want each day to have. Here's Leah's, as an example.

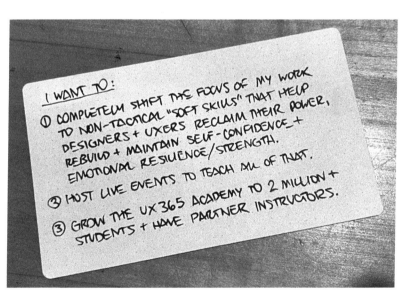

FIGURE 10.2

And here's Joe's.

If you feel stuck, here are some questions you can ask yourself:

- What kind of work do I want to be doing?
- What kind of team do I want to work with?
- What kinds of products and experiences do I want to put into the world?
- What do I want my success stories to be?
- Who do I want my allies and friends to be?
- What kind of education do I want to have? How do I want to apply that education in daily life?
- How do I want to work?
- What kind of culture do I want to be a part of and contribute to?

And then, once you've got your list, see if there's anything on it that surprises you. Odds are, you may have put down something that you didn't know mattered to you. But here's the thing: the list never lies. There's something beautifully simple and effective about giving yourself a quiet space and a few moments of reflection to discover some hard truths.

The funny thing is, once you've admitted to yourself that this is really what matters to you, it usually doesn't take as long as you think to achieve it. You'll pretty much get moving on it right away.

We'd like to close with one of the very best pieces of advice we've ever heard. When you're feeling stuck and unsure about what's next, there are two simple steps that will never fail to get you unstuck and moving forward in a positive direction:

1. Figure out what you want.
2. Give it to yourself.

Guide to the Methods in Part II

The table below lists all the methods we've included in Part II. While they're sequenced in the order they typically happen during the project lifecycle, you do *not* have to do them all or follow them in order. Use whatever makes sense within the constraints you have—and remember that something is always better than nothing.

Method	Use When	Average Time
Planning and Discovery Methods		
UX Questionnaire	How much do you know about your product and the user experience that it's intended to provide? What else do you need to know?	1–2 hours
UX Project Plan	What UX practices will you employ to design a great user experience?	2–3 hours
Stakeholder Interviews	What are the team's priorities, and how much awareness and support for UX currently exists?	5–8 hours
Opportunity Workshop	What areas of the product are most in need of improvement from a UX perspective?	3–4 hours
Project Brief	What are the expected outcomes for this user-centered design project?	2–3 hours
Strategy Workshop	What's your vision for the ideal user experience, and what do you need to focus on to bring that unique experience to life?	4–8 hours

Method	Use When	Average Time
Research Methods		
Learning Plan	What do you know, what don't you know, and how are you going to learn it?	1–2 hours
Guerilla User Research	What concerns are top of mind for your users? How do they really behave? How are people using this product today?	2 days
User Archetypes	How can you think empathetically about your customers' needs, goals, and challenges when using your product?	3–6 hours
Heuristic Markup	How does a user experience the product from beginning to end?	4–6 hours
Comparative Assessment	What are the standards and best practices that customers are likely to expect in a product like yours?	4–8 hours
Content Patterns	What content and capabilities do users have access to in your products, how is it structured, and what is the overall quality?	4–8 hours

Method	Use When	Average Time
Design Methods		
Design Brief	At a high level, how would you describe your target design solution? What are the features and personality of the product? Who is it designed for, and what activities is it intended to encourage or enable?	3–5 hours
Task Flows	How will the experience unfold over time?	1–2 hours
Sketching	What are some different visual forms the product design could take?	As much or as little time as you need (as little as 30 minutes works wonders)
Wireframes	How will the product look and function in detail?	Hours, days, or weeks, depending on the scope of the system, the volume and complexity of data and content, as well as the volume and complexity of user interaction

Method	Use When	Average Time
Testing and Validation Methods		
Interactive Prototypes	Does it work, feel, and behave as intended?	Varies based on format of prototype
Black Hat Session	What areas of the design could be improved?	30–60 minutes
Rapid Usability Test	Can people use this product as intended?	10–15 minutes per user
Five-Second Test	What impression is created by a specific screen, step, or moment within the product?	5–10 minutes per screen
UX Health Check	What's the baseline quality of the UX, and how does it change in quality over time?	1 hour on a recurring basis (weekly, monthly, quarterly, etc.)

Method	Use When	Average Time
Evangelism Methods		
Captive UX	Build awareness of user-centered design and keep people interested in your work.	1–2 hours
Mini Case Studies	Summarize your work and turn it into compelling, bite-sized stories that you can share with others.	2 hours per case study
Peer-to-Peer Learning Community	Mobilize support and knowledge within a community of interested colleagues.	Varies depending on format and role
Org Chart Evangelism	Build relationships and potential opportunities for UX in an organization.	Ongoing

INDEX

2 x 2 model, 128–131

A

A List Apart, 253
About Face: The Essentials of Interaction Design (Cooper, Reimann, Cronin, and Noessel), 167
accessibility guidelines, 40–41
Adaptive Path, User Experience Intensive Training, 125
Advancing Research Community, Rosenfeld Media, 244
Agile UX
  in Better Together model, 34, 35
  LinkedIn group, 240
alternative close, 51
analytics tracking, 47–48
anthropology, 22
Apple, Human Interface Guidelines, 153
Apple Macintosh, 17
Apple Music prototype, 204, 205
Arango, Jorge, 43, 54, 55
artifact from the future, 125–126
artificial intelligence (AI), 270
Atlassian Design System, 153
augmented reality (AR), 270
Axure RP, 45

B

back-end development, 47
Balsamiq, 187–188, 195
Better Together model, 34, 35
the "big reveal," avoiding with pre-meetings, 77
Black Hat Session method, 209–213, 221, 279
Bolt, Nate, 138
book clubs, 230, 249
bootcamp programs, 254–255
bounce rate, showing "good enough," 74
branding, and consistency, 41
Build Better Products (Klein), 48

building support for your work, 66
  common objections and responses, 82–89
  organizational issues, 75–82
  people issues, 75–78
  principles over process, 66–75
Burdett, Charles, 50
business analysis, as background for career in UX, 23
business goals, 7, 55, 260
business recipe cards, 50

C

Captive UX method, 225–227, 279
card sorting, 58
cards, for identifying UX activities, 50
career growth, 237–267
  conferences, 257–258
  continuing education, 252–253
  degree programs, 255–257
  going independent, 262–267
  making a case for your growth, 260–262
  online and local meetups, 248–252
  online professional communities, 238–248
  online resources, 253–255
  resources in your organization, 259
Carlson, Billy, 187
case studies
  developing to build support for your work, 81–82
  Mini Case Studies method, 227–230, 279
certification, in user experience, 255
checklists, 106, 107
Civic Design Community, Rosenfeld Media, 244
cognitive science, 17, 19
collaboration to generate design ideas, 61
Comparative Assessment method, 155–158, 277

compensation, for user research, 144

competitive analysis, 37

competitive assessment, 155

competitors, direct and indirect, 37, 155

complexity index, 105–106

conference presentation, 257–258

conferences, for career growth, 257–258

consent agreement, for user research, 142

consistency, and branding, 41

consultants, as organizational issue, 79–80

consulting work. *See* independent practitioner

content, in Venn diagram for IA, 55

content inventory, 159, 163

content maps, 160, 161

Content Patterns method, 159–163, 277

content strategy, 11

context, in Venn diagram for IA, 55

continuing education, for career growth, 252–253

conversion rate, 42

Cooper, Alan, 146

copywriting, 21

cost of excluding UX, 86

Costic, Vic, 80–81

Coursera, for online learning, 254

courses, for career growth, 253–255

Creative Tribes, Slack group, 244

Critical/Complex graph, 207

Crossing the Chasm (Moore), 125

customer satisfaction score (CSAT), 42

D

De Bono, Edward, 209

degree programs, for career growth, 255–257

design. *See also* methods for design constraints and endurance of, 271

in UX improvement process, 42–46

Design Brief method, 167–175, 278

Design Buddies, Discord group, 245

design libraries, 46

The Design of Everyday Things (Norman), 18

design principles, 39

of UK government, 169

design research, compared with market research, 83

Design Squad UX Community, Discord group, 246

design system, 46

design thinking, in Better Together model, 34, 35

design triage period, 199

Designer Hangout, Slack group, 243

designing, starting it, 59–62

Designing for People (Dreyfuss), 16

DesignOps Community, Rosenfeld Media, 244

diagrams, for design, 43–44

direct competition, 37, 155

Discord groups, 244–246

discovery, in UX improvement process, 36–39

Disney, Walt, 15

"done" is better than "perfect," 74

Dreyfuss, Henry, 15, 16–17

E

editing, as background for career in UX, 21

The Elements of User Experience (Garrett), 204

elevator pitch, 124–125

emotions, seven universal, 153

employment vs. self-employment, 261–262. *See also* independent practitioner

engineering, as background for career in UX, 22–23

Enterprise Experience Community, Rosenfeld Media, 244

ergonomics, 16

error rate, 42

evangelism. *See* methods for evangelism

expense of UX vs. cost of rework, 84–86, 89

experience blueprints, 180–181

Experience Dynamics, 89

F

feedback, showing "good enough," 74

feedback loops, 267

feng shui, 14

FigJam, 70

Figma, 45
Fitts, Paul, 16
Fitts's Law, 16
Five Second Test method, 216–218, 279
Floxies Community, Discord group, 246
flyers, to build awareness of UX,
    225–227
Ford, Henry, 14
freelancing. *See* independent
    practitioner
Friedman, Vitaly, 257
front-end development, 46–47

G

Garrett, Jesse James, 204
generalist vs. specialist, 262
Get Started in UX Design (GSIUXD),
    Discord group, 246
goals, business, 7, 55, 260
goals, personal, 259
Goldsworthy, James, 180
good enough, know when it is, 73–75
Google Glass, 83–84
Gothelf, Jeff, 34
Govella, Austin, 218
grant proposal writing, 260
graphic design, 22
graphical user interface, 17, 19
grid systems, 198
Griffin, John, 233
Guerilla User Research method,
    139–145, 277

H

hats, 209
    Black Hat Session method, 209–213,
      221, 279
HCI/UX Mentoring Circle, LinkedIn
    group, 241
heuristic evaluations, 151
Heuristic Markup method, 151–154, 277
Hexagon UX, Slack group, 243
human-computer interaction (HCI),
    19, 256
human factors, 16
human interface research, 18

I

IBM, Open-Source Carbon Design
    System, 153
implementation, in UX improvement
    process, 46–48
implementation collaboration and
    assistance, 47
Inclusive Design for a Digital World:
    Designing with Accessibility in Mind
    (Gilbert), 48
inclusivity guidelines, 40–41
independent practitioner, 262–267
    "consultant" or "freelancer"?, 265–266
    getting paid, 263–265
    having a contract, 265
    project briefs for deciding on job
      acceptance, 265
    time management, 266–267
indirect competition, 37, 155
industrial design, 22
informal UX network, 76–77
information architecture (IA), 8, 10
    in design of UX improvement
      process, 43
    exploring requirements, 54–58
    IA diagram of paths for users, 57–58
    Venn diagram for IA, 55
Information Architecture for the Web and
    Beyond (Rosenfeld, Morville, and
    Arango), 43, 55
informed consent, for user research, 142
inspiration libraries, 61–62
interaction design (IxD), 8, 10
Interaction Design Association (IxDA),
    LinkedIn group, 240, 250
Interaction Design Foundation (IDF)
    LinkedIn group, 241
    online learning, 254
Interactive Prototypes method,
    202–208, 279
International Usability and User
    Experience Qualification Board
    (UXQB), 255
interview tips, for user research,
    143–145
intuitive, 42–43

UX integration model, with Scrum, 34

UX Magazine, 253

UX Planet, 253

UX Project Plan method, 100–107, 276

UX Questionnaire method, 97–100, 276

UX starter library, 48

UX Support Group, Meetup group, 249

UX Team of One

   caveat to your environment, 91–92

   job description for, 26–28

   philosophy for, 1

   secret agenda of, 272

   what matters most to you, 272–274

UX This Week, LinkedIn group, 239

UX 365 Academy, for online learning, 254

UX Value Loop™, 6–7, 8, 29, 49

UX Writers & Content Designers, LinkedIn group, 241

UX writing, 11

UXD Cards, 50

UXmatters, 253

r/UXresearch, Reddit group, 248

V

Value Loop™ for UX, 6–7, 8, 29, 49

vendors, as organizational issue, 79–80

Venn diagram for IA, 55

virtual reality (VR), 270

vision artifacts, 39

visual design, 10–11, 22

W

web design, 21

Web Dev and Web Design, Discord group, 245

r/web_design, Reddit group, 247

whiteboards, use of

   in building support for your work, 70

   in design methods, 176–177, 199

"Why Software Fails" (IEEE), 89

Wilson, Thomas Ian, 32–33

wireframes, defined, 203, 204

Wireframes method, 192–199, 278

women's professional communities, 243, 246, 250

workshops

   for career growth, 253–255

   Opportunity Workshop method, 113–116, 276

   Strategy Workshop method, 120–131, 276

World Usability Day, 241

X

Xerox research center, 17

Y

Yablonski, Jon, 48, 50

Young, Indi, 38

ACKNOWLEDGMENTS

From Leah

First, thank you to Lou Rosenfeld for seeing a book in this topic, and for his guidance, patience, and support on the long road to its completion. Further kudos to Lou for having the good sense to work with the wonderful editor Marta Justak. Without Marta's expertise and tough love this book simply would not exist. Thank you, Marta, for helping me to accomplish what I never thought possible.

A thousand thank-yous to my co-author Joe Natoli for updating this book to reflect the field we work in today. It's Joe who brought this second edition to life, adding current practical wisdom and keen business sense. This book is infinitely better for it.

The visionary people at Adaptive Path taught me everything I know about user experience. Thank you to Jesse James Garrett for his leadership in shaping the field and the company. (And for writing the foreword to this book! It's humbling and fitting that your words set the tone for those that follow.) In addition to Jesse, several people from Adaptive Path deserve special thanks: Peter Merholz challenged me to find my topic and my voice. Brandon Schauer was a role model and mentor for me, probably without even realizing it. Dan Harrelson said the magic words that made me decide I could actually write this book. Henning Fischer led the way in project after project and I eagerly followed, learning from him at every step. Kate Rutter, Sarah Nelson, and Alexa Andrzejewski each in their own way modeled strong creative female leadership for me. Brian Cronin, Joanie McCollom, Pam Daghlian, and Todd Elliott provided the most critical component of all, friendship. Thank you to you all. Before Adaptive Path, there was Jeffrey Coleman, the perfect manager for a team of one. He provided the support and the space for me to find my way.

Thank you to everyone who contributed to make this book what it is. Thank you to Stephen P. Anderson for his lovely foreword in the first edition. Thank you to Andrew Maier for being the first person to offer to share his story and give me hope that others would do the same. Thanks also to Jim Ungar, Jeff White, Joe Sokohl, Jon Strande, Michael Carvin, and Louise Gruenberg who generously shared their stories and insights with me. Thank you to the 300 plus people who completed my survey and helped me learn more about common challenges for UX teams of one. Lelia Ferro, Graham Odds, Jack Holmes, James Goldsworthy, Jay Spanton, Jenny Grinblo, Mary Lojkine, Natalie Moser, Roger Attrill, Silvia Di Gianfrancesco, and Tom Randle all reviewed early drafts of the book and provided invaluable feedback that made it clearer, more informative, and just plain better. Extra special thanks to Mary Lojkine, whose thorough and thoughtful recommendations on structure rooted out unnecessary complexity and simplified the book for the better.

Thank you to Diana Kinsey, proof that one teacher truly can change a life.

Thank you to my family for the gift of sparkle. Thank you to Susy, Patty, Jane, Chrissy, Jenny and my beloved sisters, Jen and Heather. Heaven is a pool day with all of you. Thank you to my talented brothers, Ian and Joah. I love you both. Thank you to my mom Mary for raising me to be self-reliant, resourceful, and, ultimately, kind. Thank you to my brilliant children, Theo and Frances, for showing me every day what really matters in life. I love you both to the moon and around the sun and beyond the stars times infinity. Finally, thank you to my husband Chris, still the coolest, funniest, smartest guy I know after all these years.

From Joe

I am extremely grateful to Lou Rosenfeld for the invitation to contribute to this second edition of a book I was already in love with—and for his faith and trust that I was the right man for the job. I have held the utmost respect for Leah Buley's clear-eyed, no-nonsense approach to this discipline since the first edition of this book; her care for people entering and practicing in this field was evident in every word. She trusted me explicitly with her creation; as a fellow author, I can think of no greater honor.

Words fail to describe just how much of a joy editor Marta Justak has been to work with. Without her expertise, guidance, and incredibly sharp mind, this project would never have been possible—and it *never* would have gone so smoothly. And I am equally grateful to be represented so powerfully and professionally in these pages by Danielle Foster's top-tier design.

To say I am both humbled and honored that Jesse James Garrett wrote the foreword to this book is a gross understatement. Jesse's seminal book, *The Elements of User Experience*, was my introduction to this field, and the breadth, depth, and impact of his historic contributions to the field of UX are only second to his amazing warmth and generosity. Without Jesse's inspiration, example, and guidance, there is no me.

The same is true of Alan Cooper and his wife Sue. Cooper Design was the model for everything I did when I started my own firm in the late 1990s in attitude, intent, and execution. I owe these two humans more than I can explain, and their continued friendship is one of the great strokes of luck in my life.

I am deeply grateful in particular to Chuck Borowicz and John Griffin, who took time from their hectic work and family lives to review drafts of this book and deliver critical, insightful critique and feedback that made every chapter stronger. And a special shout-out is absolutely necessary to Thomas Wilson, who went above and beyond the call of duty for this project in every conceivable way.

Thanks also go to Vic Costik, John Athayde, Isaac Donkoh, Tomi Joshua, Trisha Chowdhury, Sharon Orienza, Stefanie Kruse, and Alva Henriksson—and hundreds of others across my social media networks—for sharing their stories and experiences transitioning to and working in the field. And I would be remiss if I didn't express my deep appreciation for nearly half a million students, friends, and followers across the globe: I have learned volumes from you all, and your support makes my life possible. Not a second is taken for granted.

And a very special "without whom" goes out to John Brett Buchanan, J. Charles Walker, Katie Kennedy, David Flynn, Mike Matthews, and Brian McIntyre. I will never be able to thank you enough for your wisdom, guidance, and support. Iron sharpens iron.

Above all else, I have to thank my family. My parents Richard and Donna for teaching me to believe in myself and instilling, by example, an absolute unwillingness to stay down, no matter how many times I've been knocked to the canvas. My in-laws Afi and Hassan for unconditional love and support that makes me truly believe I can be the person they see in me. And finally, the greatest thanks go to my wife Eli and my children, Julianna, Sabah, and Sophia. I will never have the words to properly explain what you all mean to me—or how truly fortunate I feel. I love you all.

ABOUT THE AUTHORS

 **Leah Buley** is a well-known researcher, designer, and author, recognized for her contributions to the field of UX through her writings, presentations, and workshops. Her research has been published in HBR, Forbes, Communication Arts, Information Age, and elsewhere. Her talks and workshops at venues like SXSW, UX Week, and UX London have a reputation for being high-energy, hands on, and just a little bit quirky.

Leah's professional experience spans agencies, startups, and Fortune 100 companies. In her 20+ years in the user experience field, she has held roles at Lovevery, InVision, Forrester, Intuit, and Adaptive Path.

At InVision she created a proprietary design maturity model based on data from over 2,000 companies globally to identify the design practices that tie to business impact. At Forrester, Leah was a principal analyst and a prominent voice for the evolving importance of design in business.

In recent years, Leah's work focuses on consumer insights and UX research. She enjoys working in-house with ambitious teams to make great products that address real human needs.

She lives in Los Angeles with her husband Chris and their children, Theo and Frances.